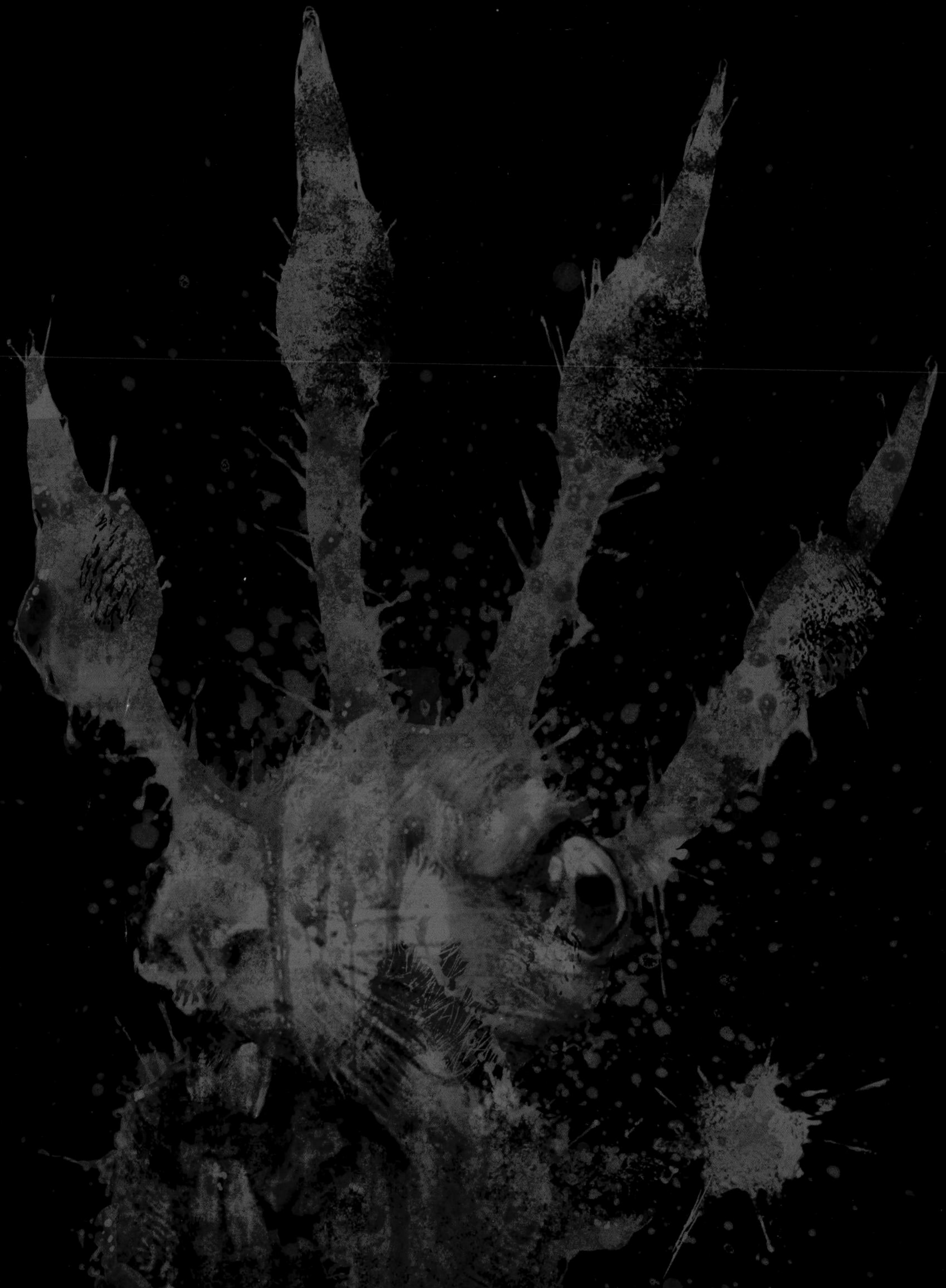

DEDICATED
TO
BELLA & ABBY

ASHLEY WITTER   ASH MACZKO

SQUARRIORS

SPRING

"AND THE MEEK SHALL INHERIT THE EARTH."

CREATED/WRITTEN/LAYOUTS
BY
ASH MACZKO

ART/LETTERS/COLORS
BY
ASHLEY WITTER

DEVIL'S DUE
1FIRST COMICS

FOR DEVIL'S DUE ENT.

FOUNDER/MANAGING PRINCIPAL — JOSH BLAYLOCK

PUBLISHING COORDINATOR — KIT CAOAGAS

LEAD DESIGNER — NICK ACCARDI

MARKETING/CROWDFUNDING COORDINATOR — KARI SMITH

ACCOUNTING — DEBBIE DAVIS

MEDIA CONTACT — PRESS@DEVILSDUE.NET

PRINTED IN UNITED STATES OF AMERICA

SQUARRIORS: VOL. 1: SPRING" 2ND PRINTING SEPTEMBER 2017. PUBLISHED BY DEVIL'S DUE / 1FIRST COMICS, LLC BY AGREEMENT WITH DEVIL'S DUE ENTERTAINMENT. OFFICE OF PUBLICATION 1658 MILWAUKEE AVE #100-5850, CHICAGO, IL 60647. SQUARRIORS, THE TIN KIN, MAW, AMONI, AND ALL ASSOCIATED CHARACTERS AND THEIR RESPECTIVE LIKENESSES ARE ™ AND © 2017

Chapter 1: Teeth and Nails

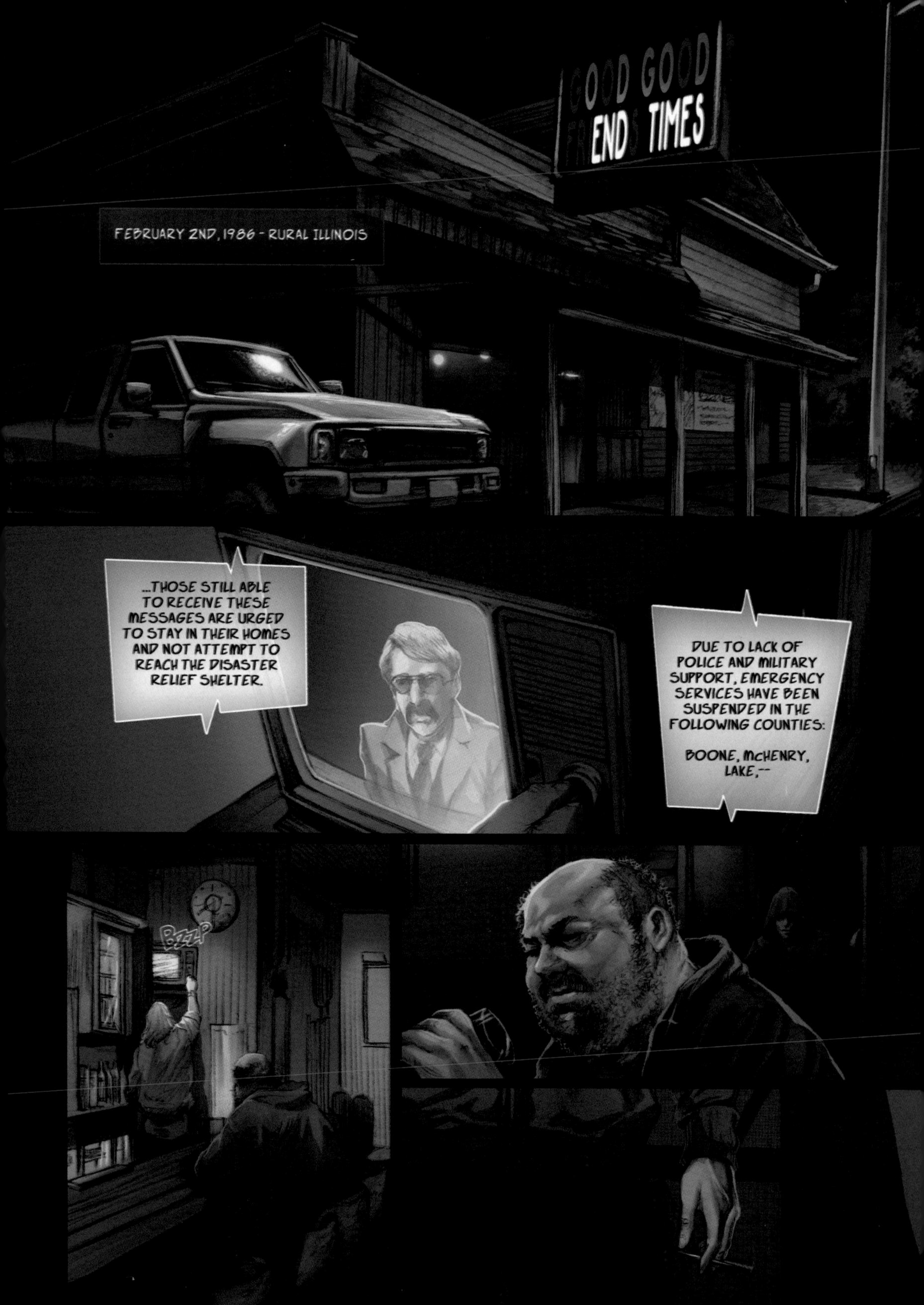

GOOD GOOD
END TIMES
FEBRUARY 2ND, 1986 - RURAL ILLINOIS
...THOSE STILL ABLE TO RECEIVE THESE MESSAGES ARE URGED TO STAY IN THEIR HOMES AND NOT ATTEMPT TO REACH THE DISASTER RELIEF SHELTER.
DUE TO LACK OF POLICE AND MILITARY SUPPORT, EMERGENCY SERVICES HAVE BEEN SUSPENDED IN THE FOLLOWING COUNTIES:
BOONE, McHENRY, LAKE,--
BZZP

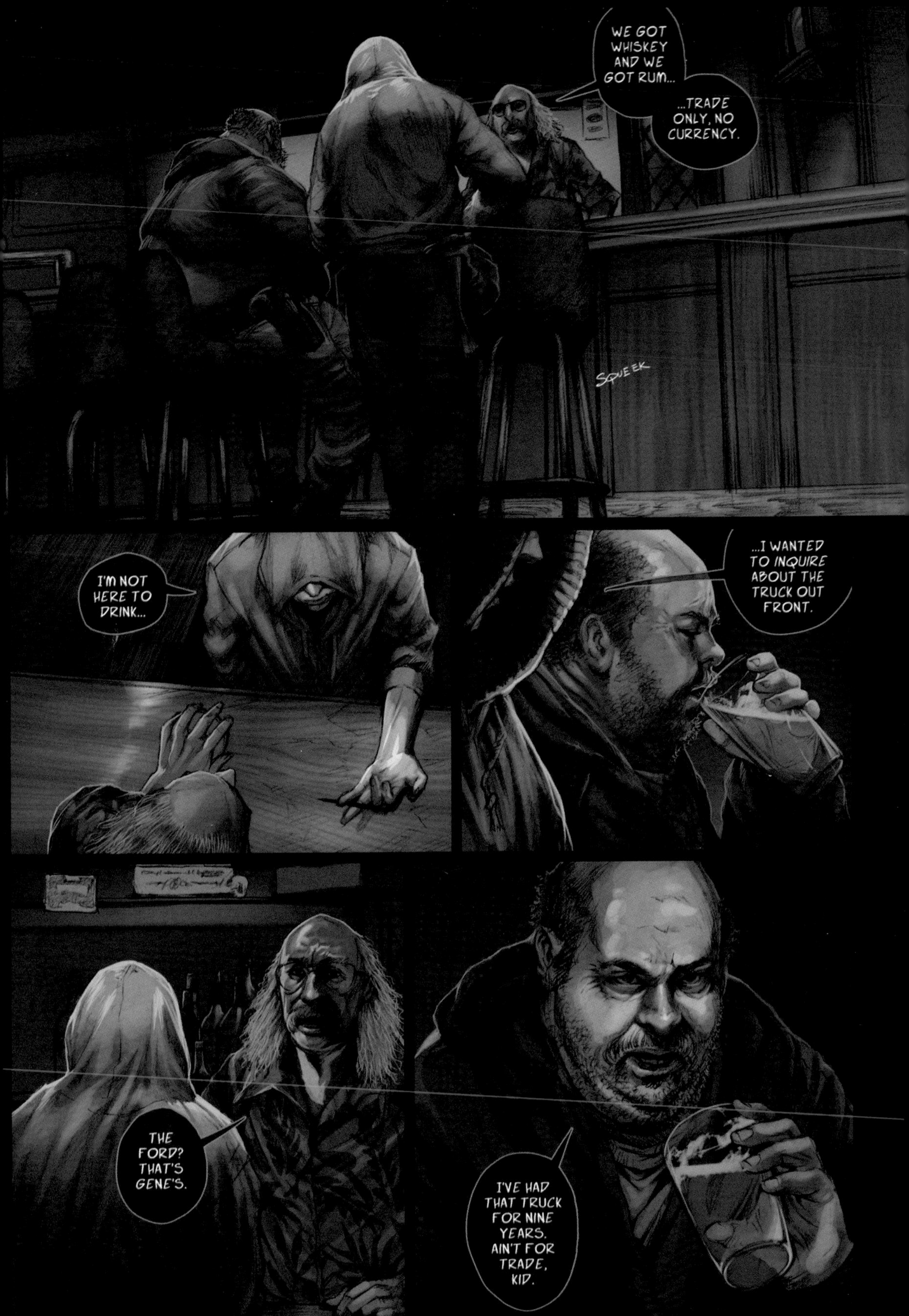
WE GOT WHISKEY AND WE GOT RUM...
...TRADE ONLY, NO CURRENCY.
SQUEEK
I'M NOT HERE TO DRINK...
...I WANTED TO INQUIRE ABOUT THE TRUCK OUT FRONT.
THE FORD? THAT'S GENE'S.
I'VE HAD THAT TRUCK FOR NINE YEARS. AIN'T FOR TRADE, KID.

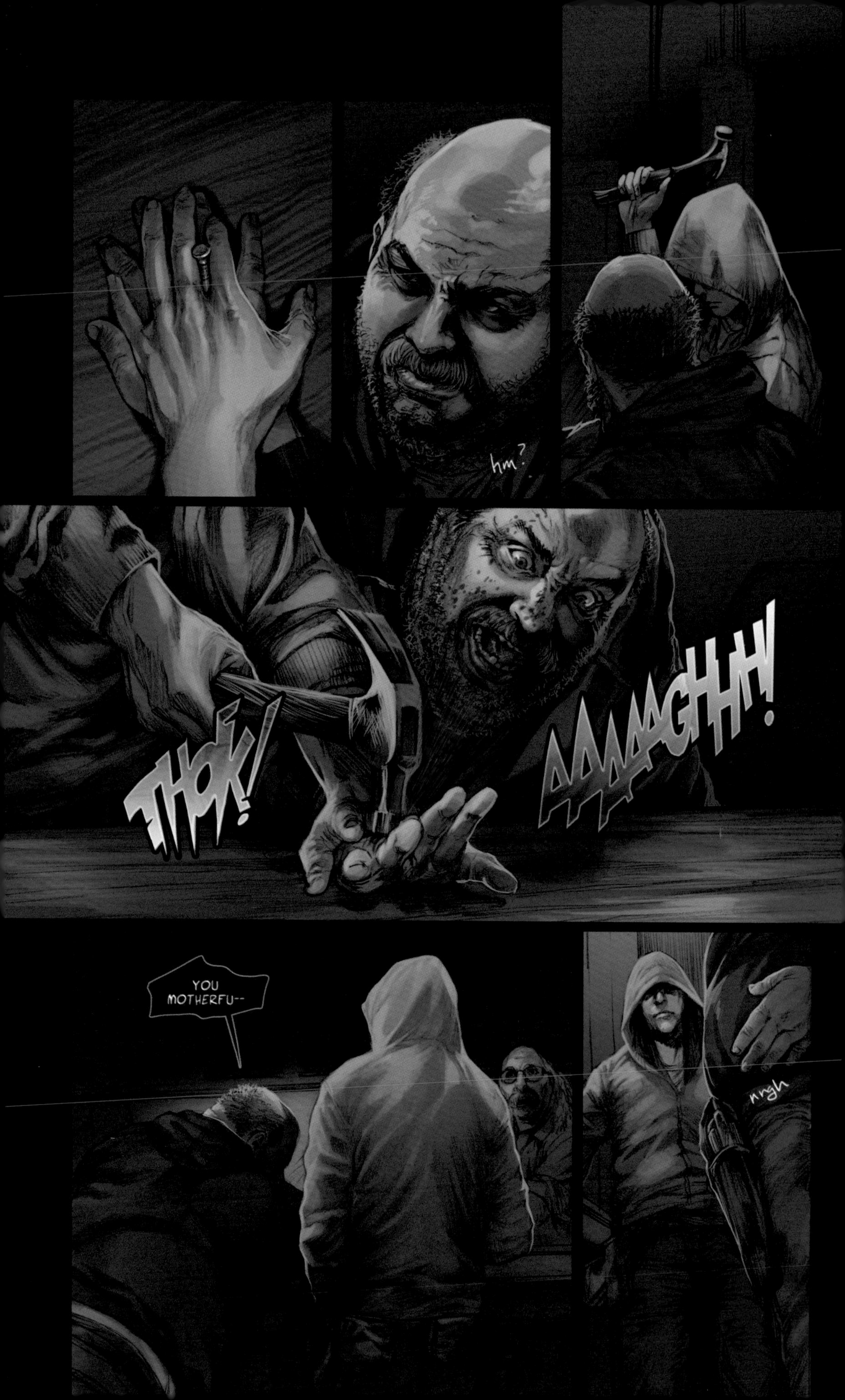
hm?
THOK!
AAAAAGHHH!
YOU MOTHERFU--
nngh

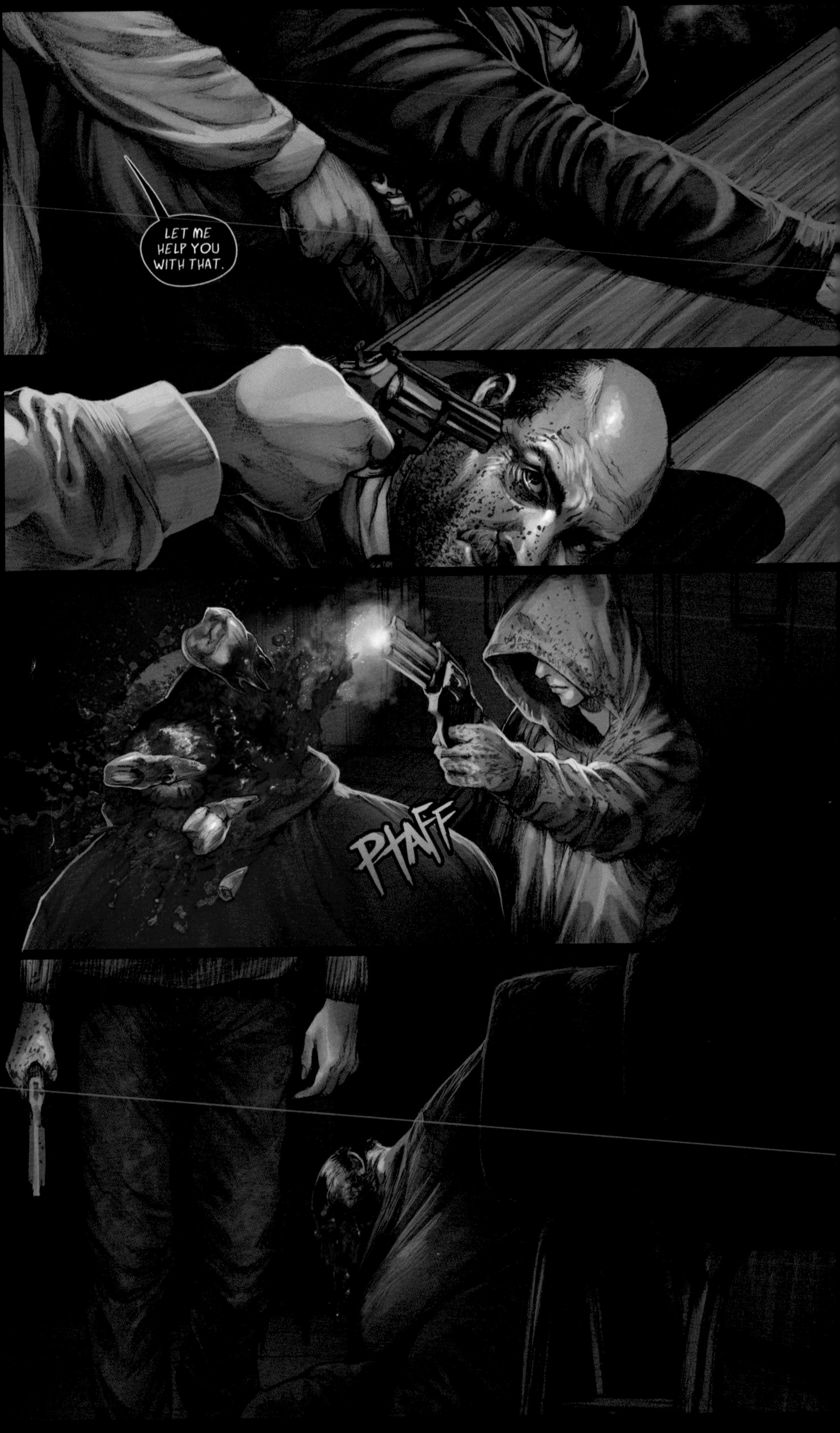
LET ME HELP YOU WITH THAT.
PTAFF

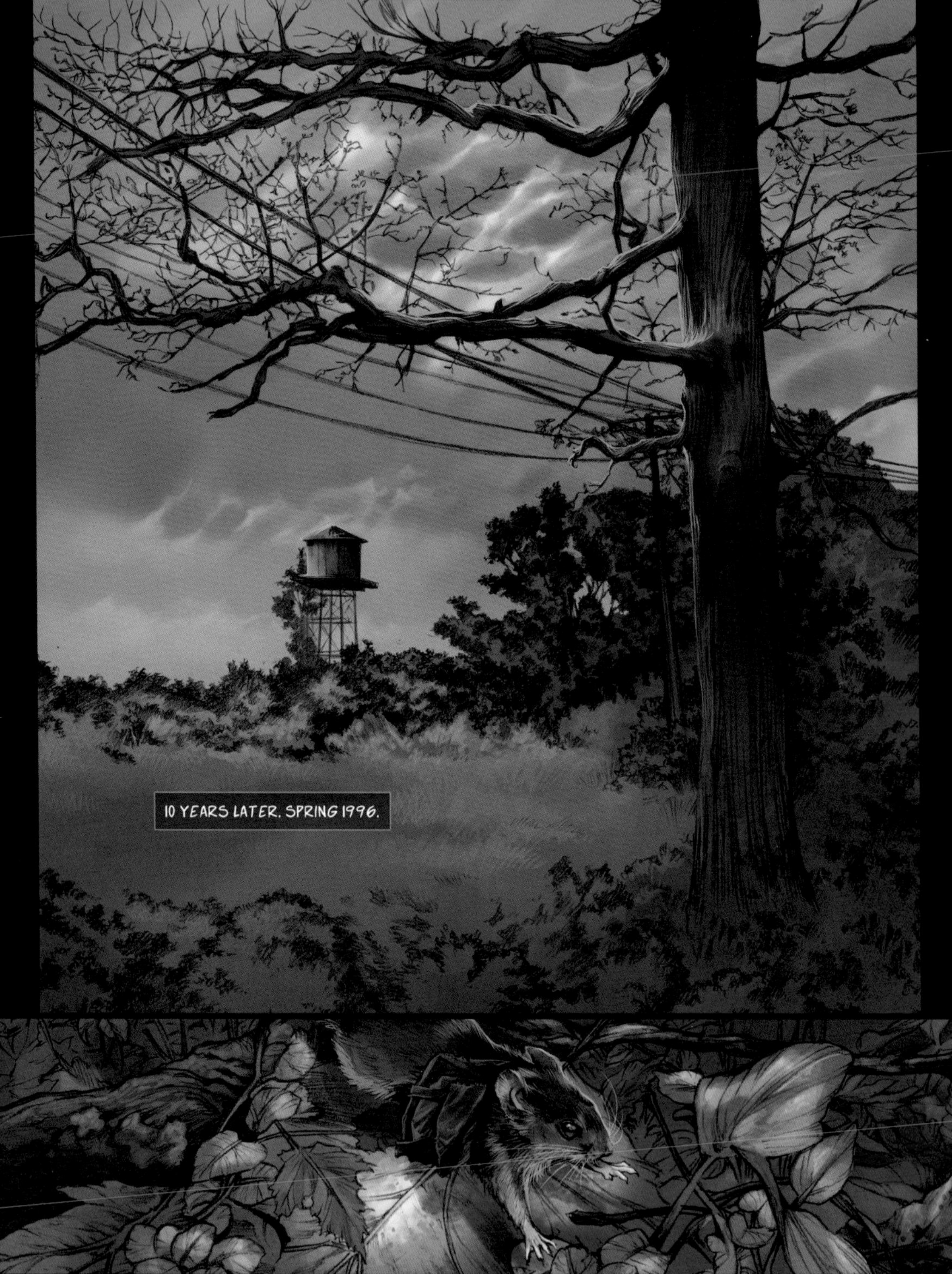
10 YEARS LATER. SPRING 1996.

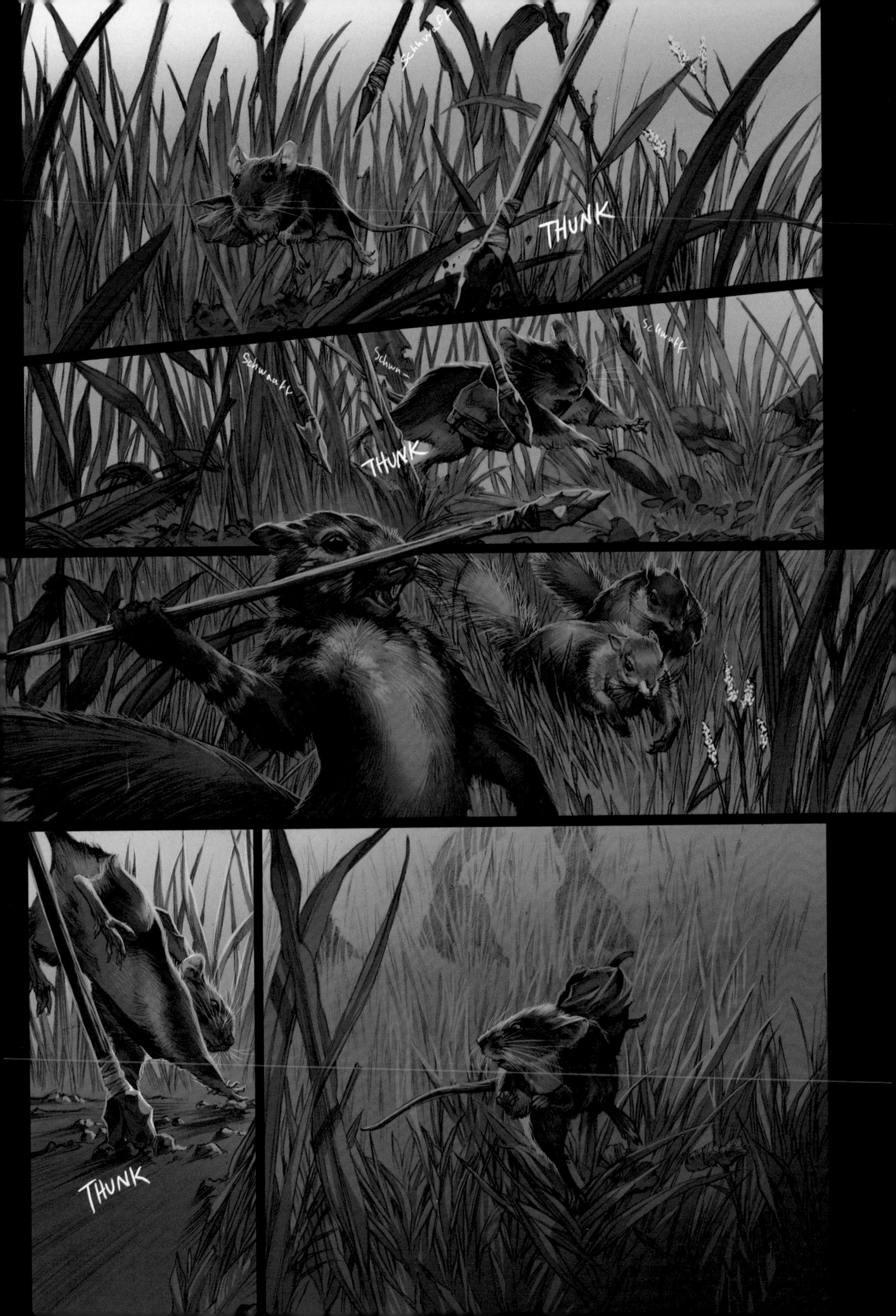

Schwaff
THUNK
Schwauff
Schwa-
Schwauff
THUNK
THUNK

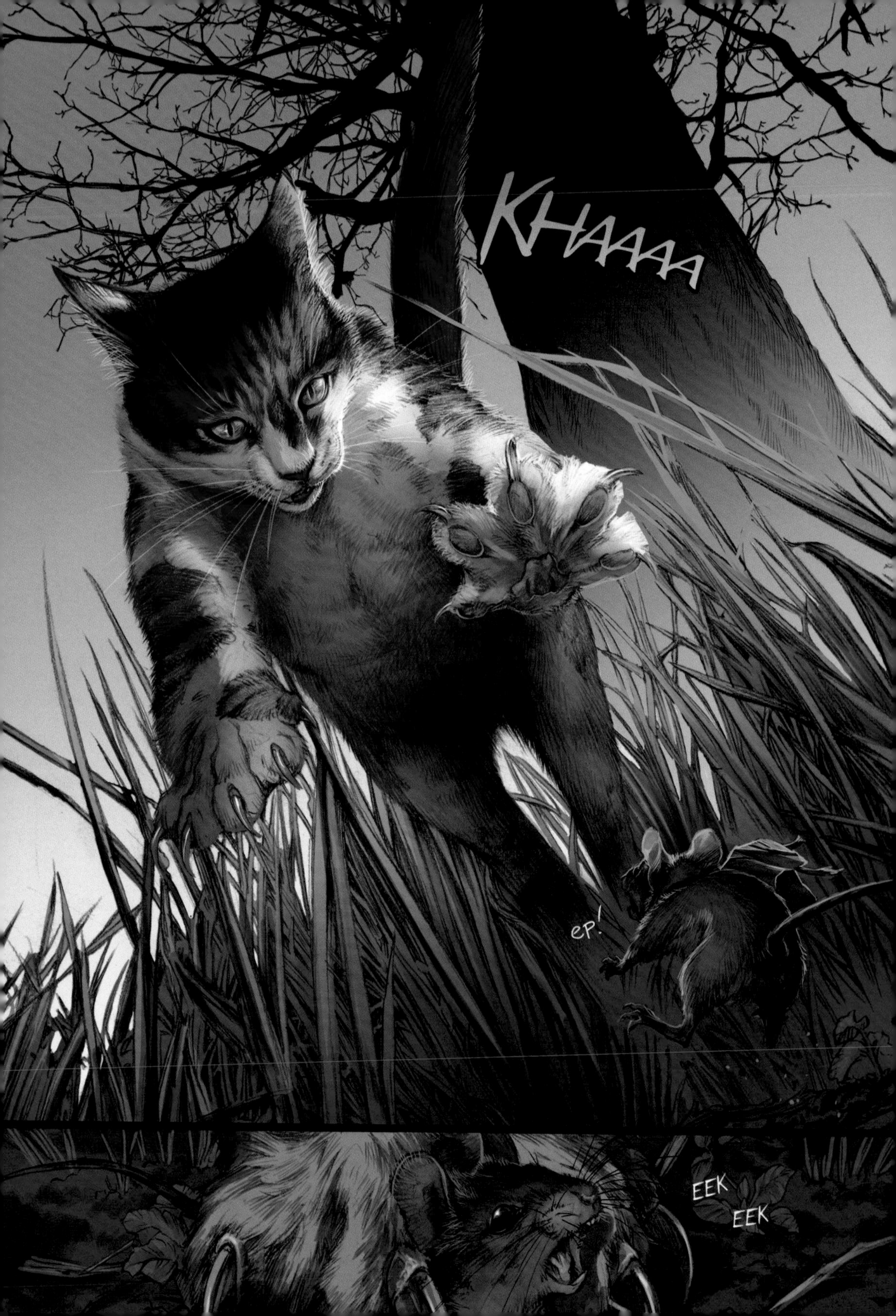
KHAAAA
eP!
EEK
EEK

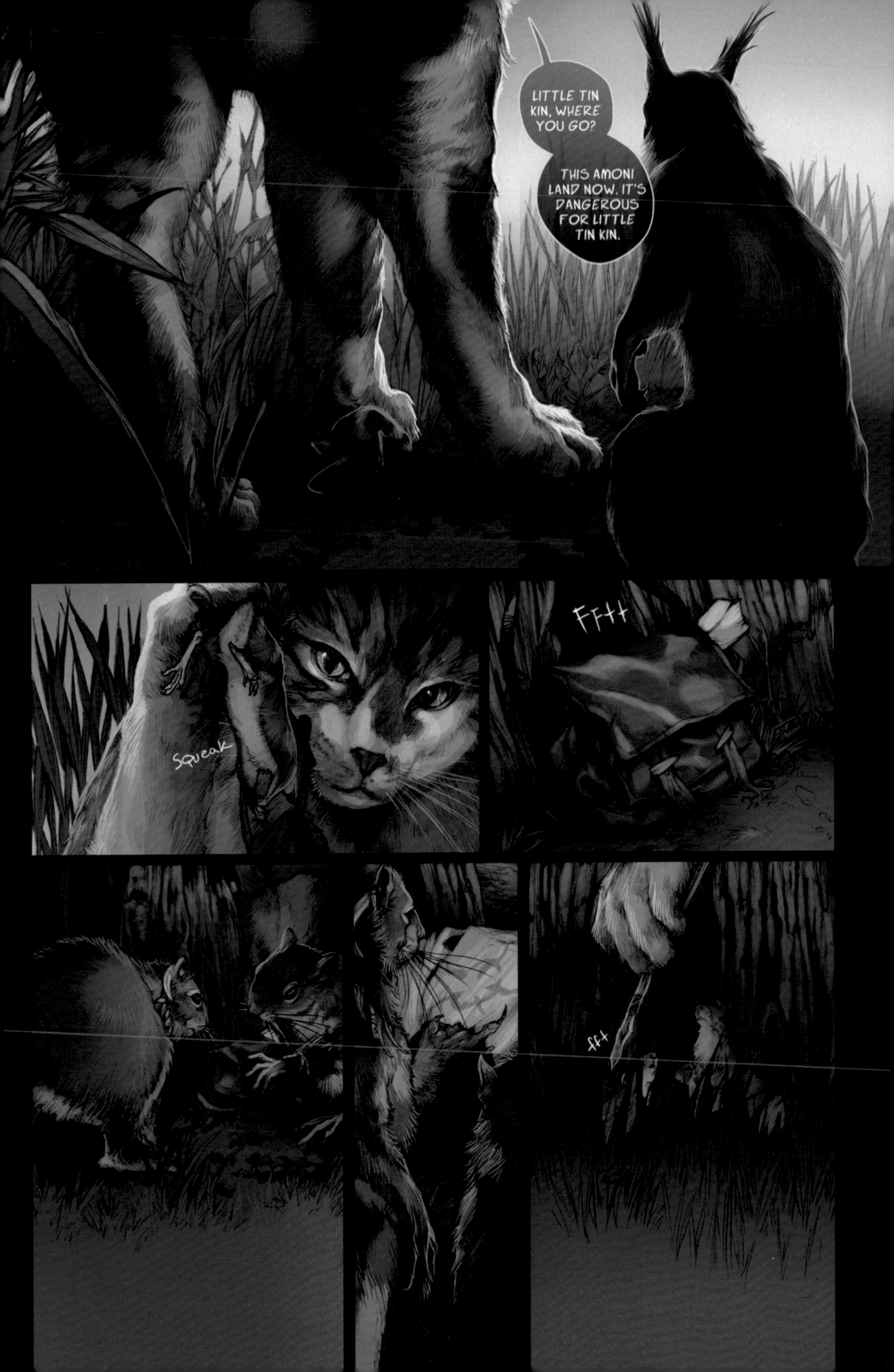
LITTLE TIN KIN, WHERE YOU GO?
THIS AMONI LAND NOW. IT'S DANGEROUS FOR LITTLE TIN KIN.
SQUEAK
FFTT
FFT

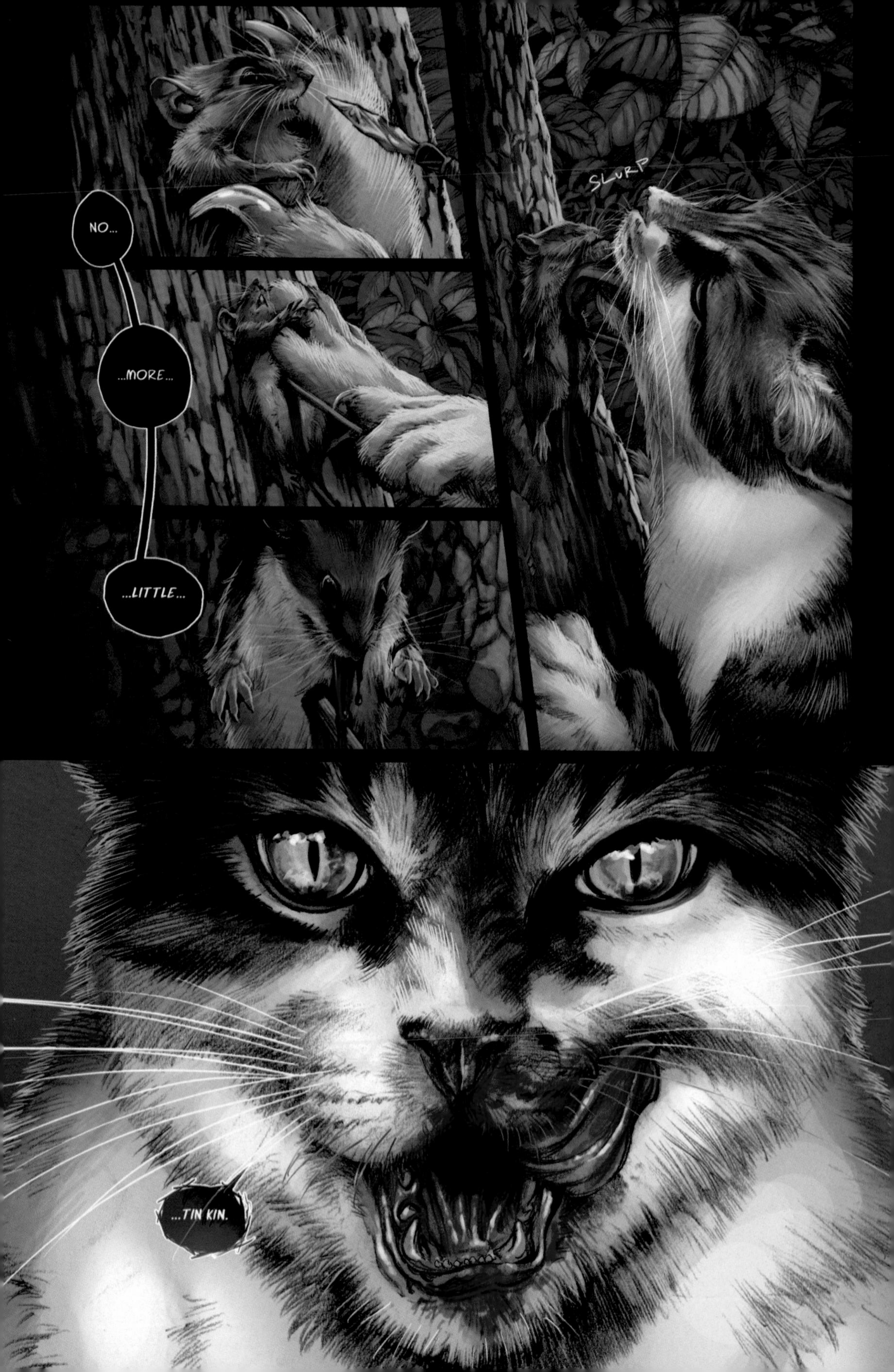
NO...
SLURP
...MORE...
...LITTLE...
...TIN KIN.

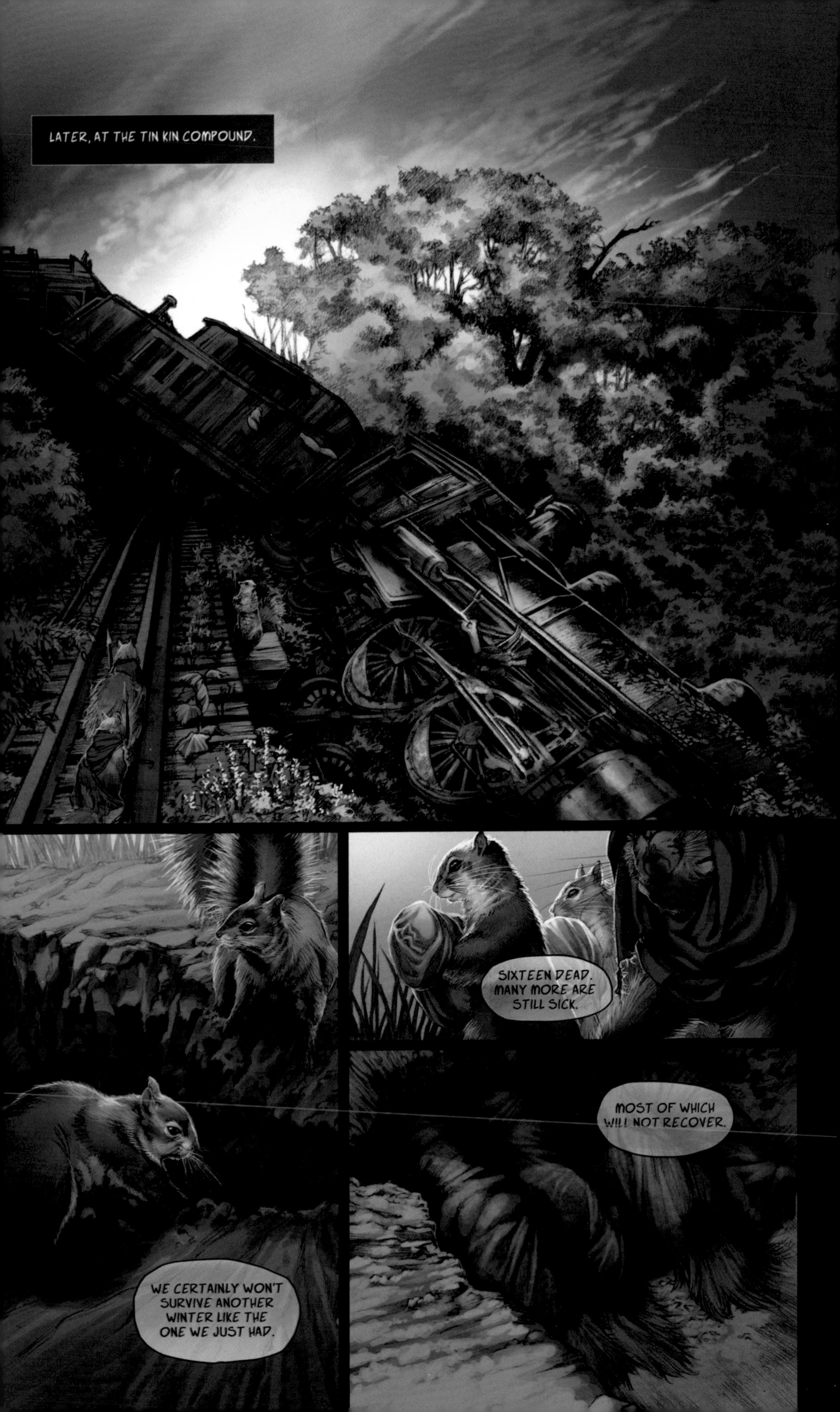
LATER, AT THE TIN KIN COMPOUND.
SIXTEEN DEAD. MANY MORE ARE STILL SICK.
MOST OF WHICH WILL NOT RECOVER.
WE CERTAINLY WON'T SURVIVE ANOTHER WINTER LIKE THE ONE WE JUST HAD.

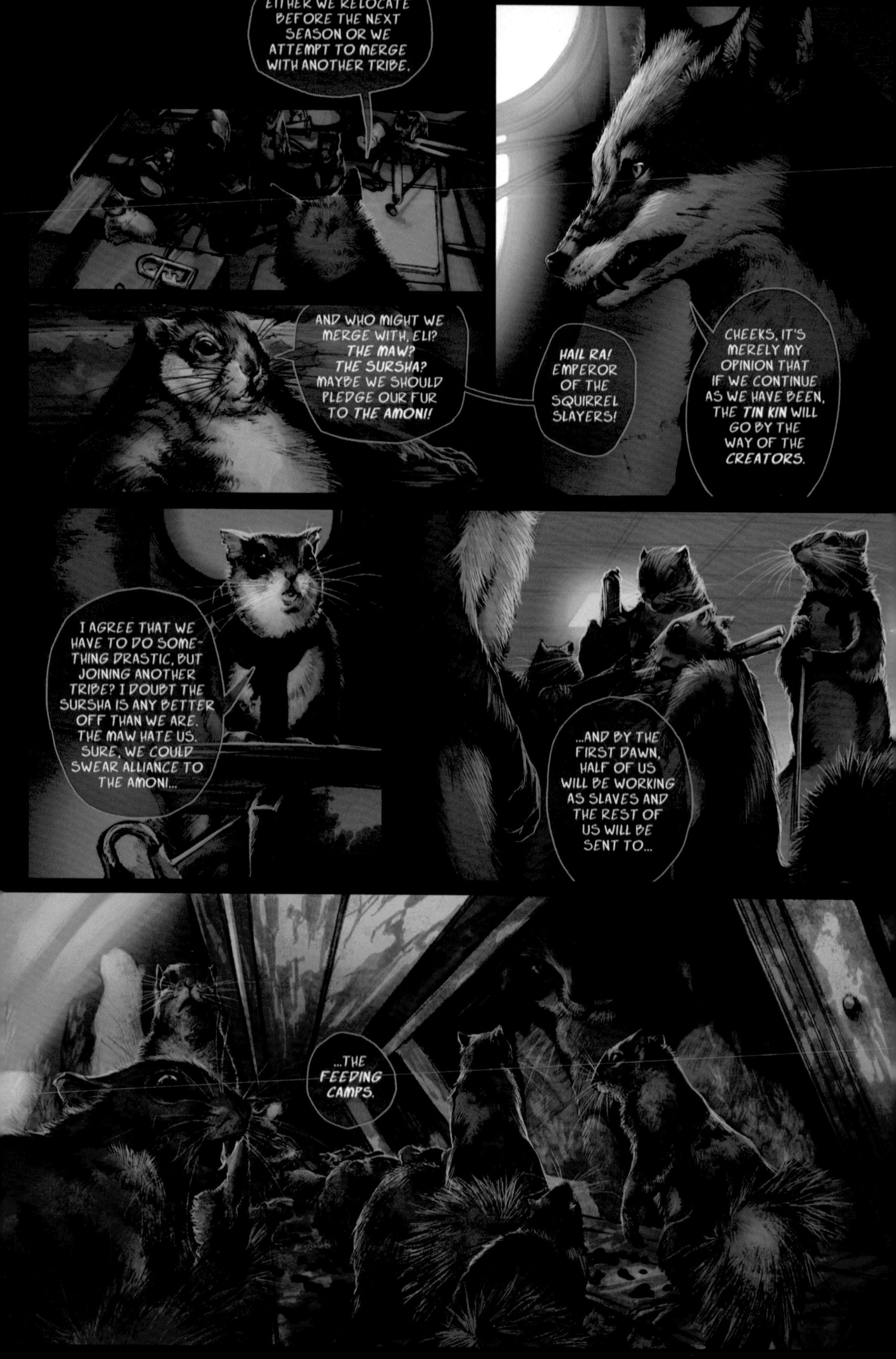
EITHER WE RELOCATE BEFORE THE NEXT SEASON OR WE ATTEMPT TO MERGE WITH ANOTHER TRIBE.
AND WHO MIGHT WE MERGE WITH, ELI? THE MAW? THE SURSHA? MAYBE WE SHOULD PLEDGE OUR FUR TO THE AMONI!
HAIL RA! EMPEROR OF THE SQUIRREL SLAYERS!
CHEEKS, IT'S MERELY MY OPINION THAT IF WE CONTINUE AS WE HAVE BEEN, THE TIN KIN WILL GO BY THE WAY OF THE CREATORS.
I AGREE THAT WE HAVE TO DO SOMETHING DRASTIC, BUT JOINING ANOTHER TRIBE? I DOUBT THE SURSHA IS ANY BETTER OFF THAN WE ARE. THE MAW HATE US. SURE, WE COULD SWEAR ALLIANCE TO THE AMONI...
...AND BY THE FIRST DAWN, HALF OF US WILL BE WORKING AS SLAVES AND THE REST OF US WILL BE SENT TO...
...THE FEEDING CAMPS.

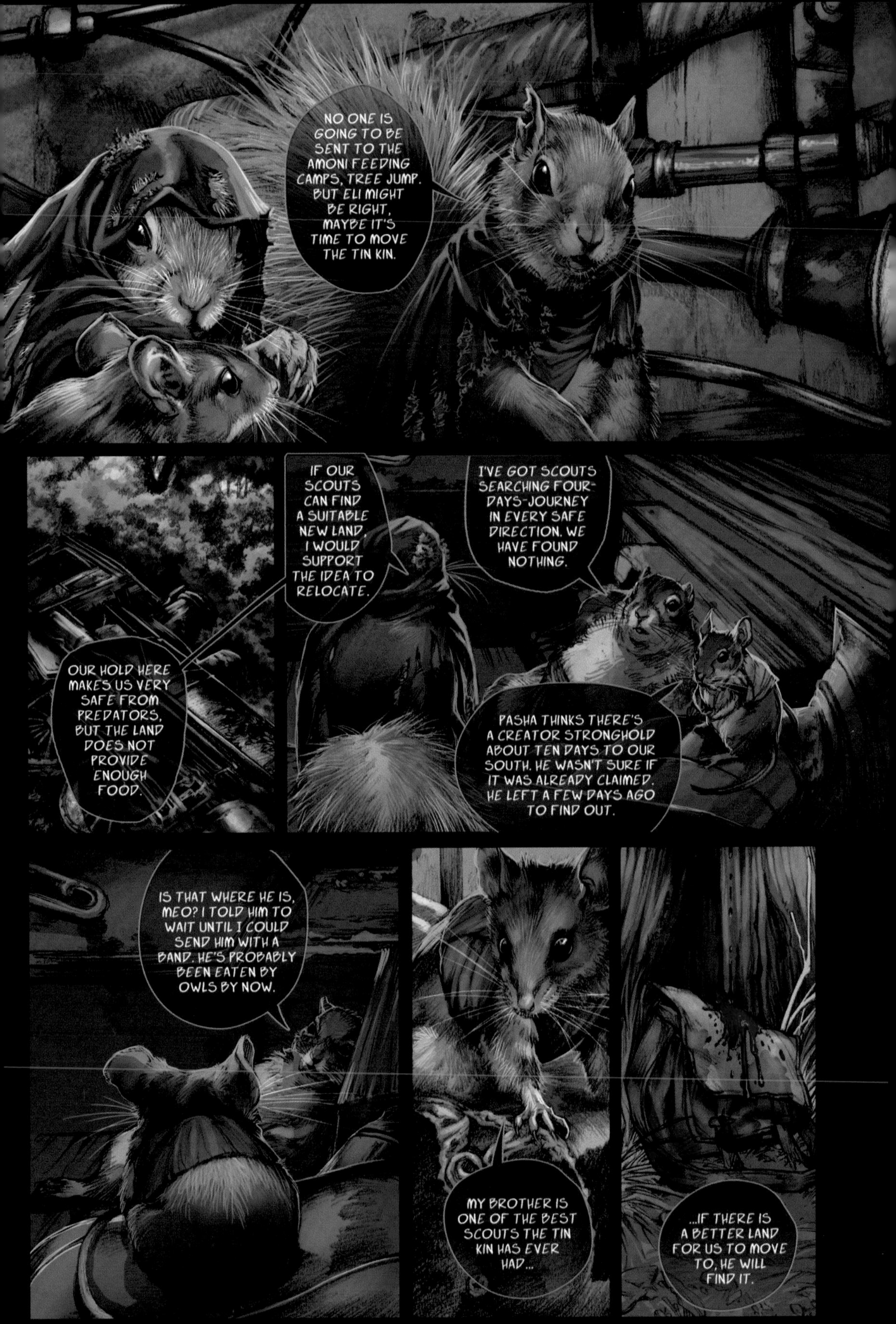
NO ONE IS GOING TO BE SENT TO THE AMONI FEEDING CAMPS, TREE JUMP. BUT ELI MIGHT BE RIGHT, MAYBE IT'S TIME TO MOVE THE TIN KIN.
OUR HOLD HERE MAKES US VERY SAFE FROM PREDATORS, BUT THE LAND DOES NOT PROVIDE ENOUGH FOOD.
IF OUR SCOUTS CAN FIND A SUITABLE NEW LAND, I WOULD SUPPORT THE IDEA TO RELOCATE.
I'VE GOT SCOUTS SEARCHING FOUR-DAYS-JOURNEY IN EVERY SAFE DIRECTION. WE HAVE FOUND NOTHING.
PASHA THINKS THERE'S A CREATOR STRONGHOLD ABOUT TEN DAYS TO OUR SOUTH. HE WASN'T SURE IF IT WAS ALREADY CLAIMED. HE LEFT A FEW DAYS AGO TO FIND OUT.
IS THAT WHERE HE IS, MEO? I TOLD HIM TO WAIT UNTIL I COULD SEND HIM WITH A BAND. HE'S PROBABLY BEEN EATEN BY OWLS BY NOW.
MY BROTHER IS ONE OF THE BEST SCOUTS THE TIN KIN HAS EVER HAD...
...IF THERE IS A BETTER LAND FOR US TO MOVE TO, HE WILL FIND IT.

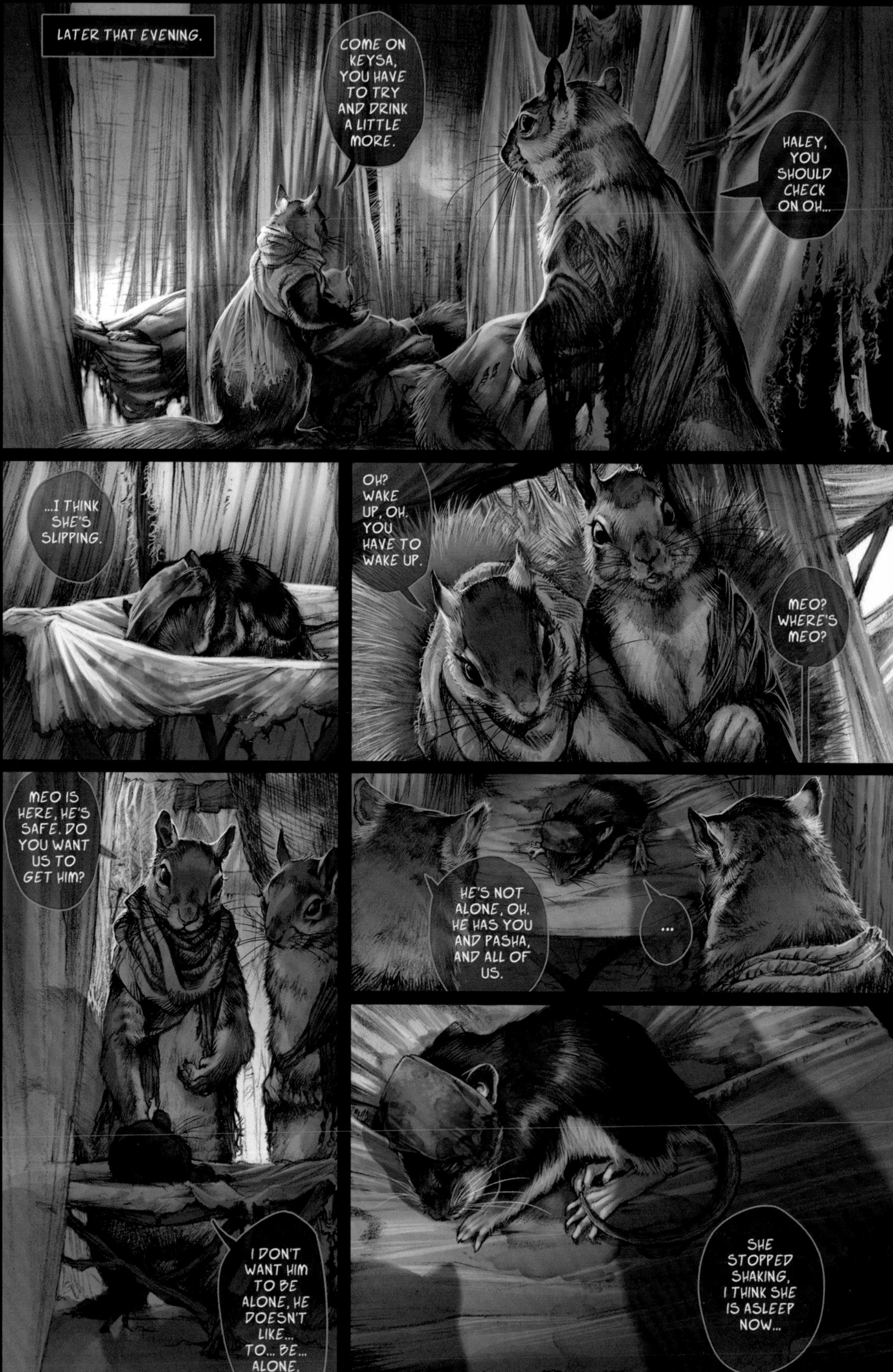
LATER THAT EVENING.
COME ON KEYSA, YOU HAVE TO TRY AND DRINK A LITTLE MORE.
HALEY, YOU SHOULD CHECK ON OH...
...I THINK SHE'S SLIPPING.
OH? WAKE UP, OH. YOU HAVE TO WAKE UP.
MEO? WHERE'S MEO?
MEO IS HERE, HE'S SAFE. DO YOU WANT US TO GET HIM?
HE'S NOT ALONE, OH. HE HAS YOU AND PASHA, AND ALL OF US.
...
I DON'T WANT HIM TO BE ALONE, HE DOESN'T LIKE... TO... BE... ALONE.
SHE STOPPED SHAKING, I THINK SHE IS ASLEEP NOW...

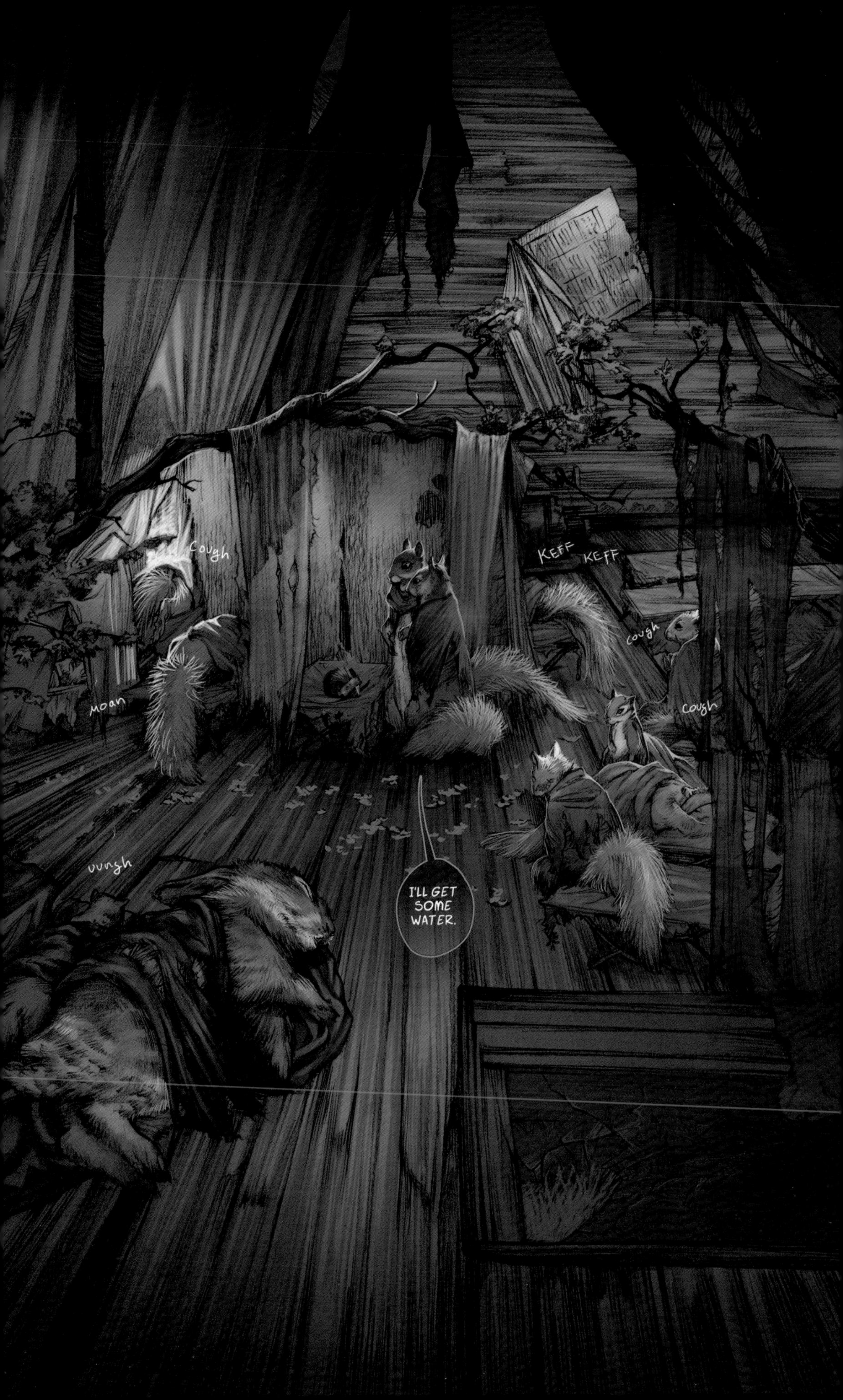
cough
KEFF KEFF
cough
moan
cough
I'LL GET SOME WATER.
uungh

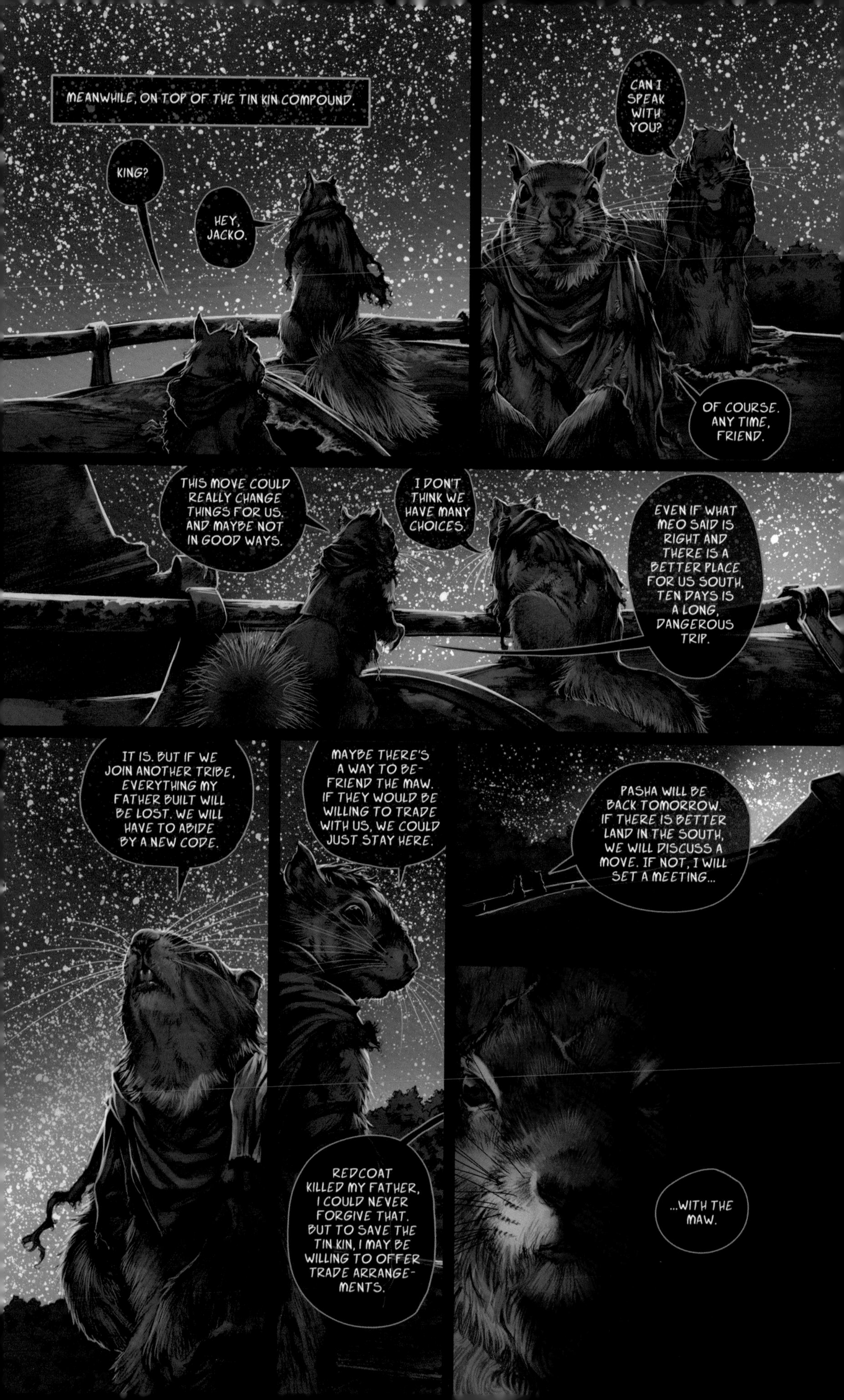
MEANWHILE, ON TOP OF THE TIN KIN COMPOUND.
KING?
HEY, JACKO.
CAN I SPEAK WITH YOU?
OF COURSE. ANY TIME, FRIEND.
THIS MOVE COULD REALLY CHANGE THINGS FOR US, AND MAYBE NOT IN GOOD WAYS.
I DON'T THINK WE HAVE MANY CHOICES.
EVEN IF WHAT MEO SAID IS RIGHT AND THERE IS A BETTER PLACE FOR US SOUTH, TEN DAYS IS A LONG, DANGEROUS TRIP.
IT IS. BUT IF WE JOIN ANOTHER TRIBE, EVERYTHING MY FATHER BUILT WILL BE LOST. WE WILL HAVE TO ABIDE BY A NEW CODE.
MAYBE THERE'S A WAY TO BE-FRIEND THE MAW. IF THEY WOULD BE WILLING TO TRADE WITH US, WE COULD JUST STAY HERE.
REDCOAT KILLED MY FATHER, I COULD NEVER FORGIVE THAT. BUT TO SAVE THE TIN KIN, I MAY BE WILLING TO OFFER TRADE ARRANGE-MENTS.
PASHA WILL BE BACK TOMORROW. IF THERE IS BETTER LAND IN THE SOUTH, WE WILL DISCUSS A MOVE. IF NOT, I WILL SET A MEETING...
...WITH THE MAW.

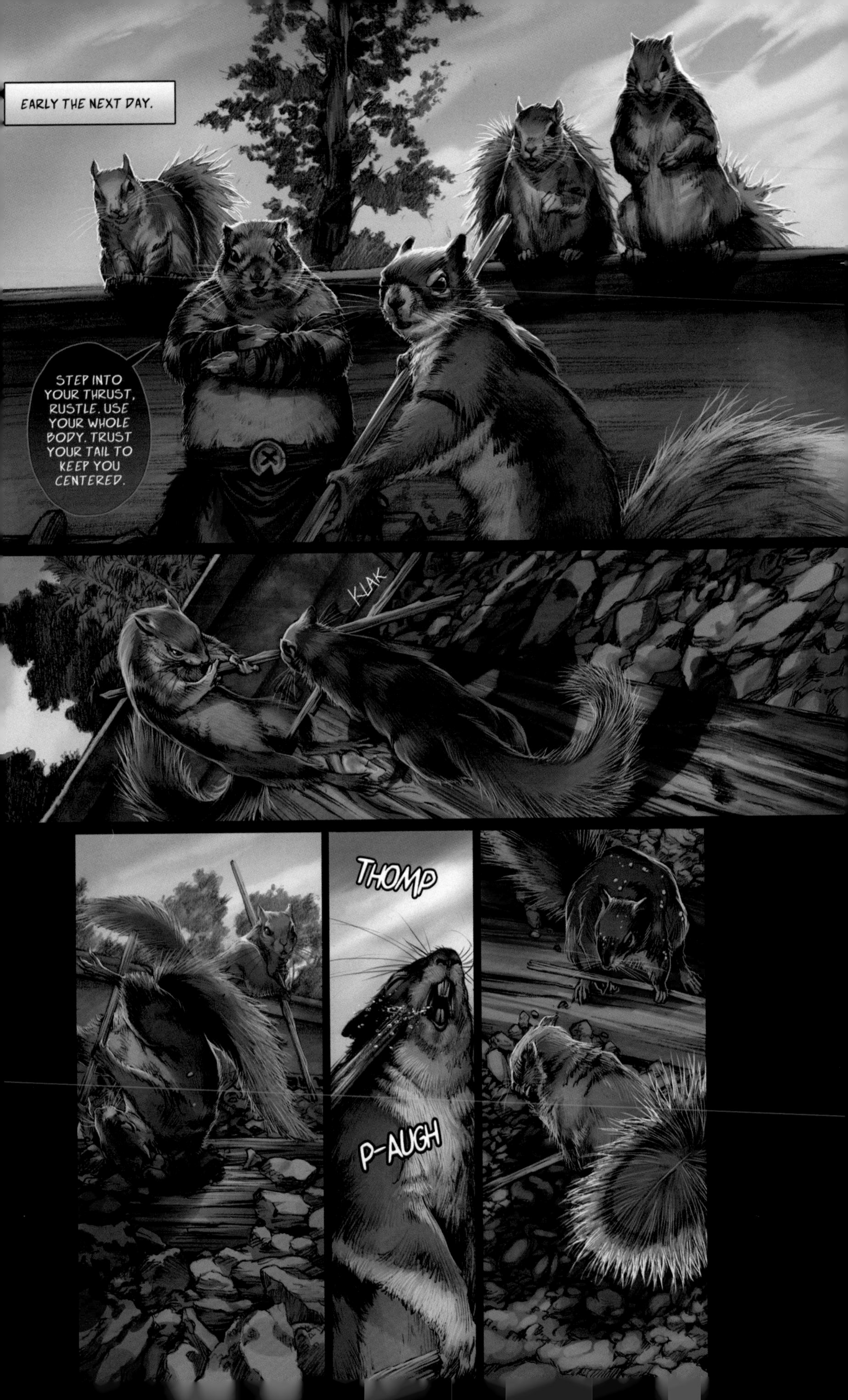
EARLY THE NEXT DAY.
STEP INTO YOUR THRUST, RUSTLE. USE YOUR WHOLE BODY. TRUST YOUR TAIL TO KEEP YOU CENTERED.
KLAK
THOMP
P-AUGH

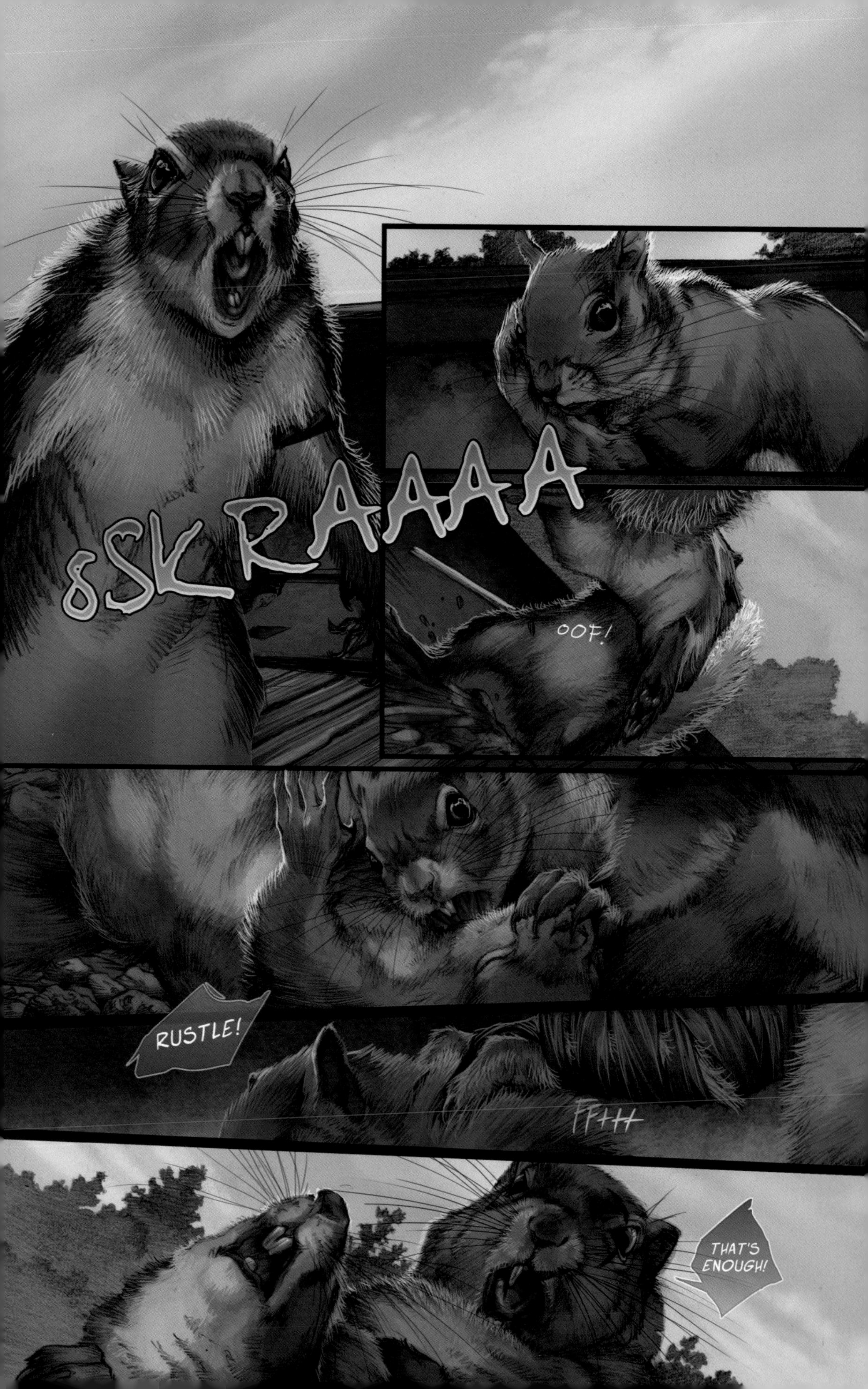
SKRAAAA
OOF!
RUSTLE!
FFTT
THAT'S ENOUGH!

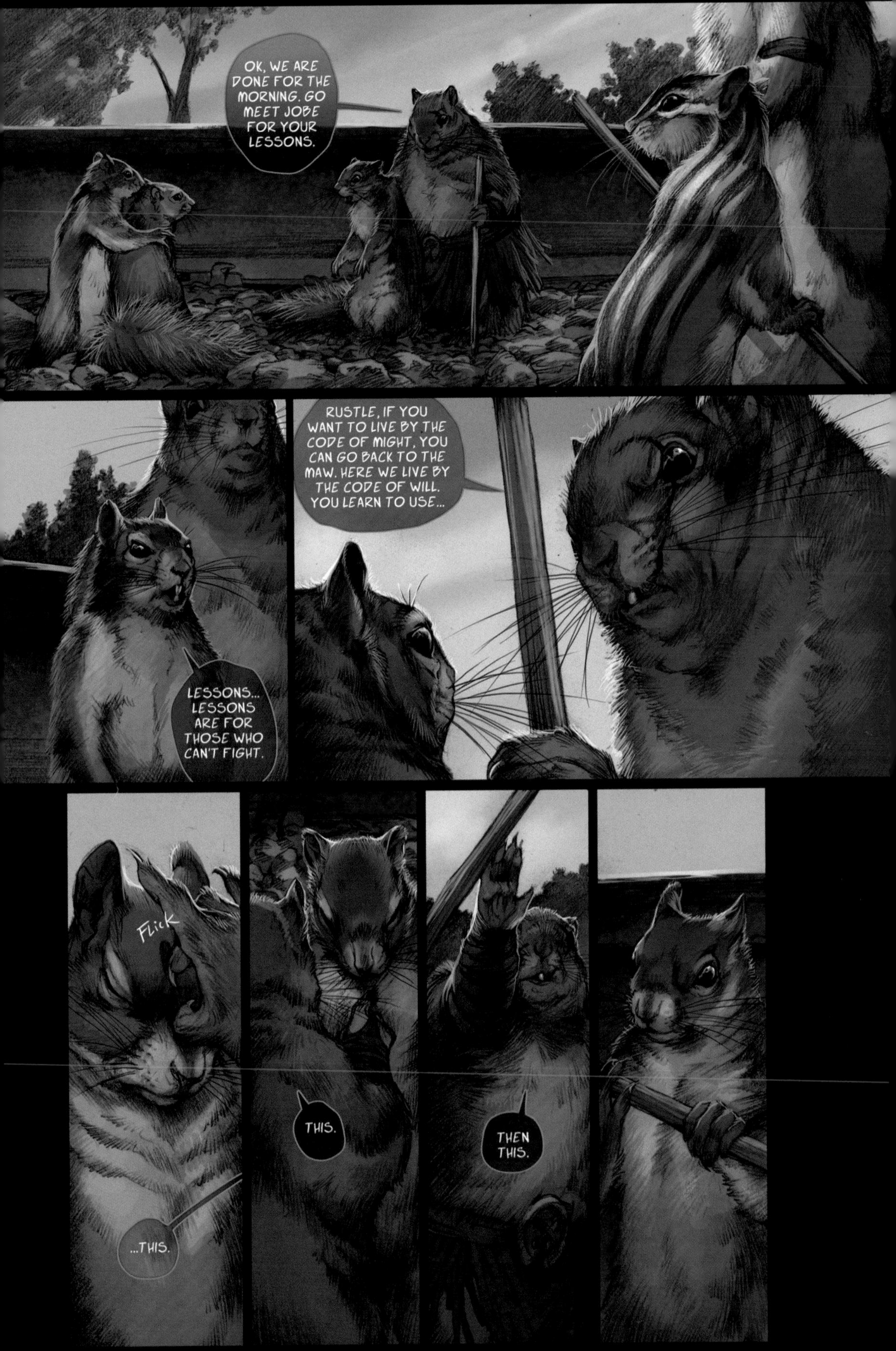

OK, WE ARE DONE FOR THE MORNING. GO MEET JOBE FOR YOUR LESSONS.
LESSONS... LESSONS ARE FOR THOSE WHO CAN'T FIGHT.
RUSTLE, IF YOU WANT TO LIVE BY THE CODE OF MIGHT, YOU CAN GO BACK TO THE MAW. HERE WE LIVE BY THE CODE OF WILL. YOU LEARN TO USE...
FLICK
...THIS.
THIS.
THEN THIS.

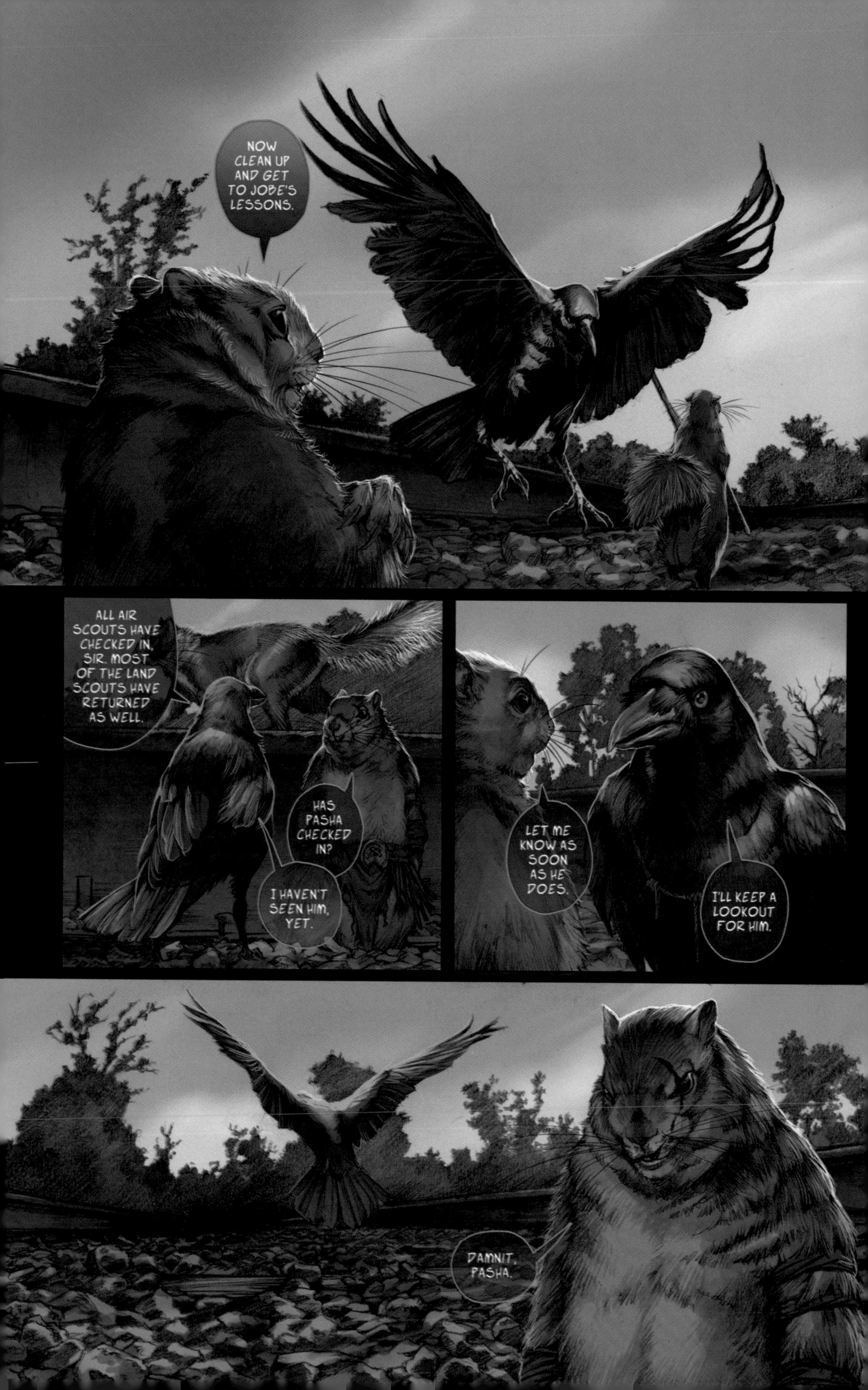
NOW CLEAN UP AND GET TO JOBE'S LESSONS.
ALL AIR SCOUTS HAVE CHECKED IN, SIR. MOST OF THE LAND SCOUTS HAVE RETURNED AS WELL.
HAS PASHA CHECKED IN?
I HAVEN'T SEEN HIM, YET.
LET ME KNOW AS SOON AS HE DOES.
I'LL KEEP A LOOKOUT FOR HIM.
DAMNIT, PASHA.

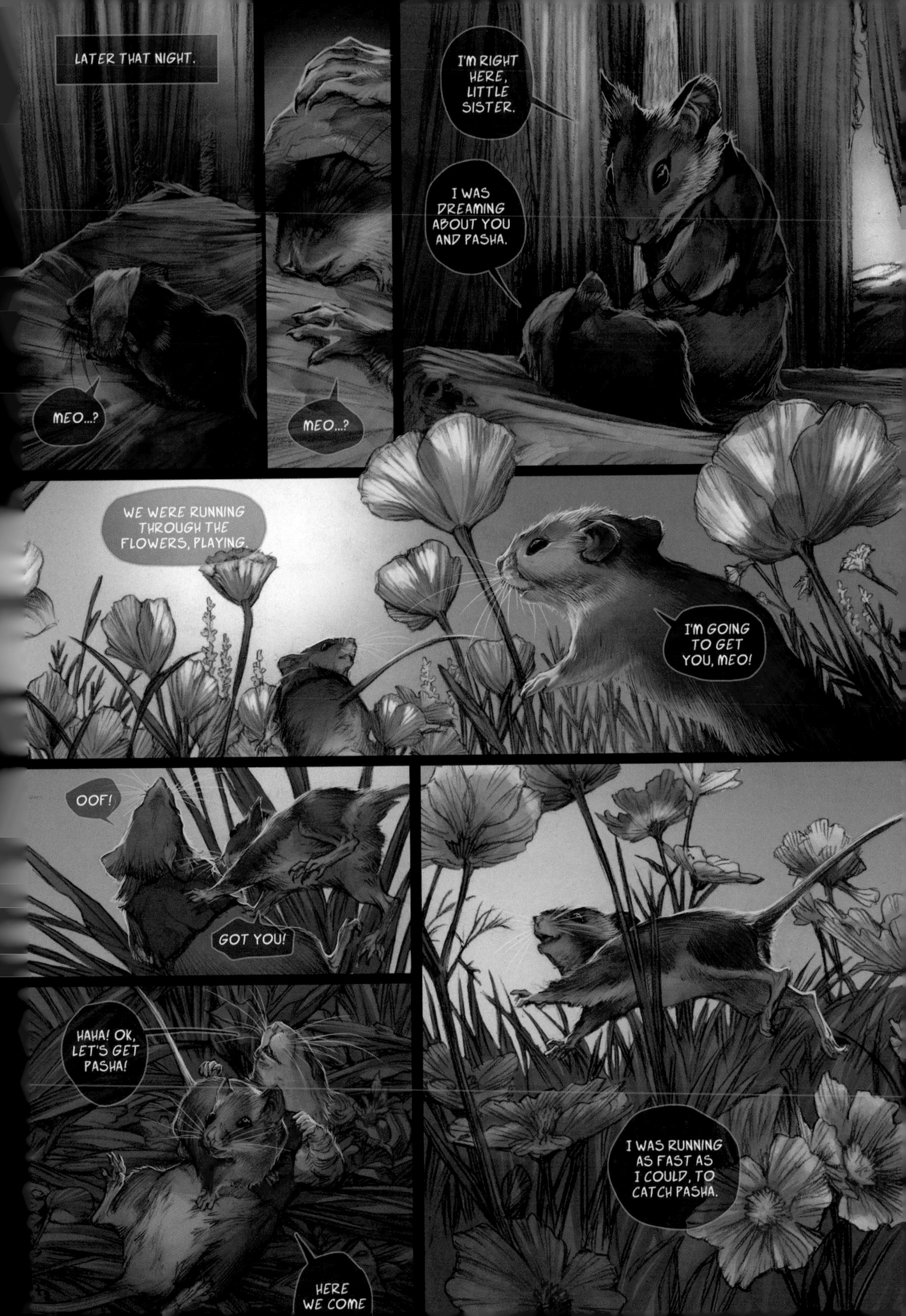
LATER THAT NIGHT.
MEO...?
MEO...?
I'M RIGHT HERE, LITTLE SISTER.
I WAS DREAMING ABOUT YOU AND PASHA.
WE WERE RUNNING THROUGH THE FLOWERS, PLAYING.
I'M GOING TO GET YOU, MEO!
OOF!
GOT YOU!
HAHA! OK, LET'S GET PASHA!
HERE WE COME
I WAS RUNNING AS FAST AS I COULD, TO CATCH PASHA.

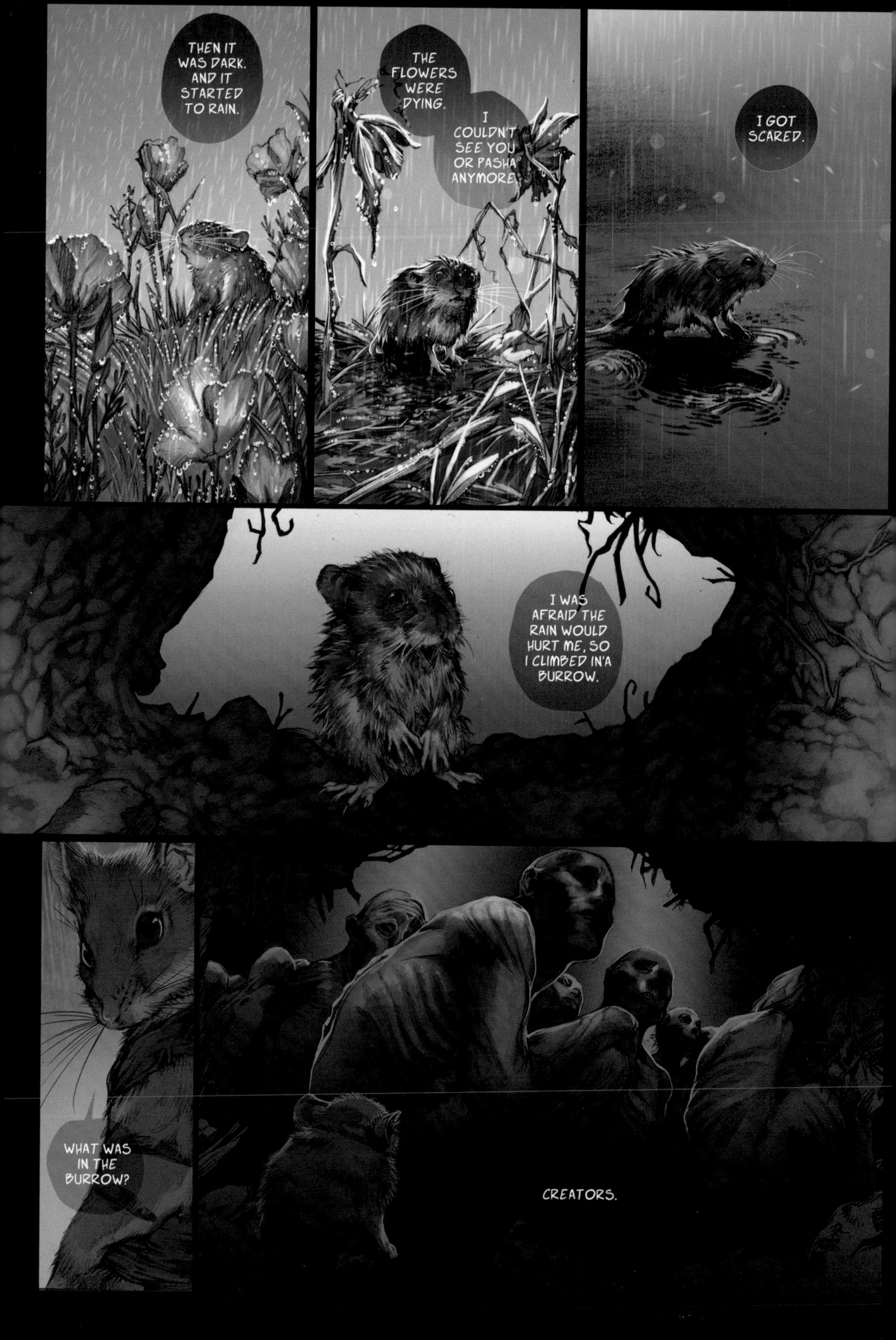

THEN IT WAS DARK. AND IT STARTED TO RAIN.
THE FLOWERS WERE DYING.
I COULDN'T SEE YOU OR PASHA ANYMORE.
I GOT SCARED.
I WAS AFRAID THE RAIN WOULD HURT ME, SO I CLIMBED IN'A BURROW.
WHAT WAS IN THE BURROW?
CREATORS.

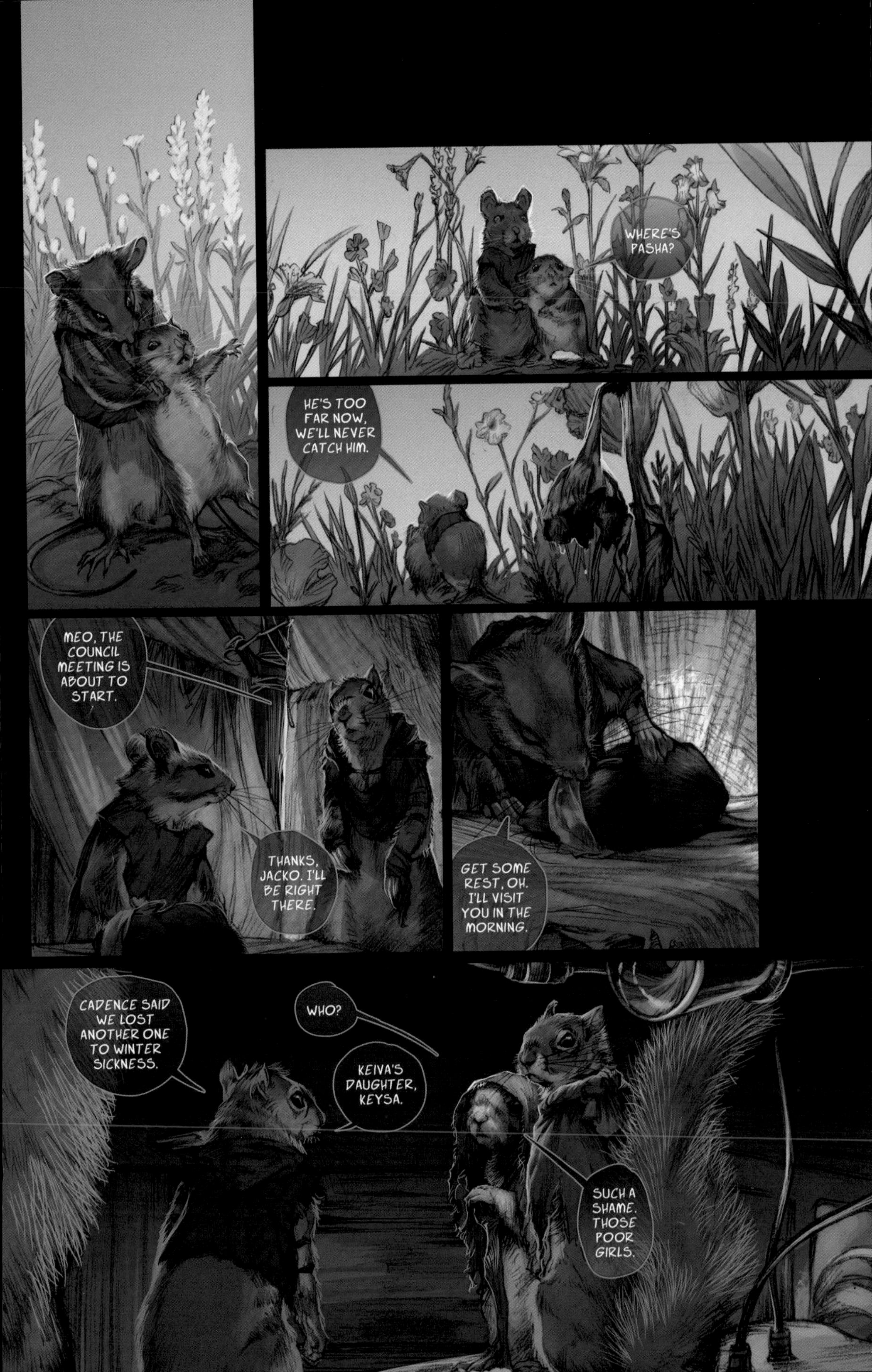
WHERE'S PASHA?
HE'S TOO FAR NOW, WE'LL NEVER CATCH HIM.
MEO, THE COUNCIL MEETING IS ABOUT TO START.
THANKS, JACKO. I'LL BE RIGHT THERE.
GET SOME REST, OH. I'LL VISIT YOU IN THE MORNING.
CADENCE SAID WE LOST ANOTHER ONE TO WINTER SICKNESS.
WHO?
KEIVA'S DAUGHTER, KEYSA.
SUCH A SHAME. THOSE POOR GIRLS.

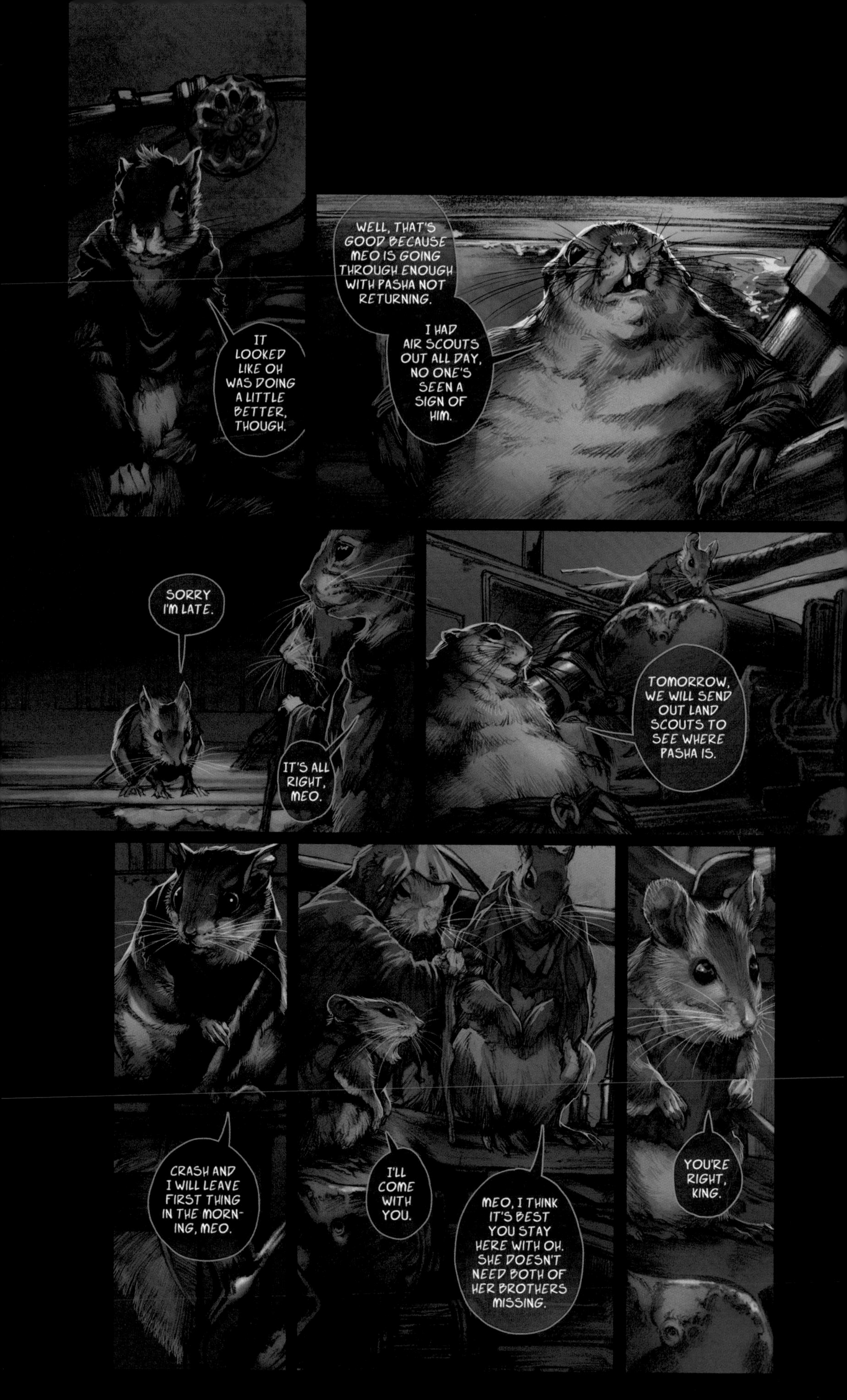
IT LOOKED LIKE OH WAS DOING A LITTLE BETTER, THOUGH.
WELL, THAT'S GOOD BECAUSE MEO IS GOING THROUGH ENOUGH WITH PASHA NOT RETURNING.
I HAD AIR SCOUTS OUT ALL DAY, NO ONE'S SEEN A SIGN OF HIM.
SORRY I'M LATE.
IT'S ALL RIGHT, MEO.
TOMORROW, WE WILL SEND OUT LAND SCOUTS TO SEE WHERE PASHA IS.
CRASH AND I WILL LEAVE FIRST THING IN THE MORN-ING, MEO.
I'LL COME WITH YOU.
MEO, I THINK IT'S BEST YOU STAY HERE WITH OH. SHE DOESN'T NEED BOTH OF HER BROTHERS MISSING.
YOU'RE RIGHT, KING.

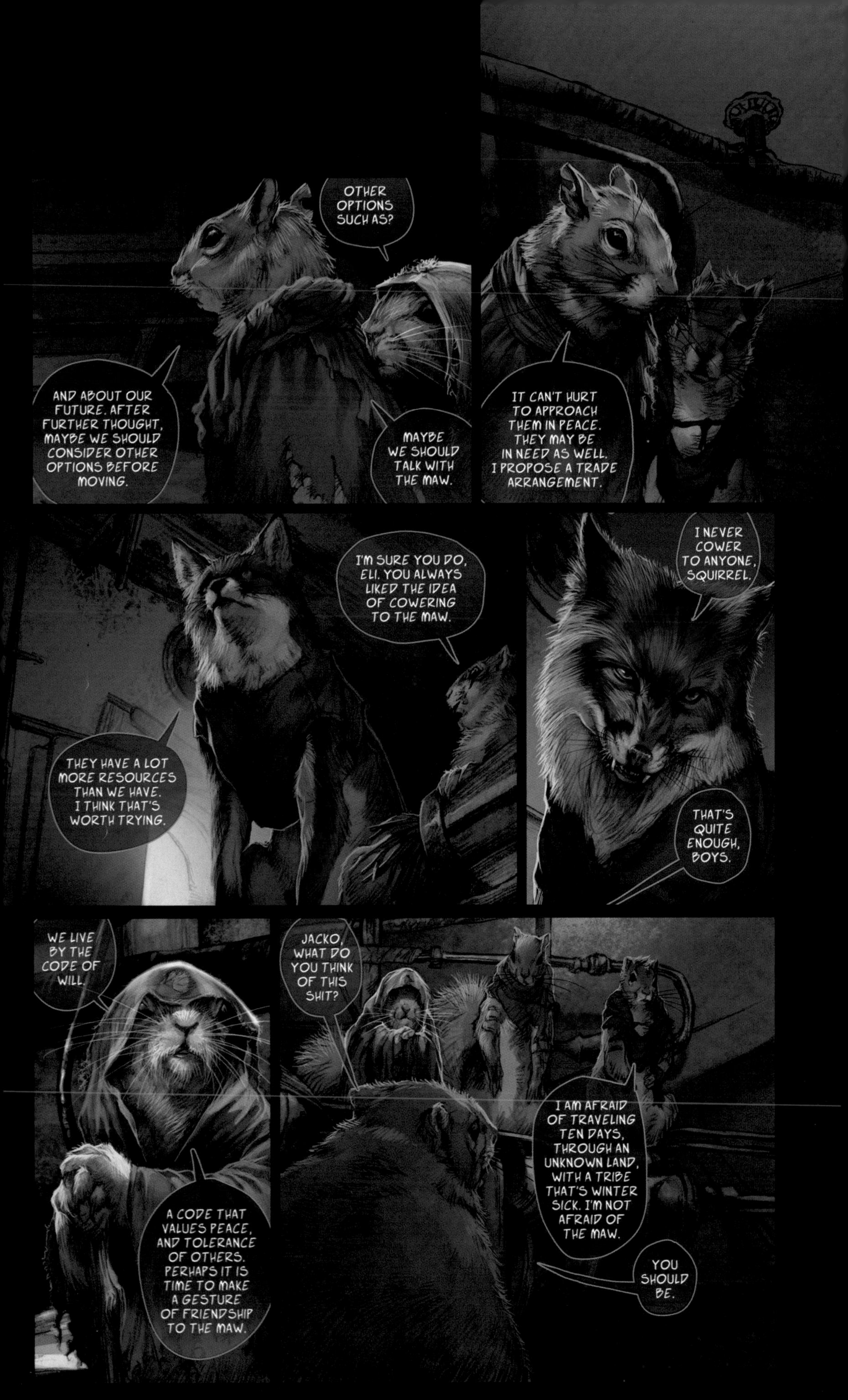
OTHER OPTIONS SUCH AS?
AND ABOUT OUR FUTURE. AFTER FURTHER THOUGHT, MAYBE WE SHOULD CONSIDER OTHER OPTIONS BEFORE MOVING.
MAYBE WE SHOULD TALK WITH THE MAW.
IT CAN'T HURT TO APPROACH THEM IN PEACE. THEY MAY BE IN NEED AS WELL. I PROPOSE A TRADE ARRANGEMENT.
I'M SURE YOU DO, ELI. YOU ALWAYS LIKED THE IDEA OF COWERING TO THE MAW.
THEY HAVE A LOT MORE RESOURCES THAN WE HAVE. I THINK THAT'S WORTH TRYING.
I NEVER COWER TO ANYONE, SQUIRREL.
THAT'S QUITE ENOUGH, BOYS.
WE LIVE BY THE CODE OF WILL.
A CODE THAT VALUES PEACE, AND TOLERANCE OF OTHERS. PERHAPS IT IS TIME TO MAKE A GESTURE OF FRIENDSHIP TO THE MAW.
JACKO, WHAT DO YOU THINK OF THIS SHIT?
I AM AFRAID OF TRAVELING TEN DAYS, THROUGH AN UNKNOWN LAND, WITH A TRIBE THAT'S WINTER SICK. I'M NOT AFRAID OF THE MAW.
YOU SHOULD BE.

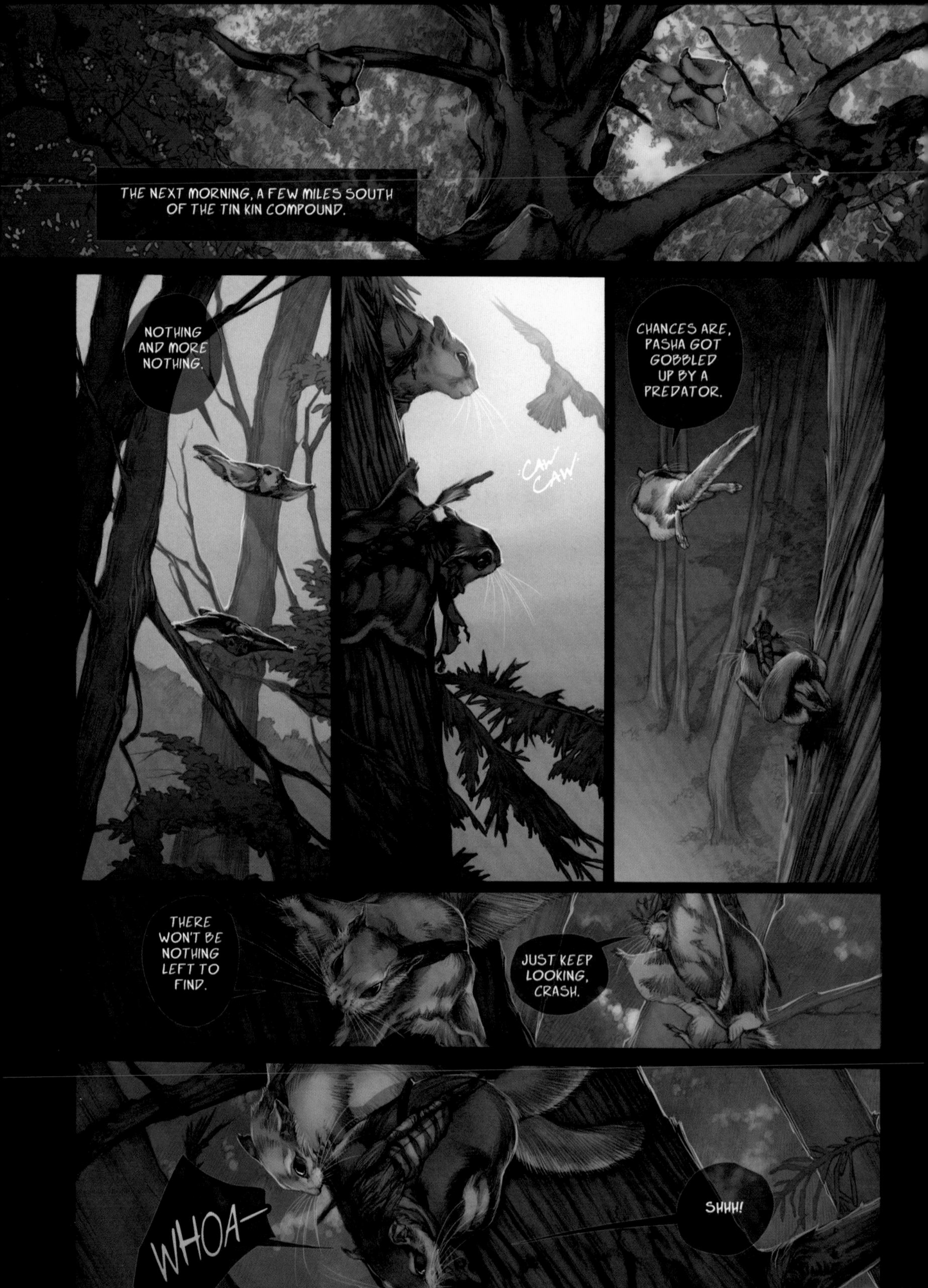
THE NEXT MORNING, A FEW MILES SOUTH OF THE TIN KIN COMPOUND.
NOTHING AND MORE NOTHING.
CAW CAW
CHANCES ARE, PASHA GOT GOBBLED UP BY A PREDATOR.
THERE WON'T BE NOTHING LEFT TO FIND.
JUST KEEP LOOKING, CRASH.
WHOA—
SHHH!

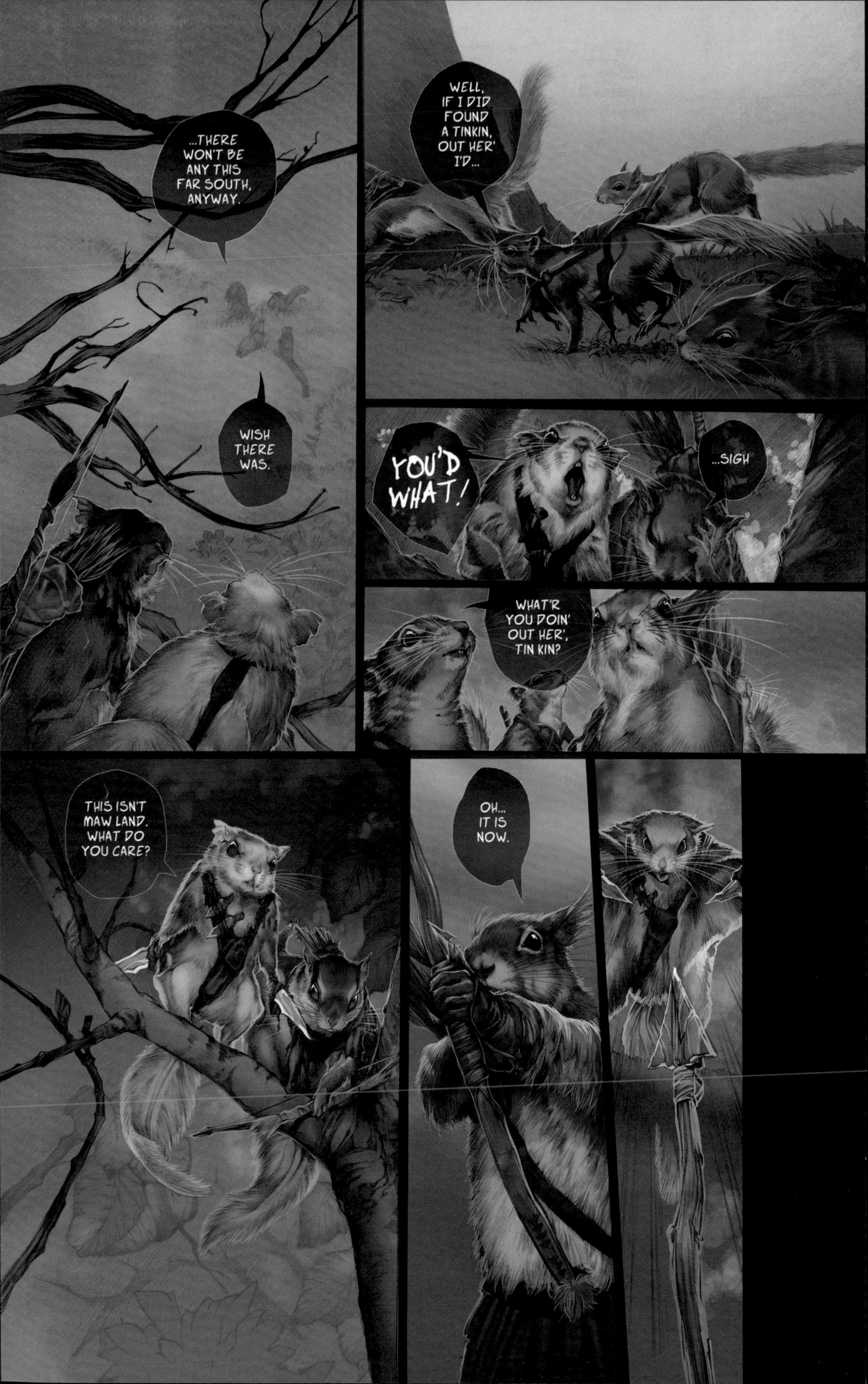

...THERE WON'T BE ANY THIS FAR SOUTH, ANYWAY.
WISH THERE WAS.
WELL, IF I DID FOUND A TINKIN, OUT HER' I'D...
YOU'D WHAT!
...SIGH
WHAT'R YOU DOIN' OUT HER', TIN KIN?
THIS ISN'T MAW LAND. WHAT DO YOU CARE?
OH... IT IS NOW.

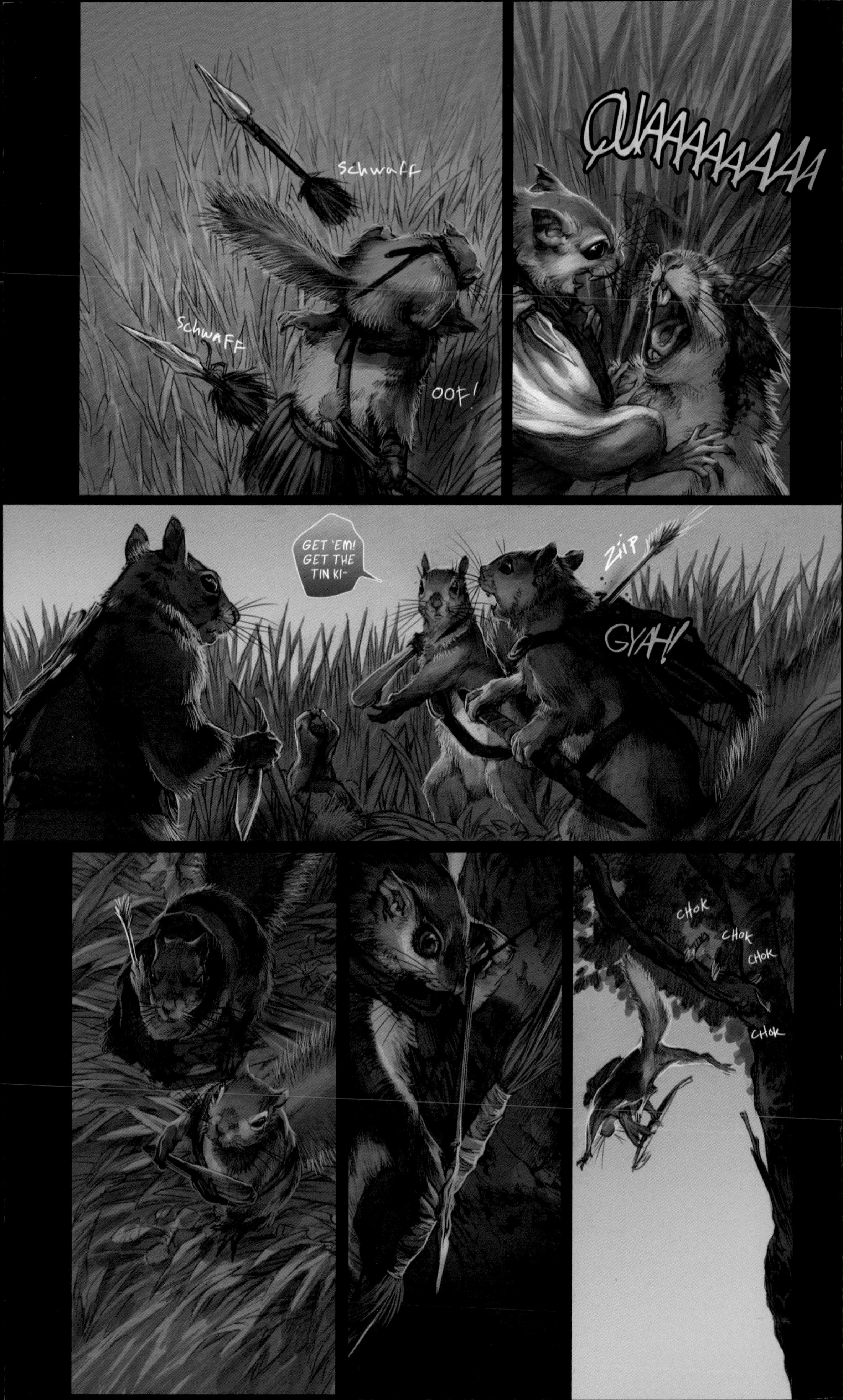

SCHWAFF
SCHWAFF
OOF!
QUAAAAAAAAA
GET 'EM! GET THE TIN KI-
ZIP
GYAH!
CHOK
CHOK
CHOK
CHOK

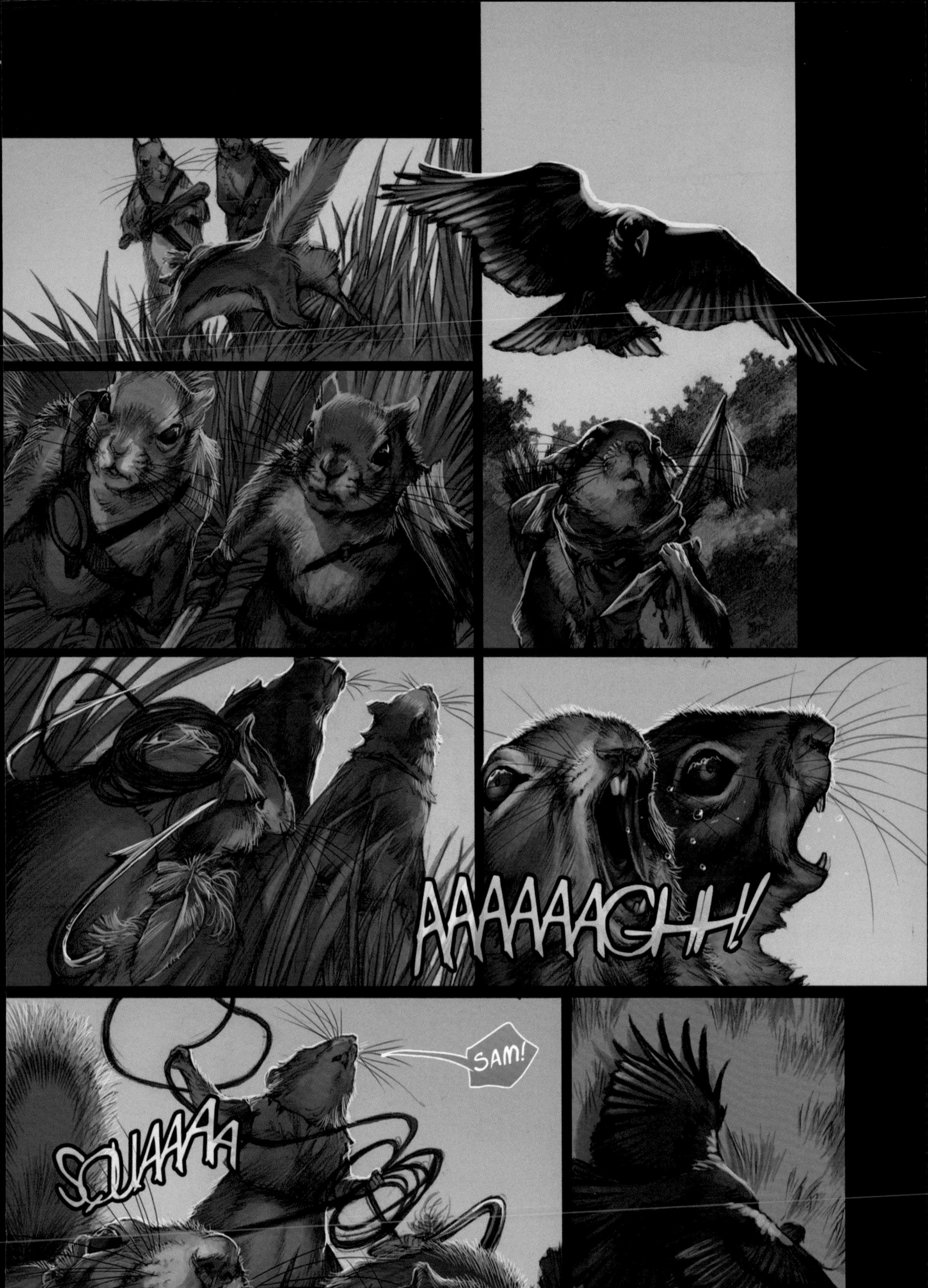
AAAAAAGHH!
SAM!
SQUAAAA

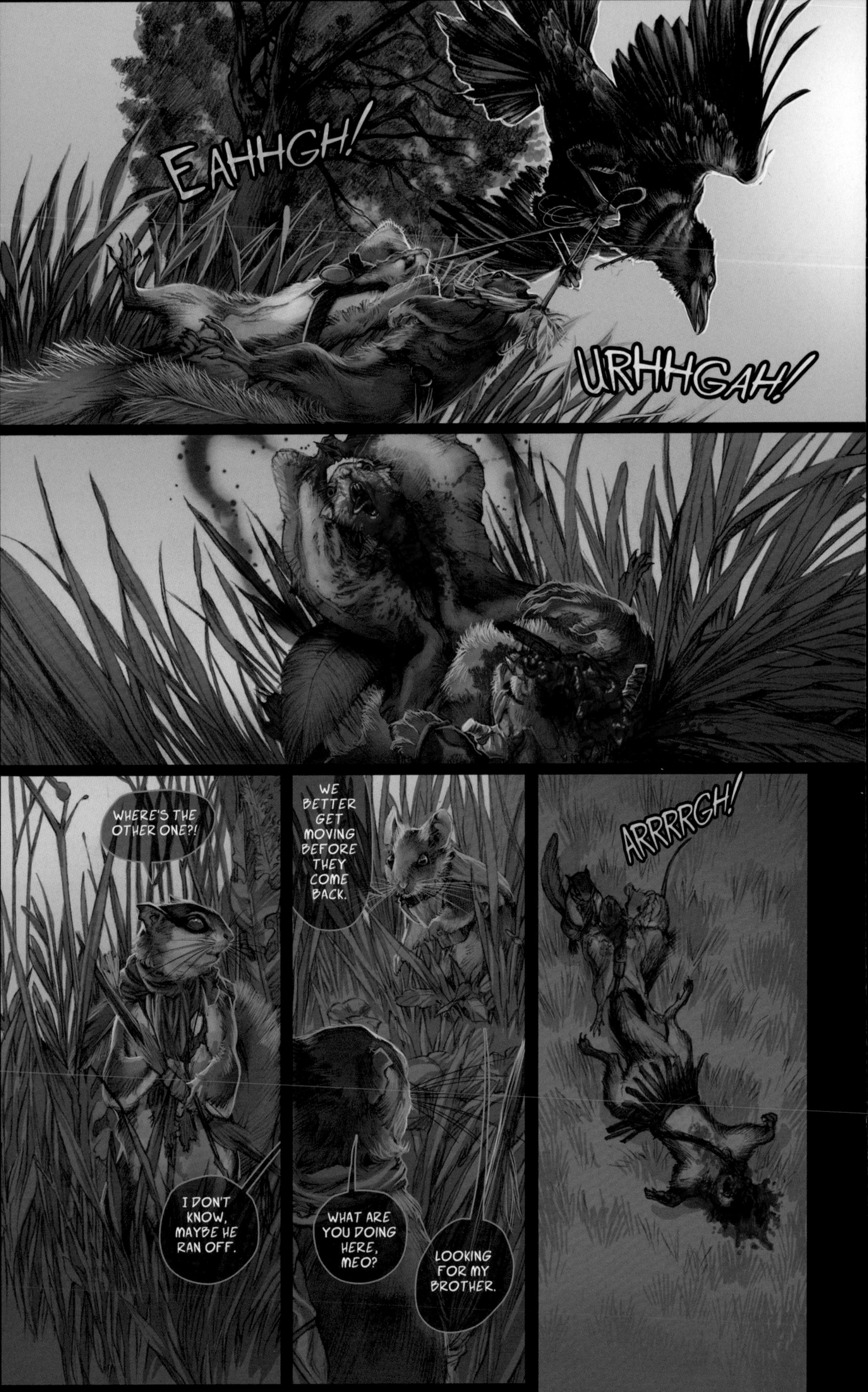
EAHHGH!
URHHGAH!
WHERE'S THE OTHER ONE?!
I DON'T KNOW, MAYBE HE RAN OFF.
WE BETTER GET MOVING BEFORE THEY COME BACK.
WHAT ARE YOU DOING HERE, MEO?
LOOKING FOR MY BROTHER.
ARRRRGH!

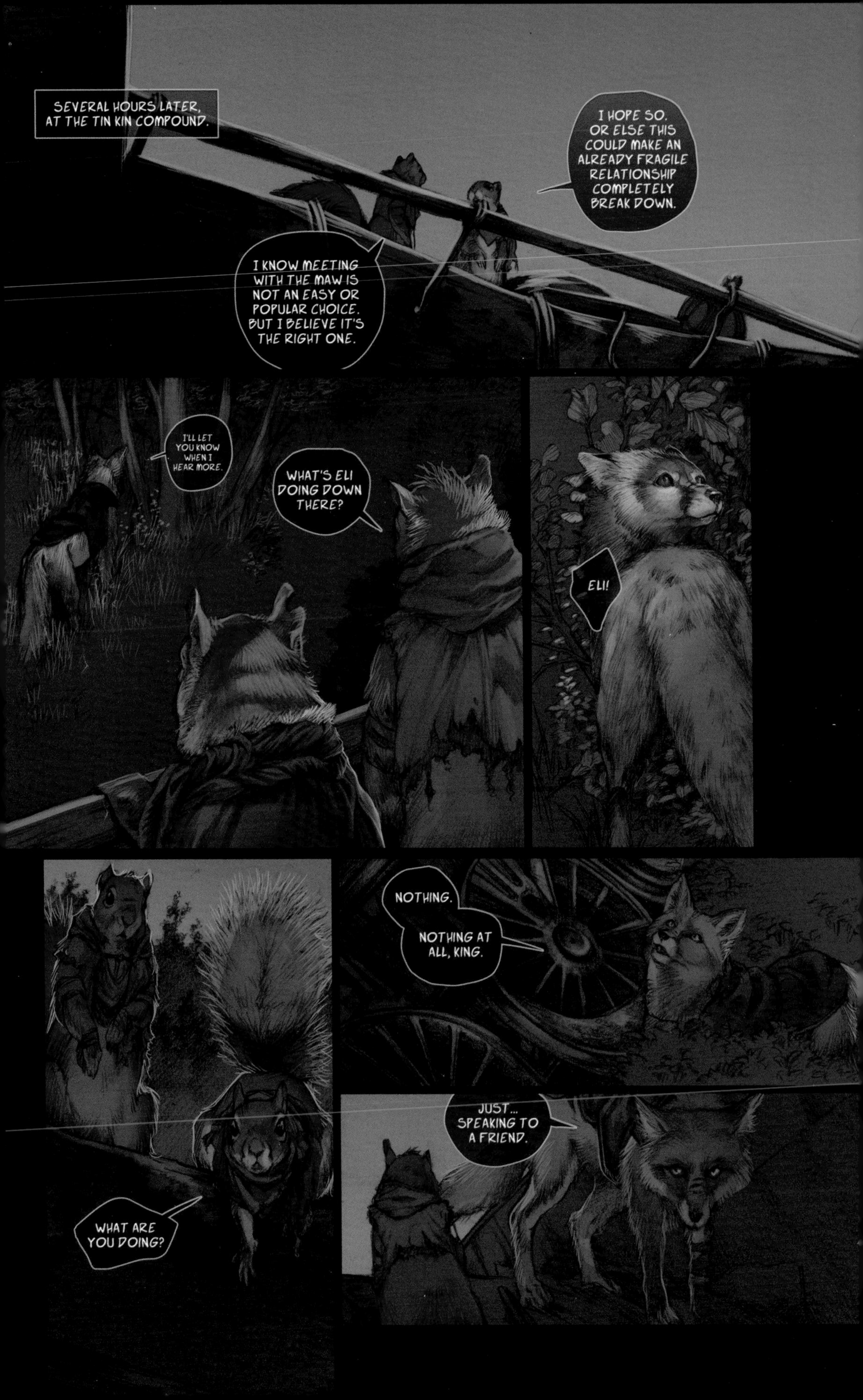
SEVERAL HOURS LATER, AT THE TIN KIN COMPOUND.
I KNOW MEETING WITH THE MAW IS NOT AN EASY OR POPULAR CHOICE. BUT I BELIEVE IT'S THE RIGHT ONE.
I HOPE SO. OR ELSE THIS COULD MAKE AN ALREADY FRAGILE RELATIONSHIP COMPLETELY BREAK DOWN.
I'LL LET YOU KNOW WHEN I HEAR MORE.
WHAT'S ELI DOING DOWN THERE?
ELI!
WHAT ARE YOU DOING?
NOTHING.
NOTHING AT ALL, KING.
JUST... SPEAKING TO A FRIEND.

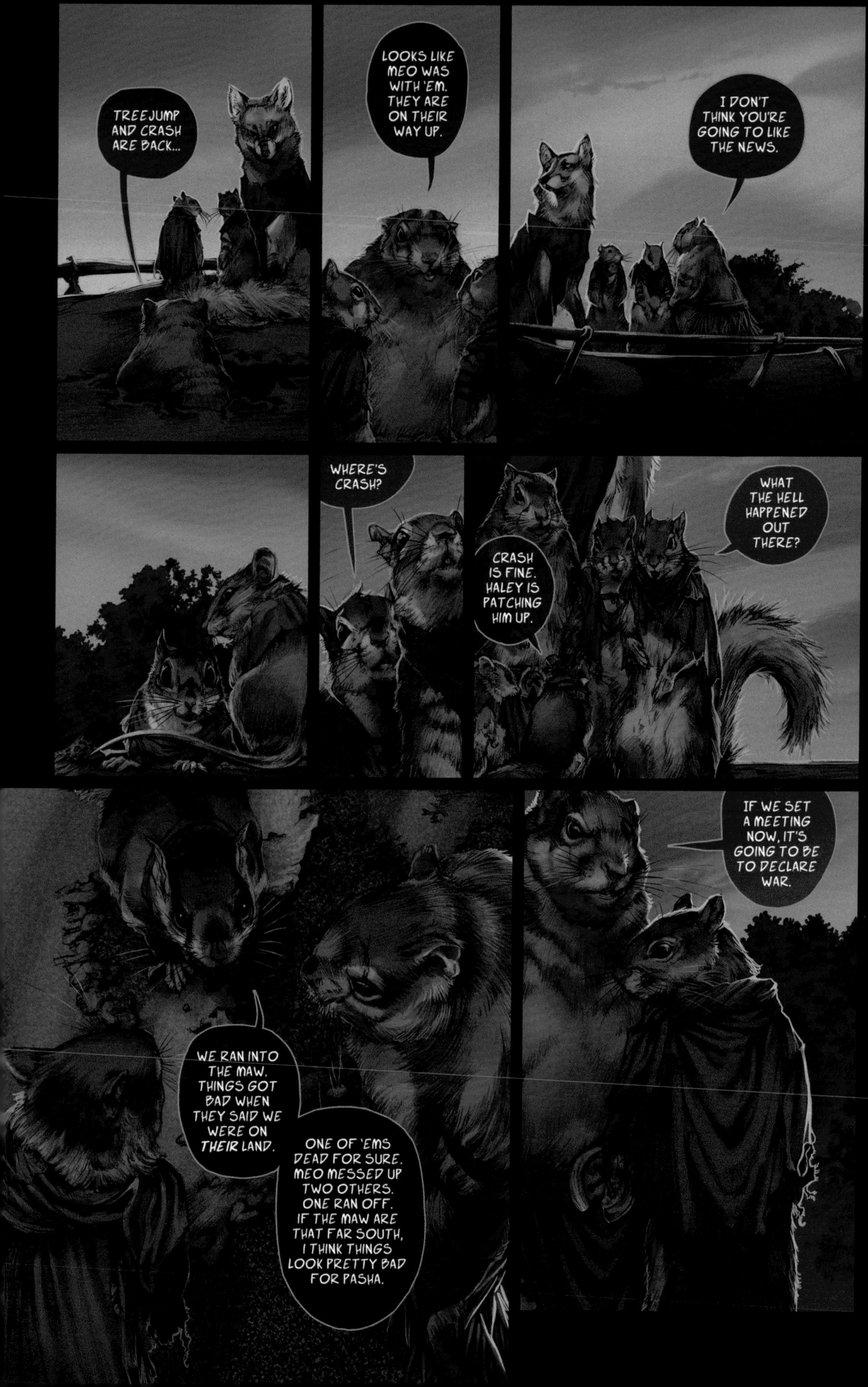
TREEJUMP AND CRASH ARE BACK...
LOOKS LIKE MEO WAS WITH 'EM. THEY ARE ON THEIR WAY UP.
I DON'T THINK YOU'RE GOING TO LIKE THE NEWS.
WHERE'S CRASH?
CRASH IS FINE. HALEY IS PATCHING HIM UP.
WHAT THE HELL HAPPENED OUT THERE?
WE RAN INTO THE MAW. THINGS GOT BAD WHEN THEY SAID WE WERE ON *THEIR* LAND.
ONE OF 'EMS DEAD FOR SURE. MEO MESSED UP TWO OTHERS. ONE RAN OFF. IF THE MAW ARE THAT FAR SOUTH, I THINK THINGS LOOK PRETTY BAD FOR PASHA.
IF WE SET A MEETING NOW, IT'S GOING TO BE TO DECLARE WAR.

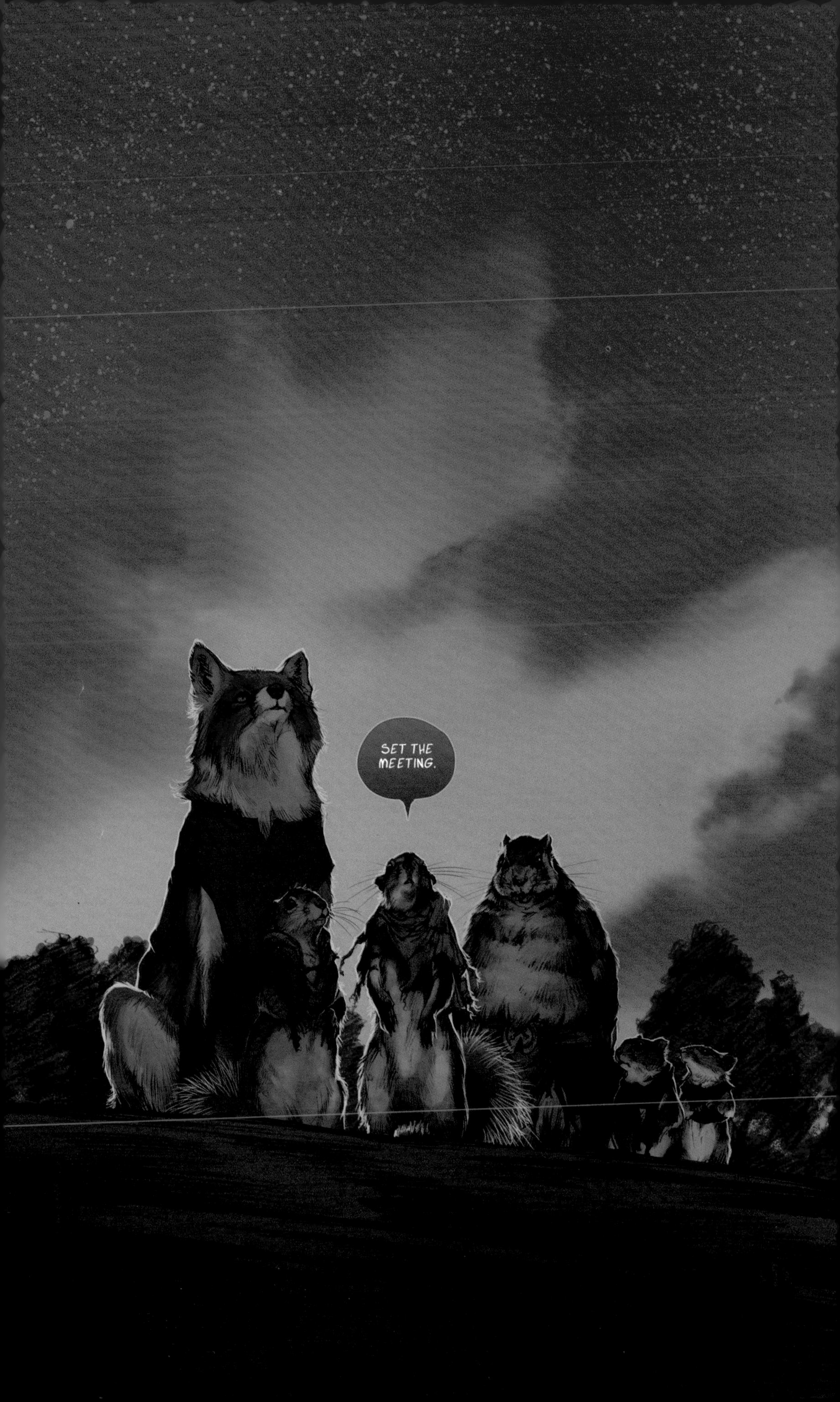
SET THE MEETING.

Chapter 2: Fragile

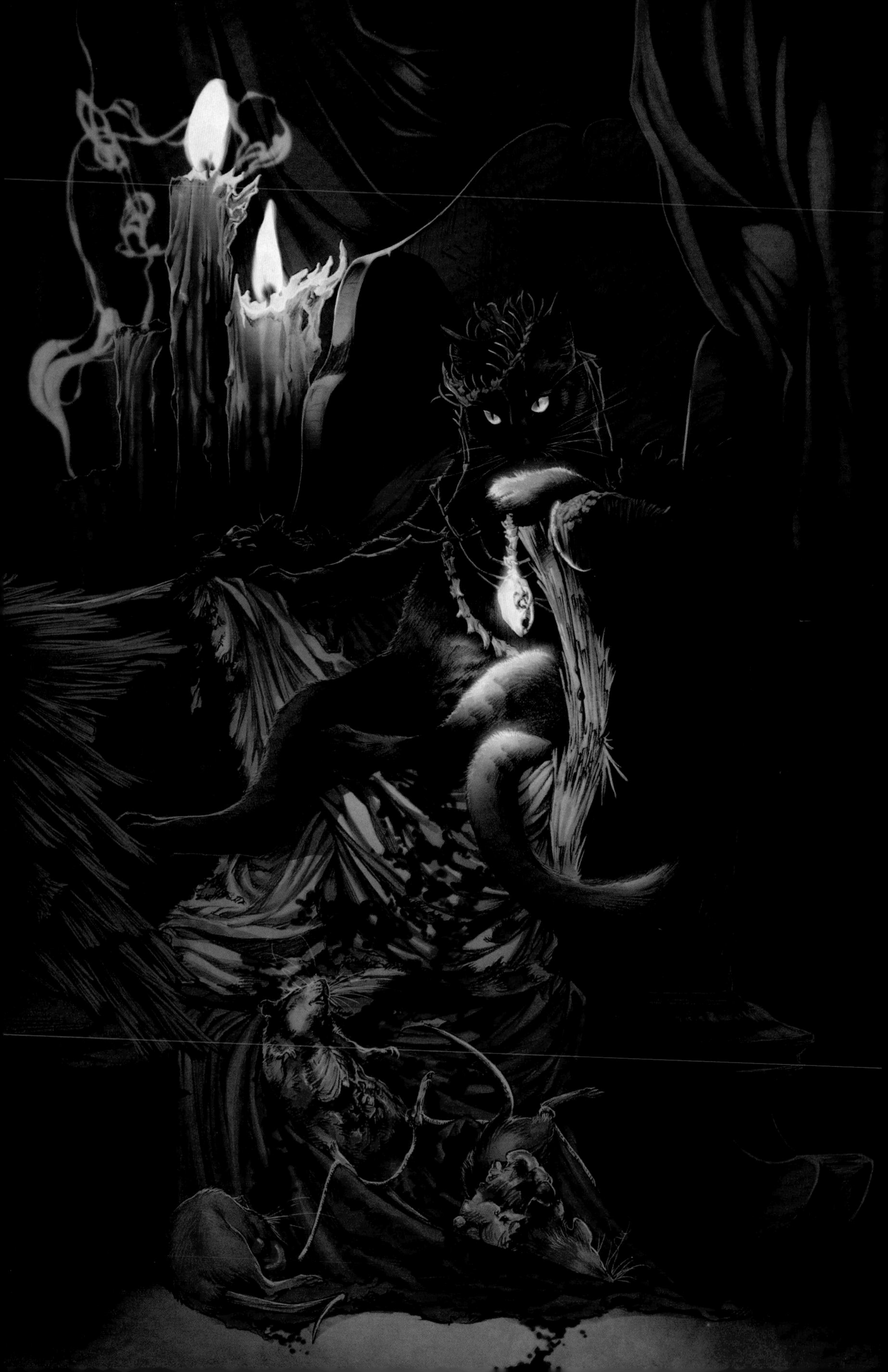

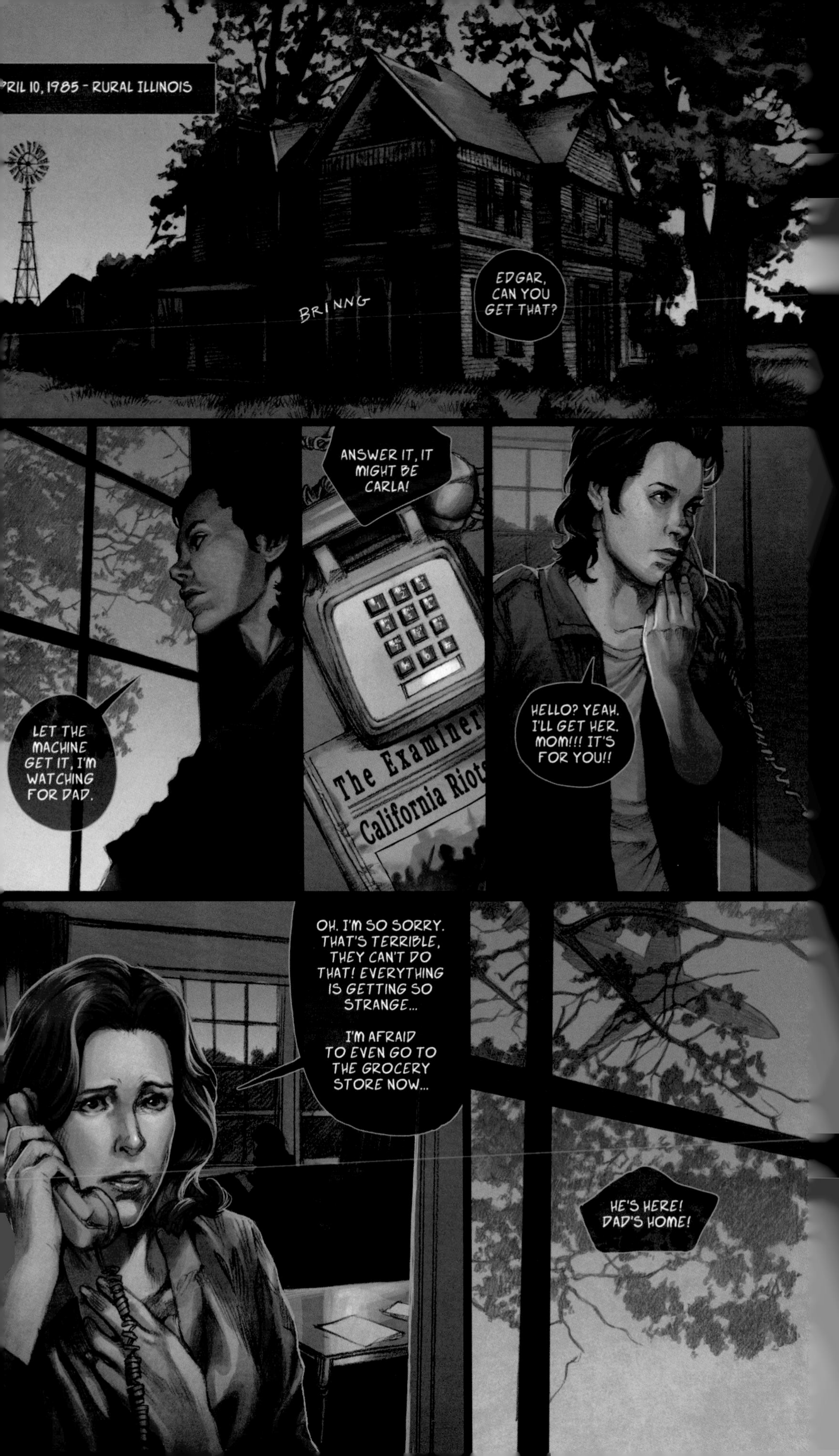

RIL 10, 1985 - RURAL ILLINOIS
BRINNG
EDGAR, CAN YOU GET THAT?
LET THE MACHINE GET IT, I'M WATCHING FOR DAD.
ANSWER IT, IT MIGHT BE CARLA!
The Examiner
California Riots
HELLO? YEAH. I'LL GET HER. MOM!!! IT'S FOR YOU!!
OH. I'M SO SORRY. THAT'S TERRIBLE, THEY CAN'T DO THAT! EVERYTHING IS GETTING SO STRANGE...
I'M AFRAID TO EVEN GO TO THE GROCERY STORE NOW...
HE'S HERE! DAD'S HOME!

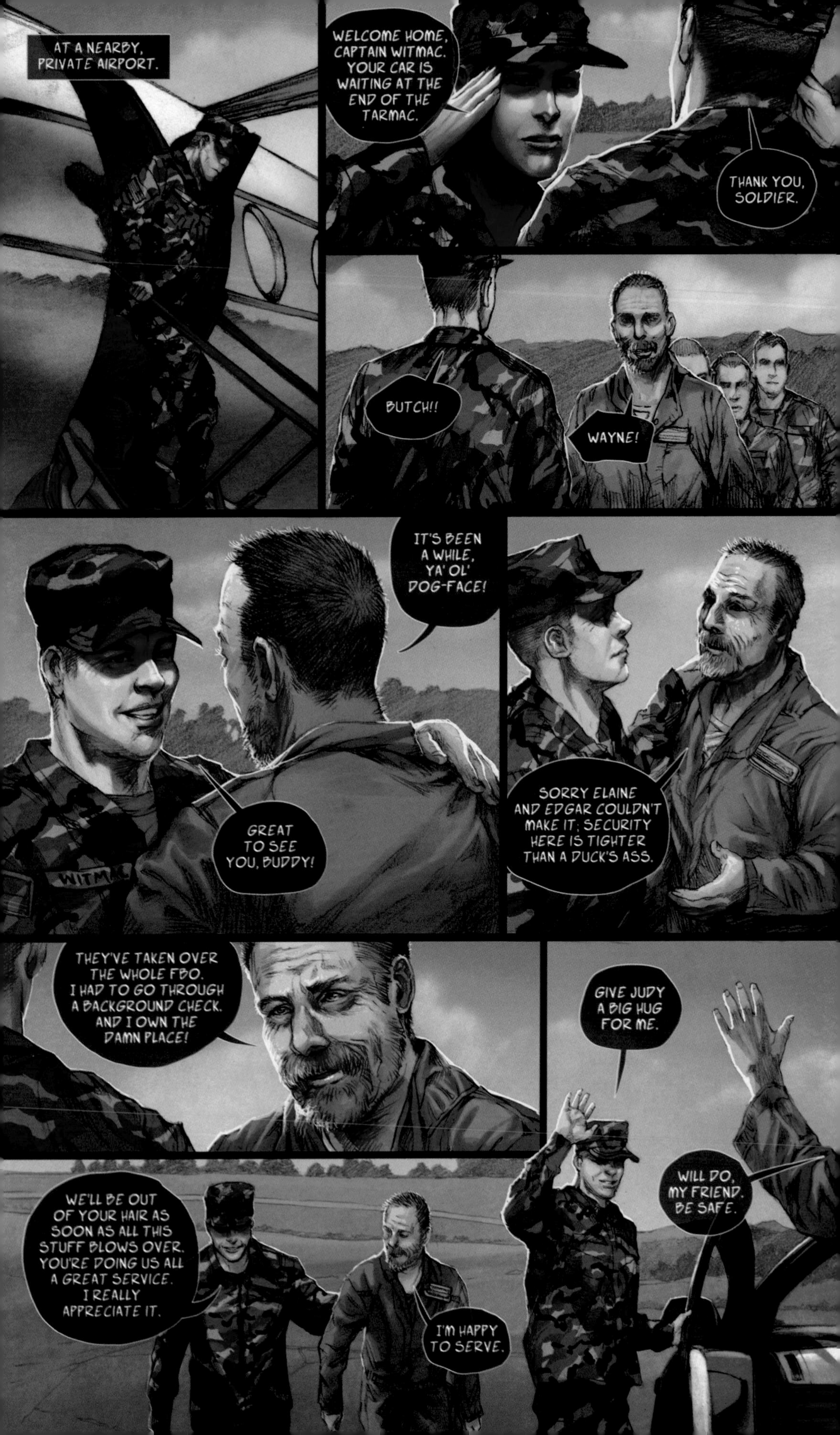
AT A NEARBY, PRIVATE AIRPORT.
WELCOME HOME, CAPTAIN WITMAC. YOUR CAR IS WAITING AT THE END OF THE TARMAC.
THANK YOU, SOLDIER.
BUTCH!!
WAYNE!
IT'S BEEN A WHILE, YA' OL' DOG-FACE!
GREAT TO SEE YOU, BUDDY!
WITMA
SORRY ELAINE AND EDGAR COULDN'T MAKE IT; SECURITY HERE IS TIGHTER THAN A DUCK'S ASS.
THEY'VE TAKEN OVER THE WHOLE FBO. I HAD TO GO THROUGH A BACKGROUND CHECK. AND I OWN THE DAMN PLACE!
WE'LL BE OUT OF YOUR HAIR AS SOON AS ALL THIS STUFF BLOWS OVER. YOU'RE DOING US ALL A GREAT SERVICE. I REALLY APPRECIATE IT.
I'M HAPPY TO SERVE.
GIVE JUDY A BIG HUG FOR ME.
WILL DO, MY FRIEND. BE SAFE.

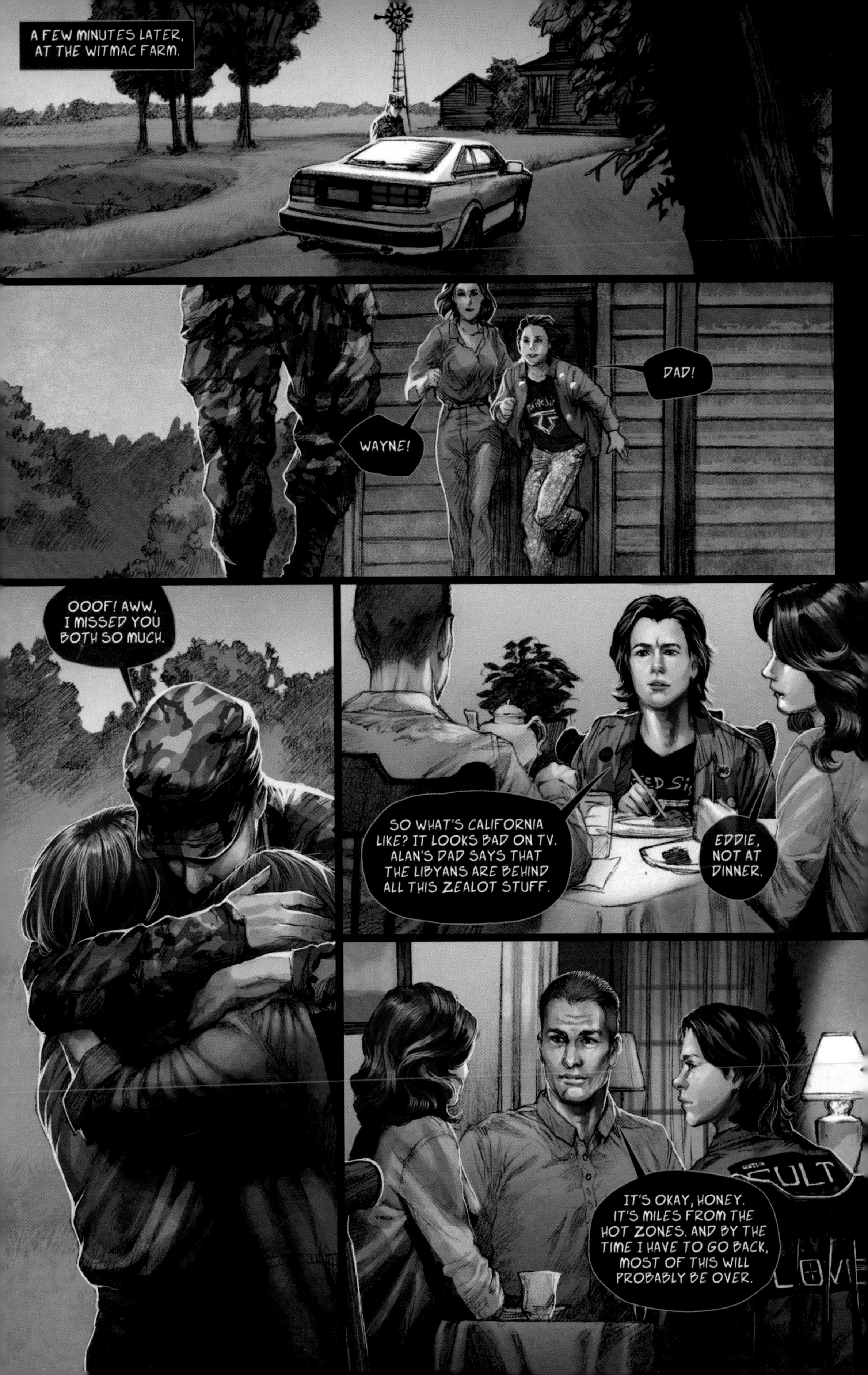

A FEW MINUTES LATER, AT THE WITMAC FARM.
DAD!
WAYNE!
OOOF! AWW, I MISSED YOU BOTH SO MUCH.
SO WHAT'S CALIFORNIA LIKE? IT LOOKS BAD ON TV. ALAN'S DAD SAYS THAT THE LIBYANS ARE BEHIND ALL THIS ZEALOT STUFF.
EDDIE, NOT AT DINNER.
IT'S OKAY, HONEY. IT'S MILES FROM THE HOT ZONES. AND BY THE TIME I HAVE TO GO BACK, MOST OF THIS WILL PROBABLY BE OVER.

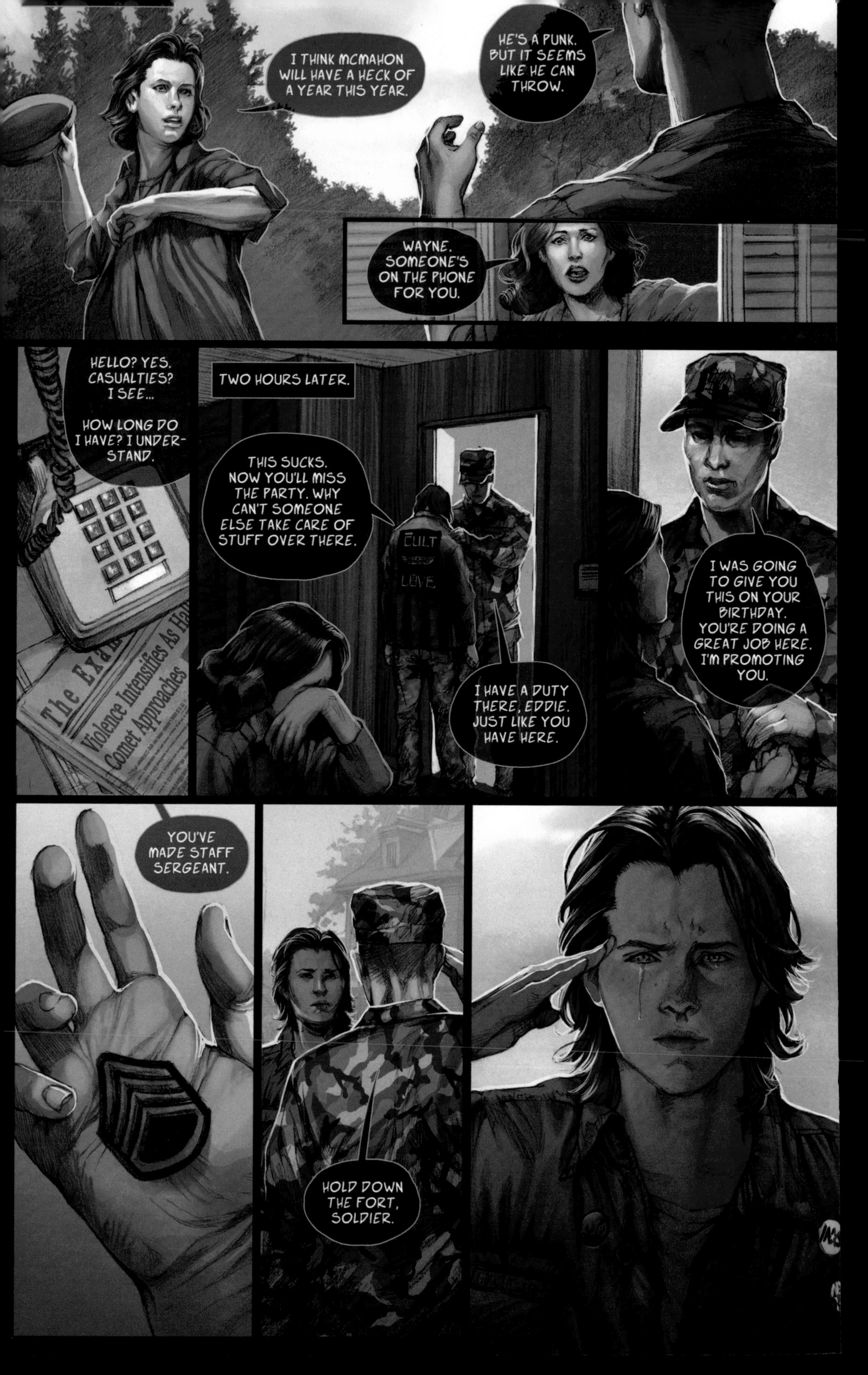
I THINK MCMAHON WILL HAVE A HECK OF A YEAR THIS YEAR.
HE'S A PUNK. BUT IT SEEMS LIKE HE CAN THROW.
WAYNE. SOMEONE'S ON THE PHONE FOR YOU.
HELLO? YES. CASUALTIES? I SEE...
HOW LONG DO I HAVE? I UNDERSTAND.
The Exa
Violence Intensifies As Ha
Comet Approaches
TWO HOURS LATER.
THIS SUCKS. NOW YOU'LL MISS THE PARTY. WHY CAN'T SOMEONE ELSE TAKE CARE OF STUFF OVER THERE.
CULT
LOVE
I HAVE A DUTY THERE, EDDIE. JUST LIKE YOU HAVE HERE.
I WAS GOING TO GIVE YOU THIS ON YOUR BIRTHDAY. YOU'RE DOING A GREAT JOB HERE. I'M PROMOTING YOU.
YOU'VE MADE STAFF SERGEANT.
HOLD DOWN THE FORT, SOLDIER.

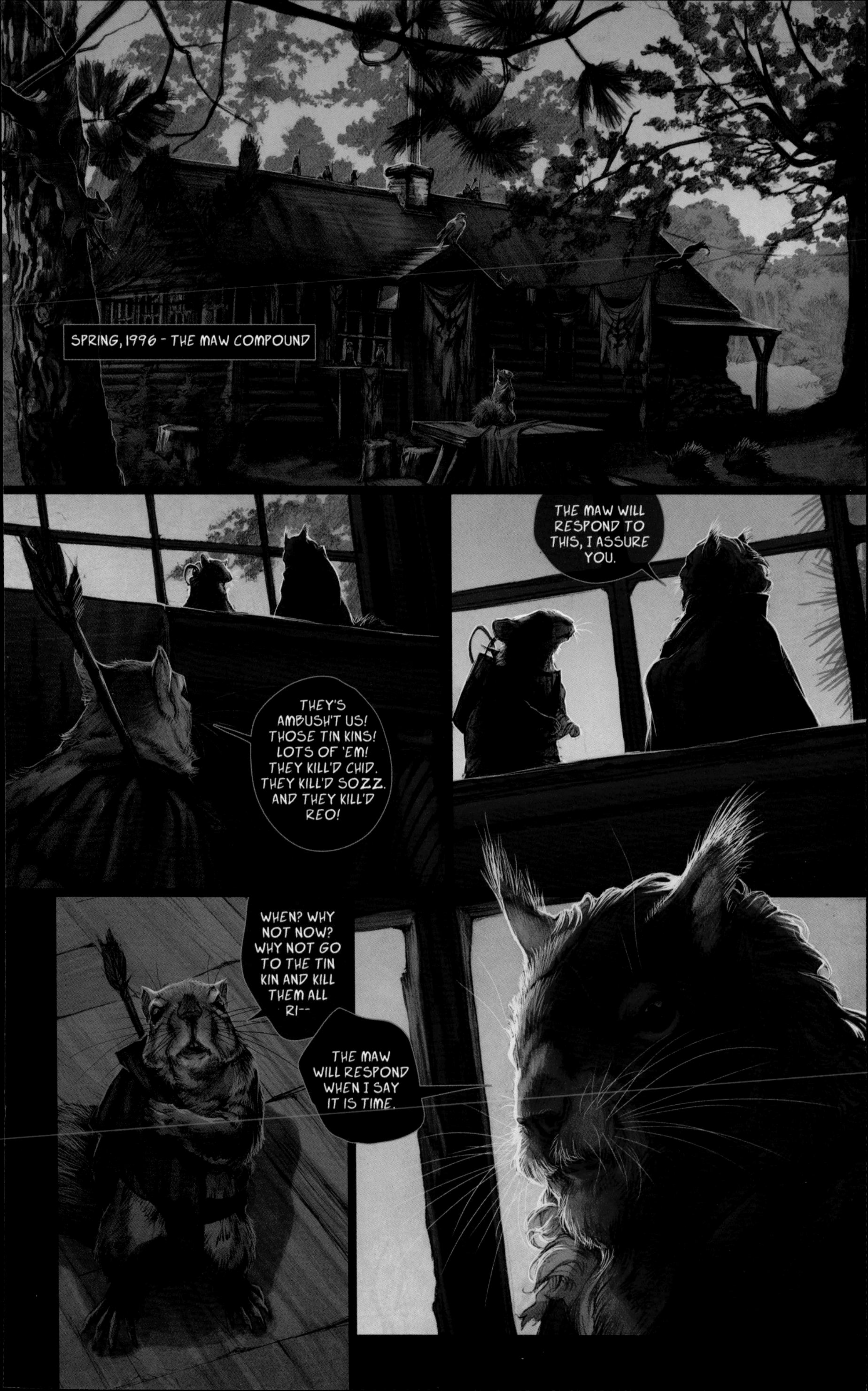
SPRING, 1996 - THE MAW COMPOUND
THEY'S AMBUSH'T US! THOSE TIN KINS! LOTS OF 'EM! THEY KILL'D CHID. THEY KILL'D SOZZ. AND THEY KILL'D REO!
THE MAW WILL RESPOND TO THIS, I ASSURE YOU.
WHEN? WHY NOT NOW? WHY NOT GO TO THE TIN KIN AND KILL THEM ALL RI--
THE MAW WILL RESPOND WHEN I SAY IT IS TIME.

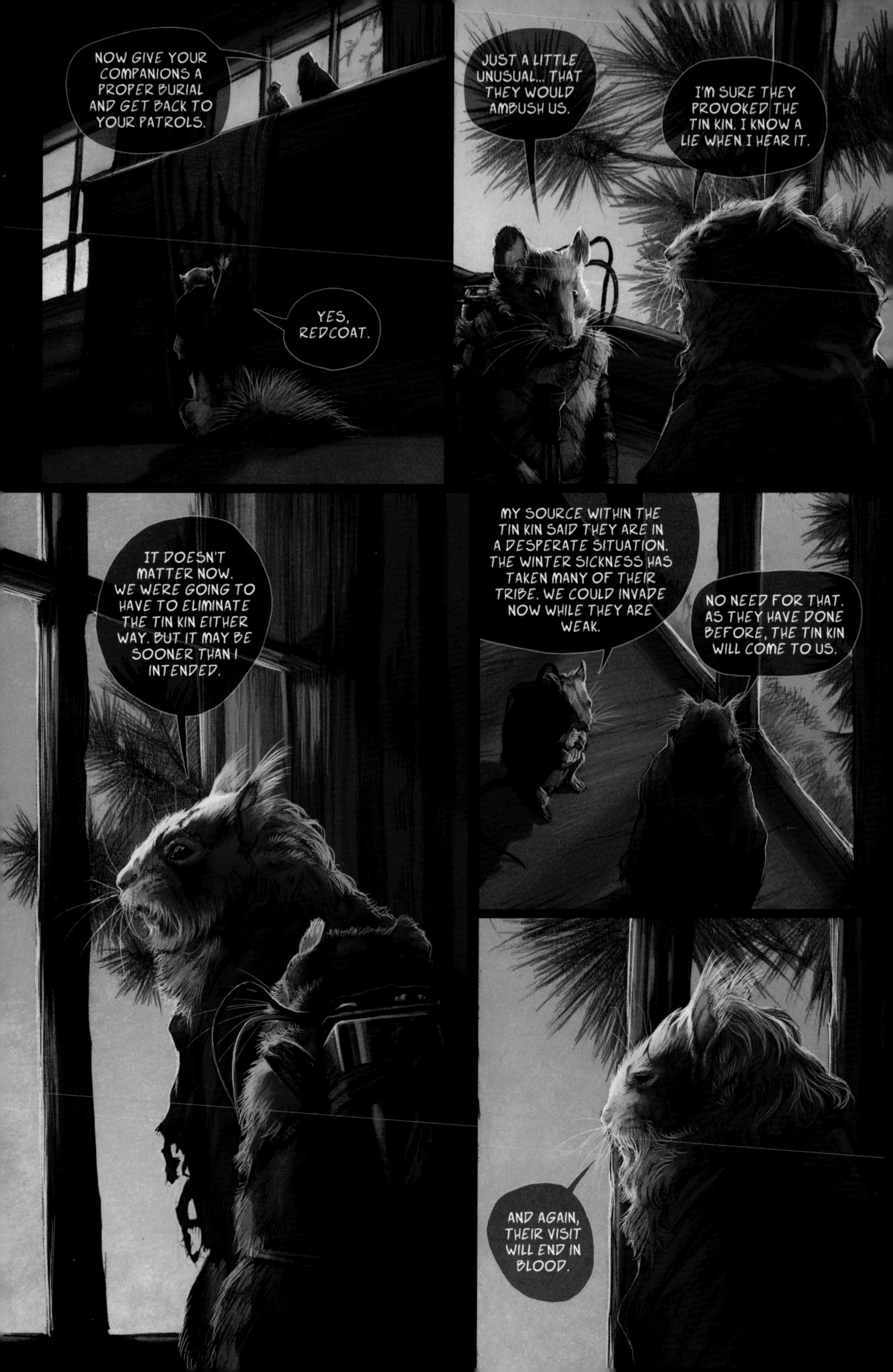
NOW GIVE YOUR COMPANIONS A PROPER BURIAL AND GET BACK TO YOUR PATROLS.
YES, REDCOAT.
JUST A LITTLE UNUSUAL... THAT THEY WOULD AMBUSH US.
I'M SURE THEY PROVOKED THE TIN KIN. I KNOW A LIE WHEN I HEAR IT.
IT DOESN'T MATTER NOW. WE WERE GOING TO HAVE TO ELIMINATE THE TIN KIN EITHER WAY. BUT IT MAY BE SOONER THAN I INTENDED.
MY SOURCE WITHIN THE TIN KIN SAID THEY ARE IN A DESPERATE SITUATION. THE WINTER SICKNESS HAS TAKEN MANY OF THEIR TRIBE. WE COULD INVADE NOW WHILE THEY ARE WEAK.
NO NEED FOR THAT. AS THEY HAVE DONE BEFORE, THE TIN KIN WILL COME TO US.
AND AGAIN, THEIR VISIT WILL END IN BLOOD.

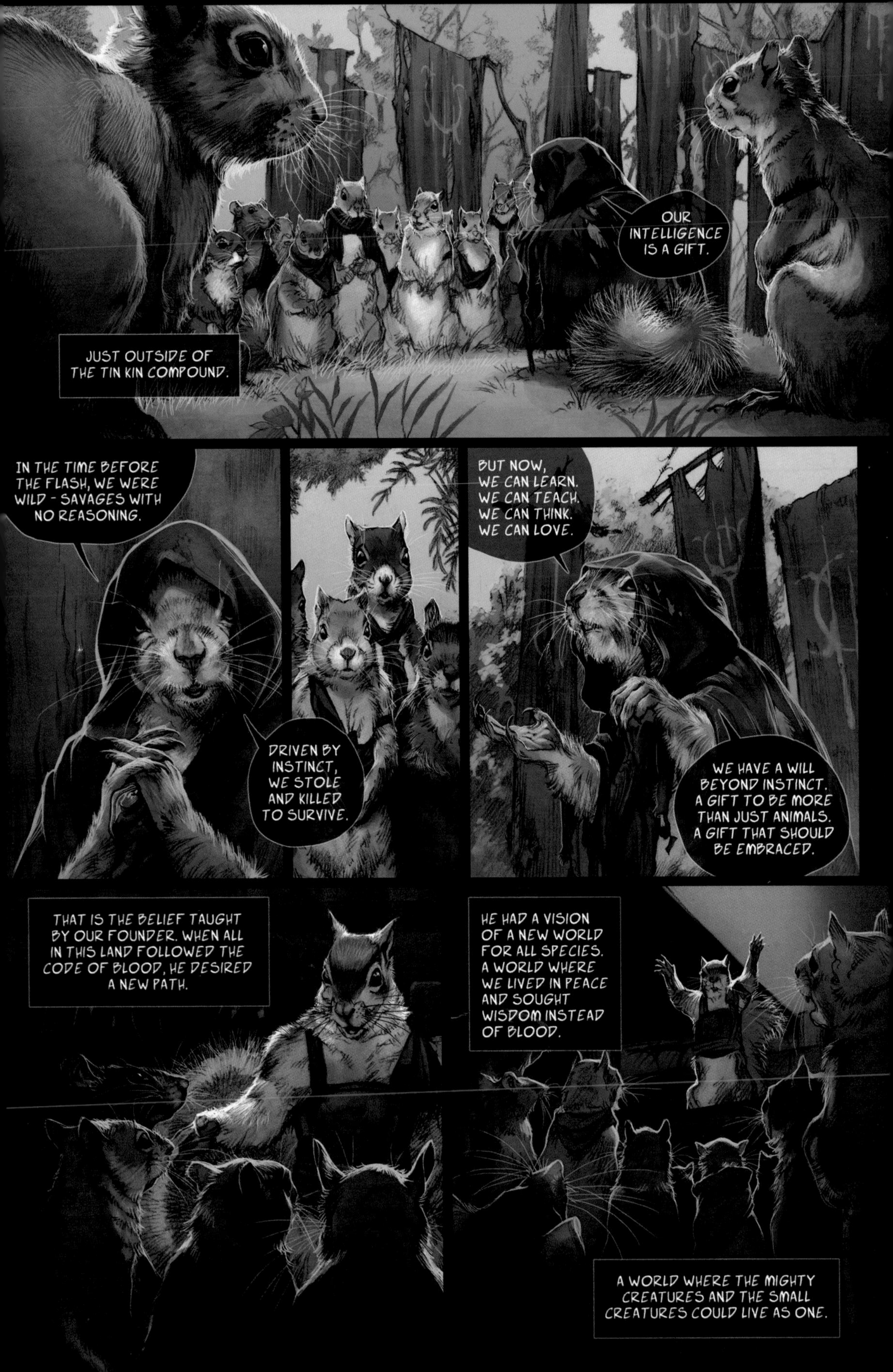
OUR INTELLIGENCE IS A GIFT.
JUST OUTSIDE OF THE TIN KIN COMPOUND.
IN THE TIME BEFORE THE FLASH, WE WERE WILD - SAVAGES WITH NO REASONING.
DRIVEN BY INSTINCT, WE STOLE AND KILLED TO SURVIVE.
BUT NOW, WE CAN LEARN. WE CAN TEACH. WE CAN THINK. WE CAN LOVE.
WE HAVE A WILL BEYOND INSTINCT. A GIFT TO BE MORE THAN JUST ANIMALS. A GIFT THAT SHOULD BE EMBRACED.
THAT IS THE BELIEF TAUGHT BY OUR FOUNDER. WHEN ALL IN THIS LAND FOLLOWED THE CODE OF BLOOD, HE DESIRED A NEW PATH.
HE HAD A VISION OF A NEW WORLD FOR ALL SPECIES. A WORLD WHERE WE LIVED IN PEACE AND SOUGHT WISDOM INSTEAD OF BLOOD.
A WORLD WHERE THE MIGHTY CREATURES AND THE SMALL CREATURES COULD LIVE AS ONE.

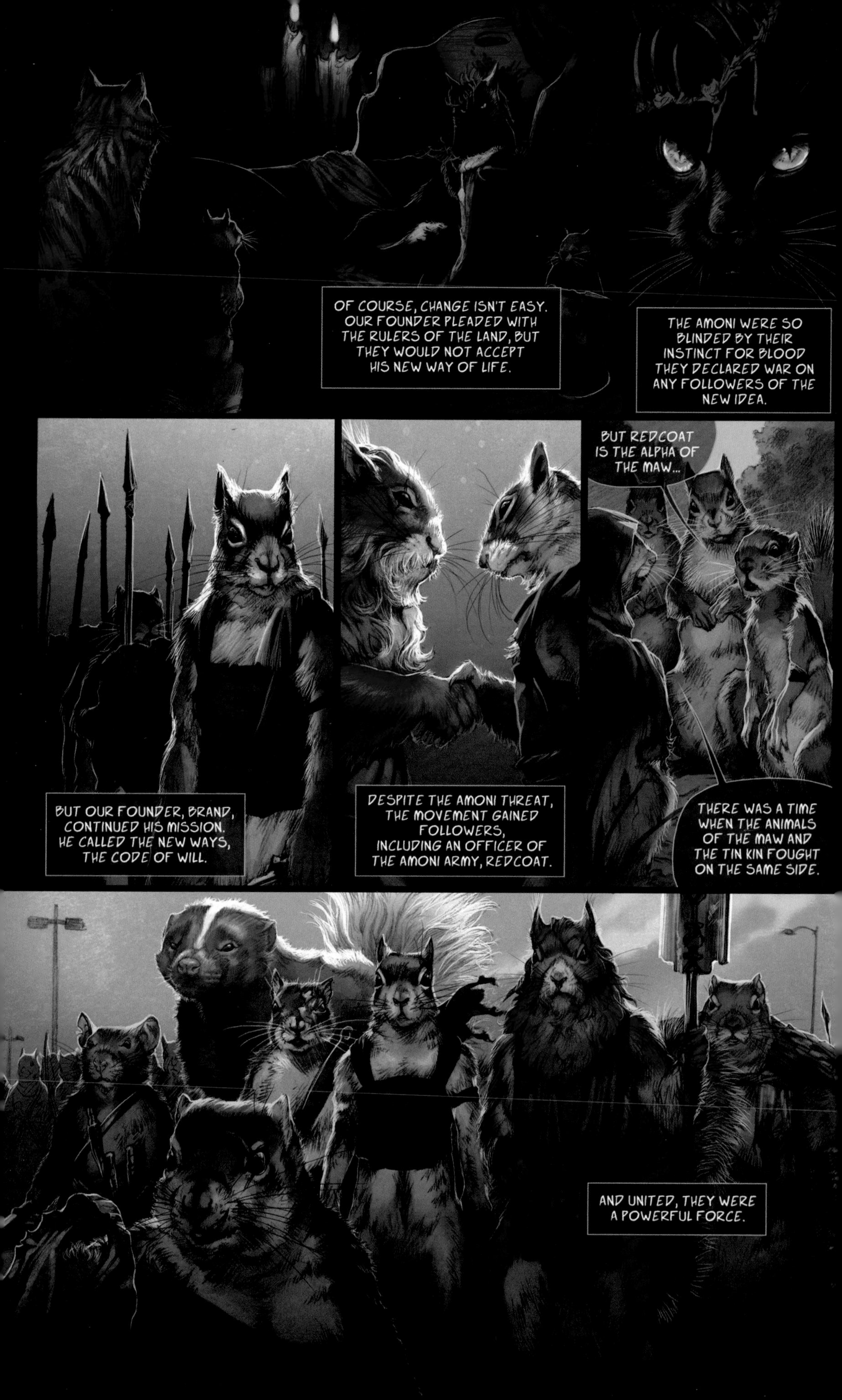
OF COURSE, CHANGE ISN'T EASY. OUR FOUNDER PLEADED WITH THE RULERS OF THE LAND, BUT THEY WOULD NOT ACCEPT HIS NEW WAY OF LIFE.
THE AMONI WERE SO BLINDED BY THEIR INSTINCT FOR BLOOD THEY DECLARED WAR ON ANY FOLLOWERS OF THE NEW IDEA.
BUT OUR FOUNDER, BRAND, CONTINUED HIS MISSION. HE CALLED THE NEW WAYS, THE CODE OF WILL.
DESPITE THE AMONI THREAT, THE MOVEMENT GAINED FOLLOWERS, INCLUDING AN OFFICER OF THE AMONI ARMY, REDCOAT.
BUT REDCOAT IS THE ALPHA OF THE MAW...
THERE WAS A TIME WHEN THE ANIMALS OF THE MAW AND THE TIN KIN FOUGHT ON THE SAME SIDE.
AND UNITED, THEY WERE A POWERFUL FORCE.

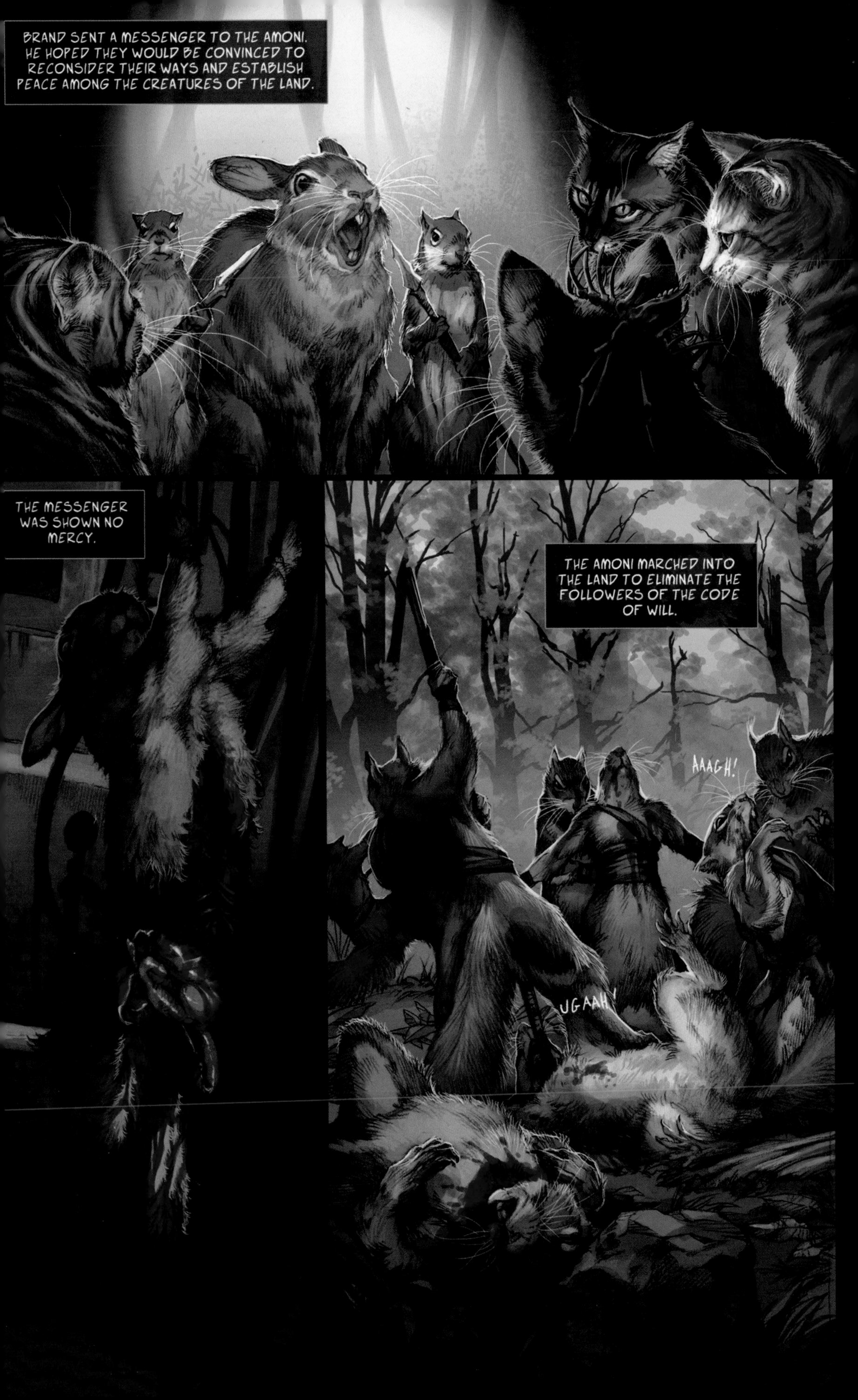
BRAND SENT A MESSENGER TO THE AMONI. HE HOPED THEY WOULD BE CONVINCED TO RECONSIDER THEIR WAYS AND ESTABLISH PEACE AMONG THE CREATURES OF THE LAND.
THE MESSENGER WAS SHOWN NO MERCY.
THE AMONI MARCHED INTO THE LAND TO ELIMINATE THE FOLLOWERS OF THE CODE OF WILL.
AAAGH!
UGAAH!

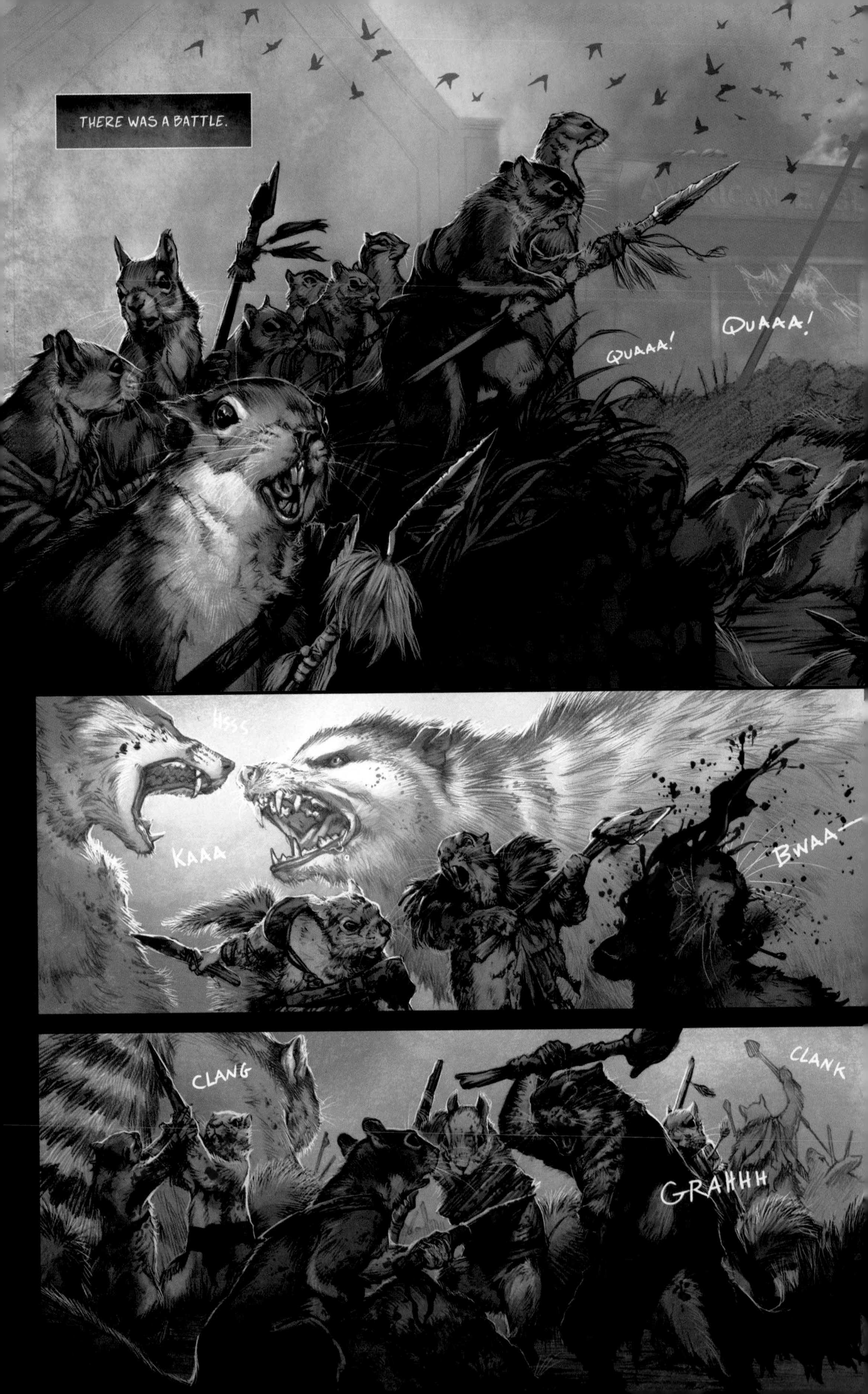
THERE WAS A BATTLE.
QUAAA!
QUAAA!
HSSS
KAAA
BWAA—
CLANG
CLANK
GRAHHH

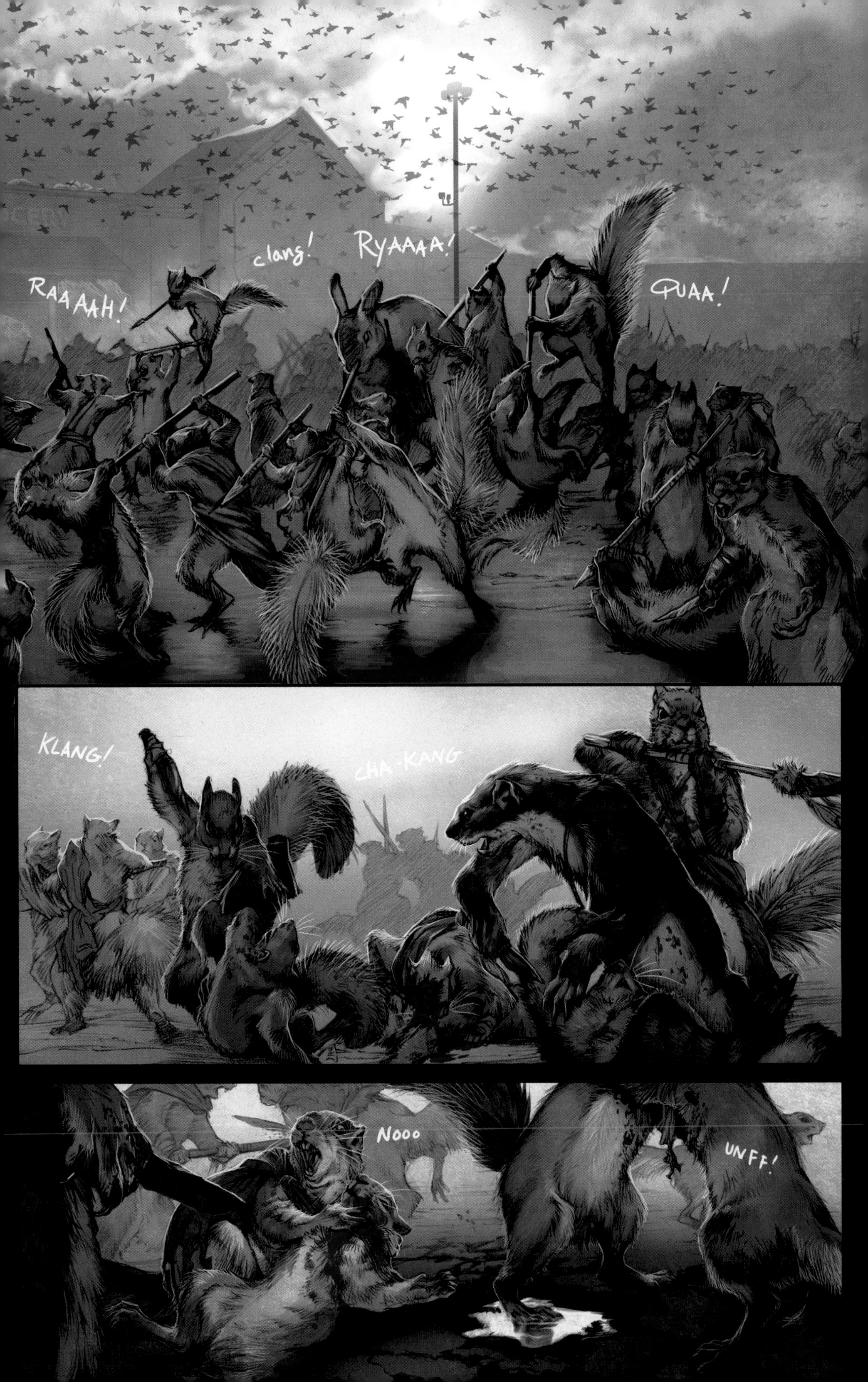
RAAAAH!
clang!
RYAAAA!
QUAA!
KLANG!
CHA-KANG
Nooo
UNFF!

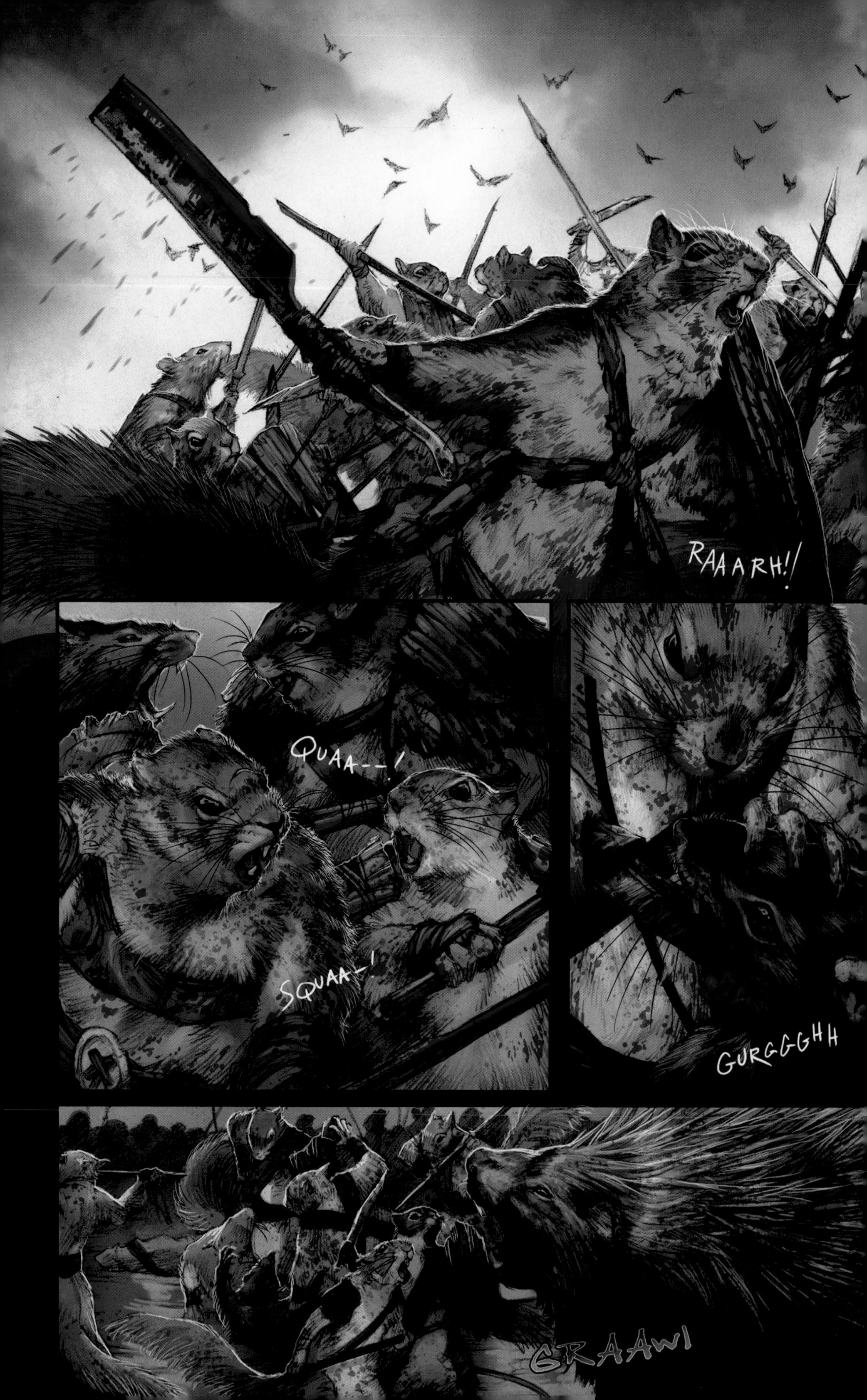
RAAARH!!
QUAA--!
SQUAA-!
GURGGGHH
GRAAW!

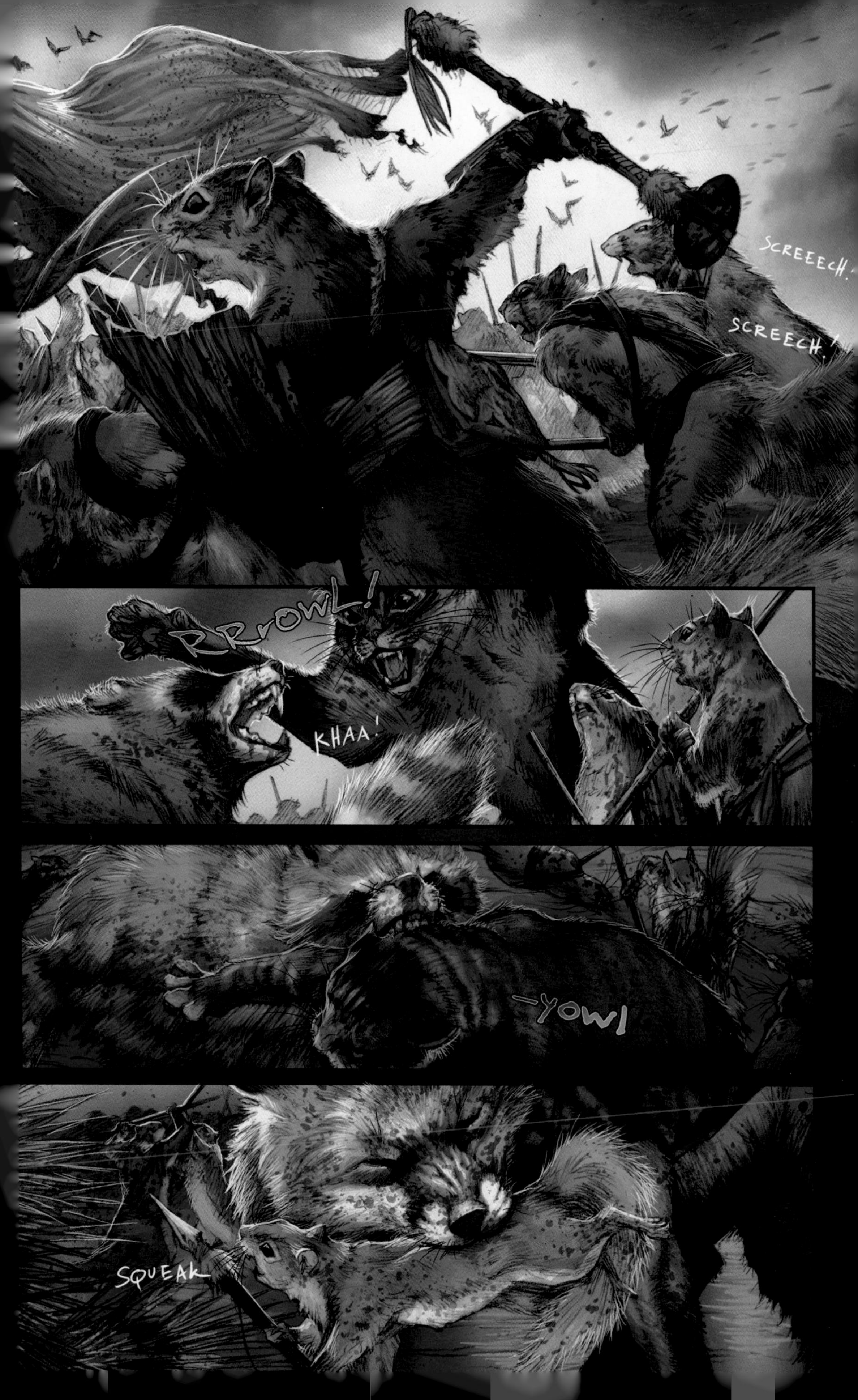
SCREEECH!
SCREECH!
RRrowL!
KHAA!
-YOWl
SQUEAK

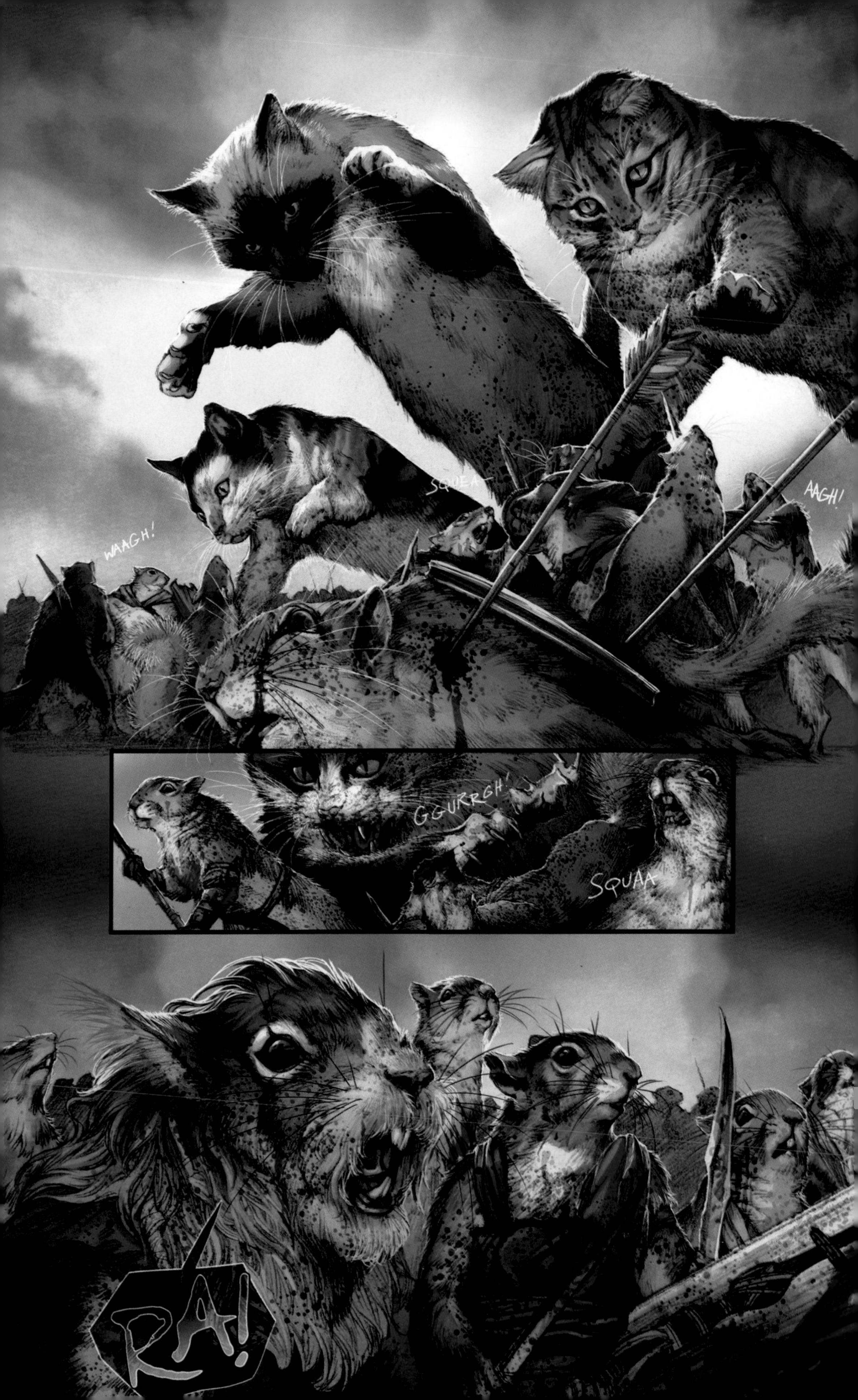
SQUEA
AAGH!
WAAGH!
GGURRGH!
SQUAA
RA!

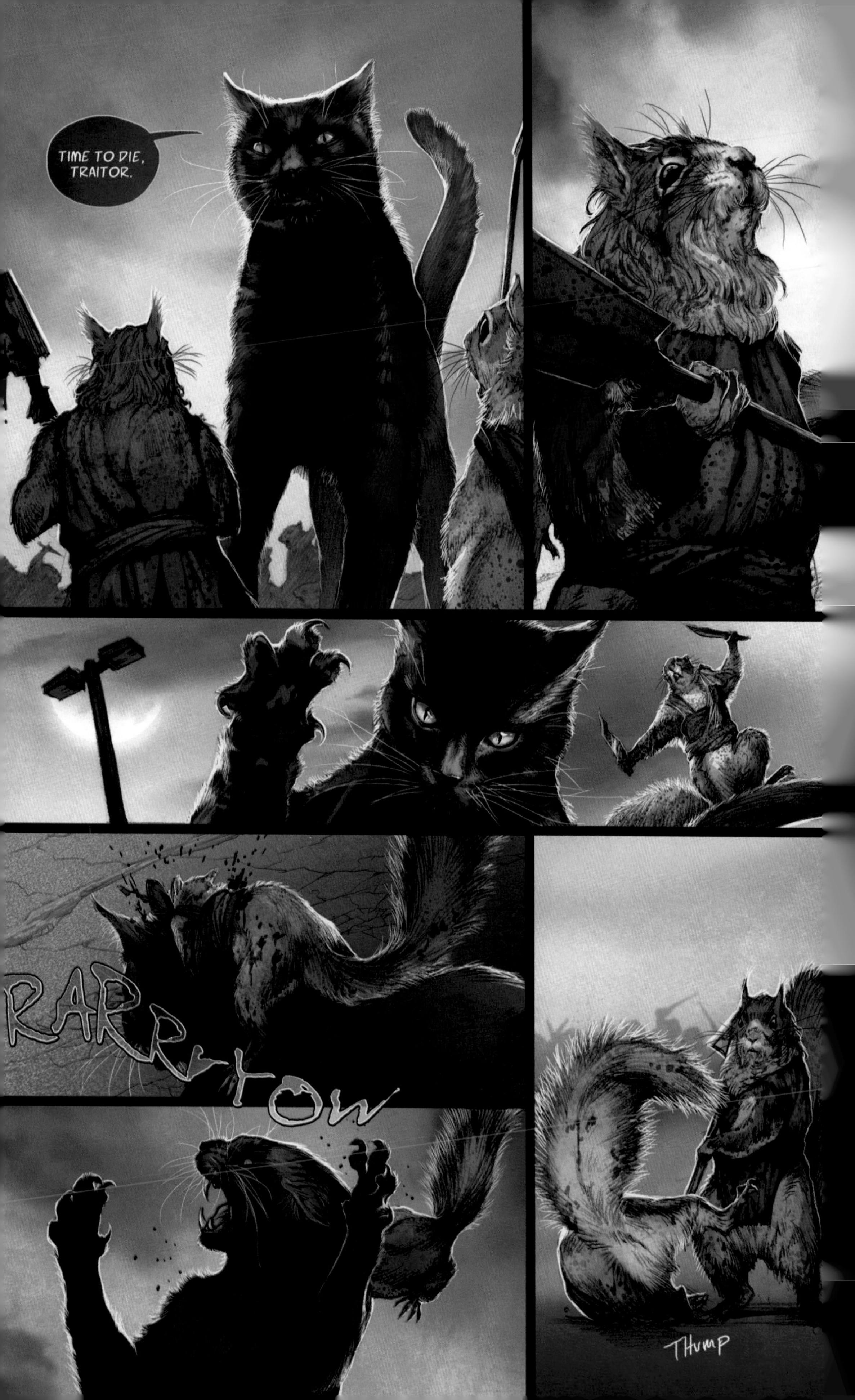
TIME TO DIE, TRAITOR.
RARRrOW
THump

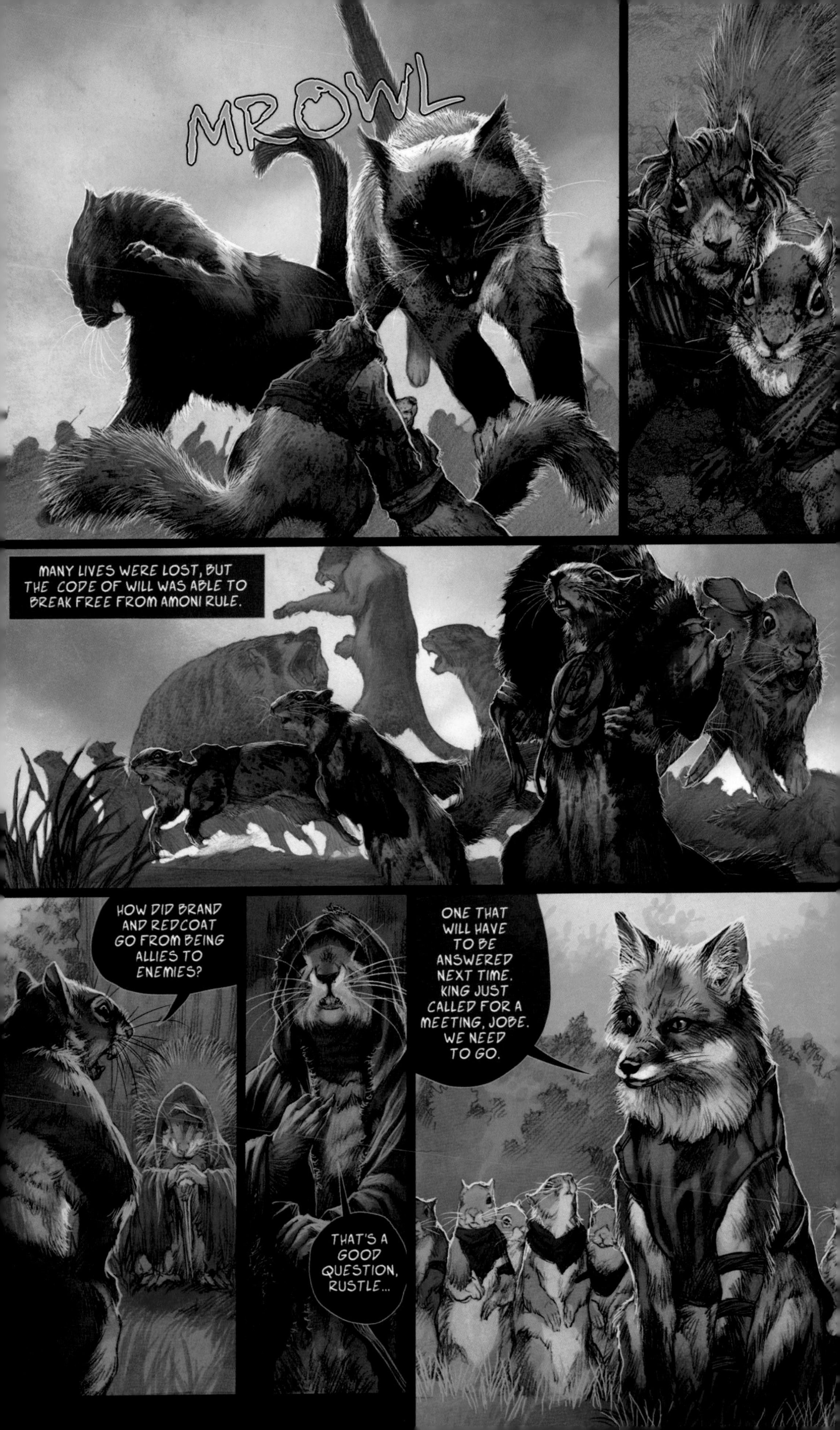
MROWL
MANY LIVES WERE LOST, BUT THE CODE OF WILL WAS ABLE TO BREAK FREE FROM AMONI RULE.
HOW DID BRAND AND REDCOAT GO FROM BEING ALLIES TO ENEMIES?
THAT'S A GOOD QUESTION, RUSTLE...
ONE THAT WILL HAVE TO BE ANSWERED NEXT TIME. KING JUST CALLED FOR A MEETING, JOBE. WE NEED TO GO.

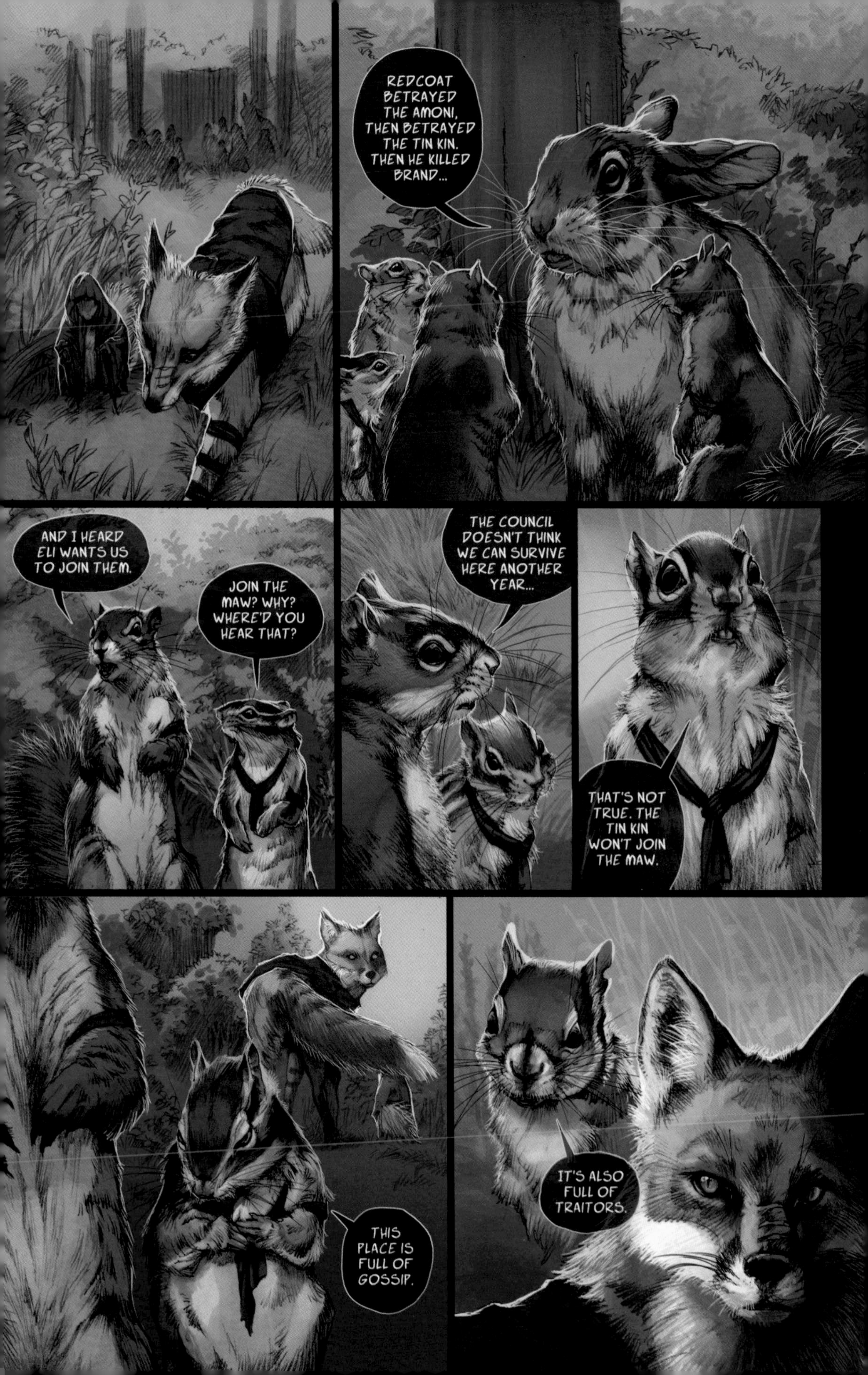
REDCOAT BETRAYED THE AMONI, THEN BETRAYED THE TIN KIN. THEN HE KILLED BRAND...
AND I HEARD ELI WANTS US TO JOIN THEM.
JOIN THE MAW? WHY? WHERE'D YOU HEAR THAT?
THE COUNCIL DOESN'T THINK WE CAN SURVIVE HERE ANOTHER YEAR...
THAT'S NOT TRUE. THE TIN KIN WON'T JOIN THE MAW.
THIS PLACE IS FULL OF GOSSIP.
IT'S ALSO FULL OF TRAITORS.

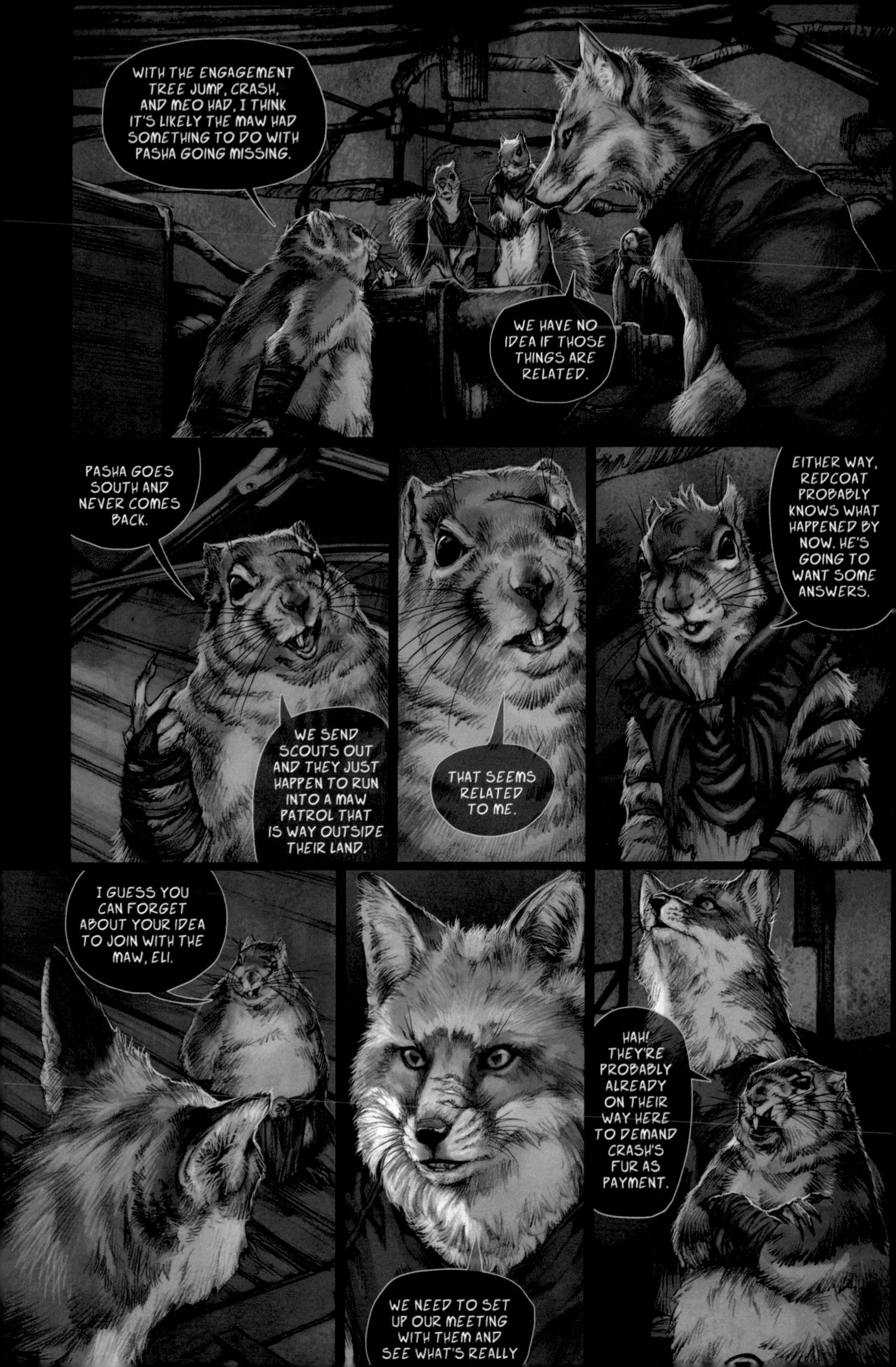
WITH THE ENGAGEMENT TREE JUMP, CRASH, AND MEO HAD, I THINK IT'S LIKELY THE MAW HAD SOMETHING TO DO WITH PASHA GOING MISSING.
WE HAVE NO IDEA IF THOSE THINGS ARE RELATED.
PASHA GOES SOUTH AND NEVER COMES BACK.
WE SEND SCOUTS OUT AND THEY JUST HAPPEN TO RUN INTO A MAW PATROL THAT IS WAY OUTSIDE THEIR LAND.
THAT SEEMS RELATED TO ME.
EITHER WAY, REDCOAT PROBABLY KNOWS WHAT HAPPENED BY NOW. HE'S GOING TO WANT SOME ANSWERS.
I GUESS YOU CAN FORGET ABOUT YOUR IDEA TO JOIN WITH THE MAW, ELI.
WE NEED TO SET UP OUR MEETING WITH THEM AND SEE WHAT'S REALLY
HAH! THEY'RE PROBABLY ALREADY ON THEIR WAY HERE TO DEMAND CRASH'S FUR AS PAYMENT.

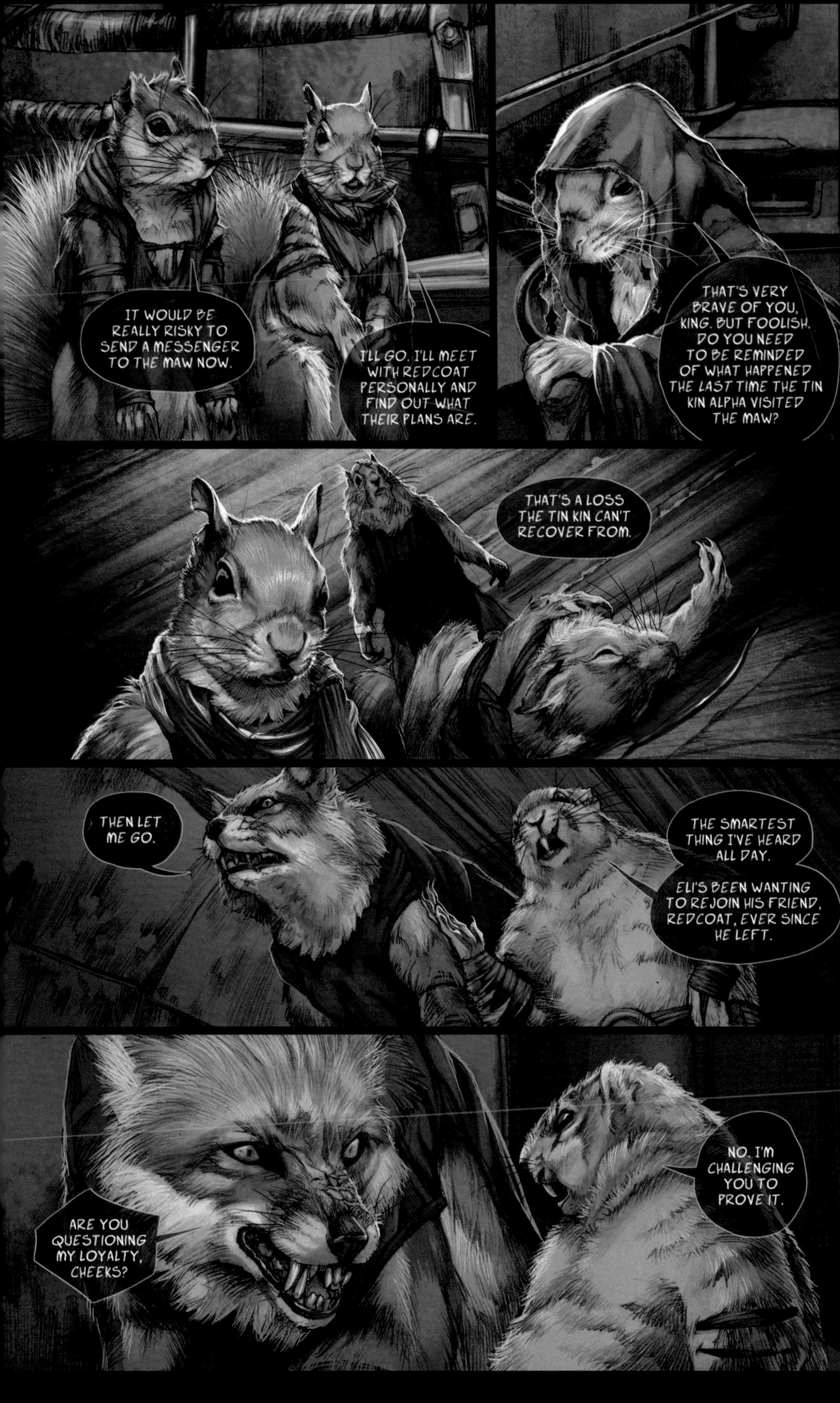
IT WOULD BE REALLY RISKY TO SEND A MESSENGER TO THE MAW NOW.
I'LL GO. I'LL MEET WITH REDCOAT PERSONALLY AND FIND OUT WHAT THEIR PLANS ARE.
THAT'S VERY BRAVE OF YOU, KING. BUT FOOLISH. DO YOU NEED TO BE REMINDED OF WHAT HAPPENED THE LAST TIME THE TIN KIN ALPHA VISITED THE MAW?
THAT'S A LOSS THE TIN KIN CAN'T RECOVER FROM.
THEN LET ME GO.
THE SMARTEST THING I'VE HEARD ALL DAY.
ELI'S BEEN WANTING TO REJOIN HIS FRIEND, REDCOAT, EVER SINCE HE LEFT.
ARE YOU QUESTIONING MY LOYALTY, CHEEKS?
NO. I'M CHALLENGING YOU TO PROVE IT.

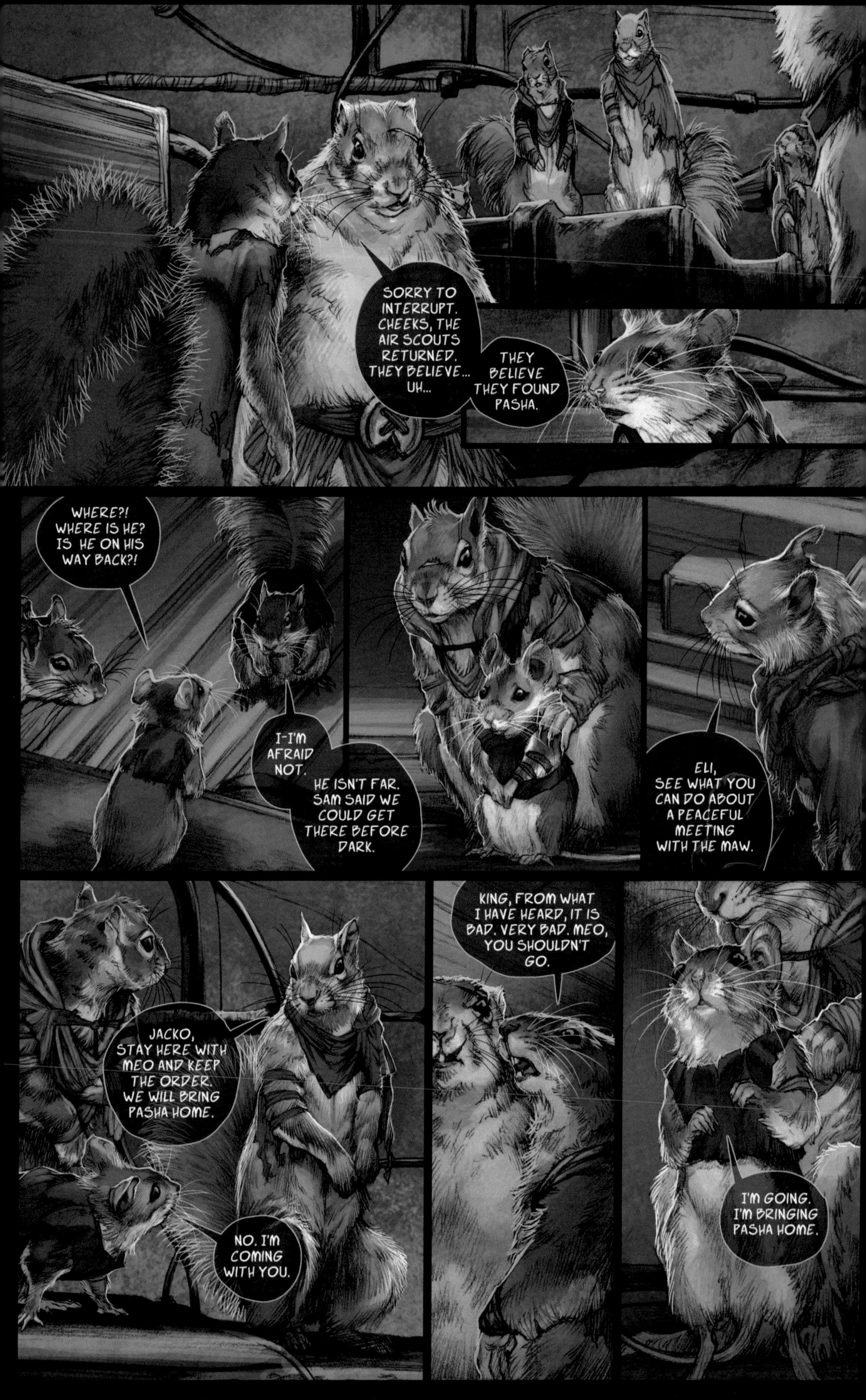
SORRY TO INTERRUPT. CHEEKS, THE AIR SCOUTS RETURNED. THEY BELIEVE... UH...
THEY BELIEVE THEY FOUND PASHA.
WHERE?! WHERE IS HE? IS HE ON HIS WAY BACK?!
I-I'M AFRAID NOT.
HE ISN'T FAR. SAM SAID WE COULD GET THERE BEFORE DARK.
ELI, SEE WHAT YOU CAN DO ABOUT A PEACEFUL MEETING WITH THE MAW.
JACKO, STAY HERE WITH MEO AND KEEP THE ORDER. WE WILL BRING PASHA HOME.
NO. I'M COMING WITH YOU.
KING, FROM WHAT I HAVE HEARD, IT IS BAD. VERY BAD. MEO, YOU SHOULDN'T GO.
I'M GOING. I'M BRINGING PASHA HOME.

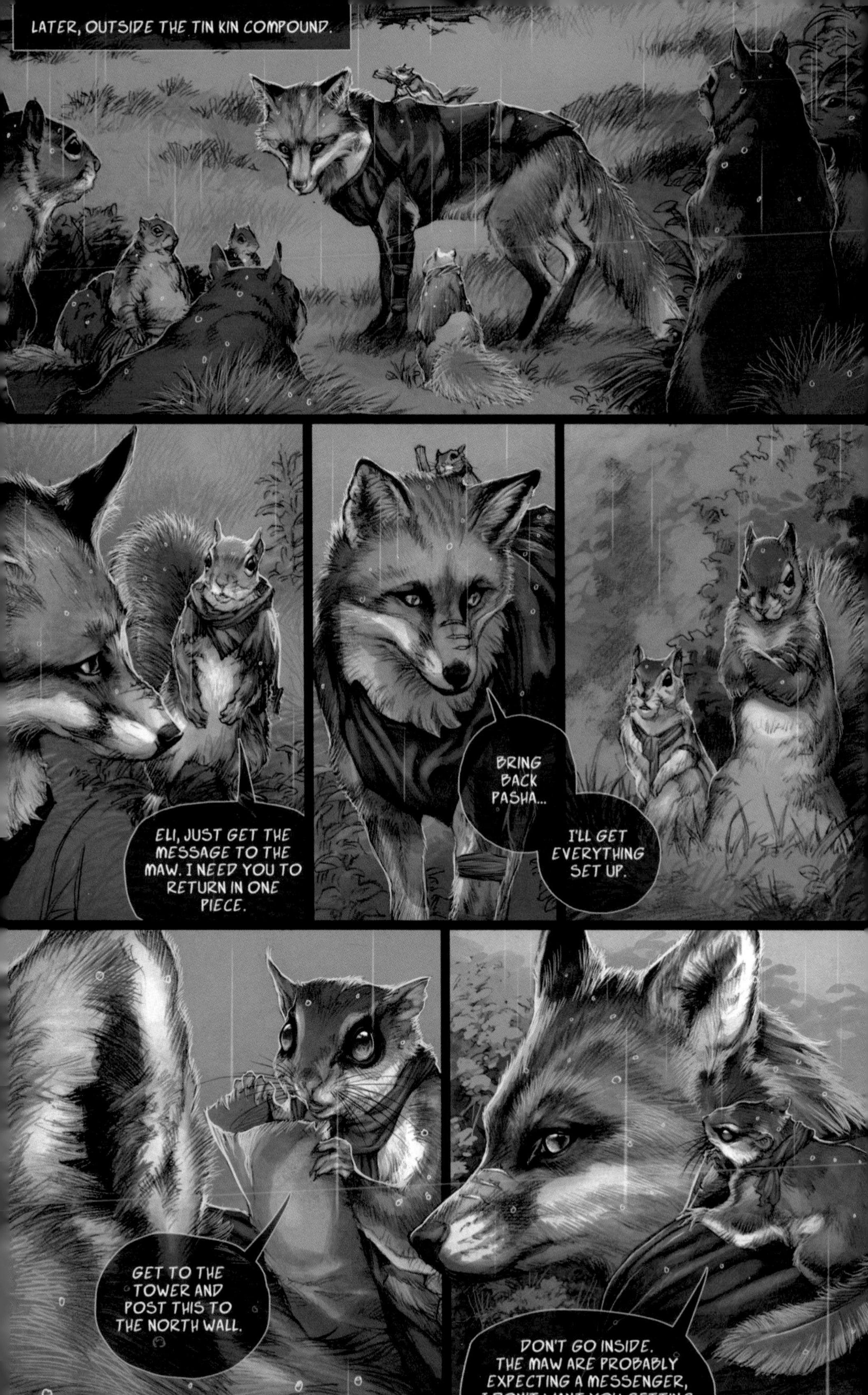
LATER, OUTSIDE THE TIN KIN COMPOUND.
ELI, JUST GET THE MESSAGE TO THE MAW. I NEED YOU TO RETURN IN ONE PIECE.
BRING BACK PASHA...
I'LL GET EVERYTHING SET UP.
GET TO THE TOWER AND POST THIS TO THE NORTH WALL.
DON'T GO INSIDE. THE MAW ARE PROBABLY EXPECTING A MESSENGER, I DON'T WANT YOU GETTING AMBUSHED BY GHOST OR SOME OTHER SCUM.

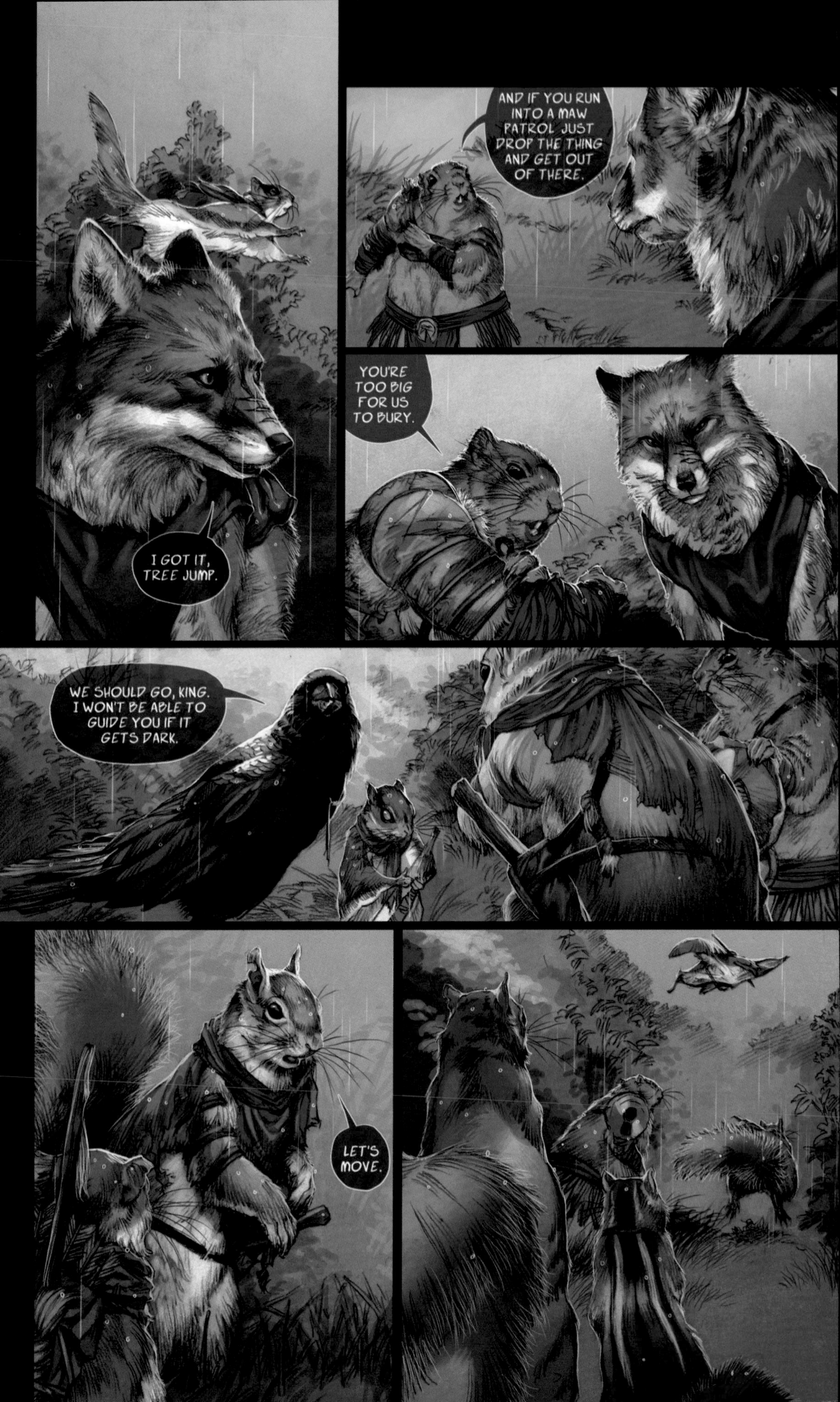
AND IF YOU RUN INTO A MAW PATROL JUST DROP THE THING AND GET OUT OF THERE.
I GOT IT, TREE JUMP.
YOU'RE TOO BIG FOR US TO BURY.
WE SHOULD GO, KING. I WON'T BE ABLE TO GUIDE YOU IF IT GETS DARK.
LET'S MOVE.

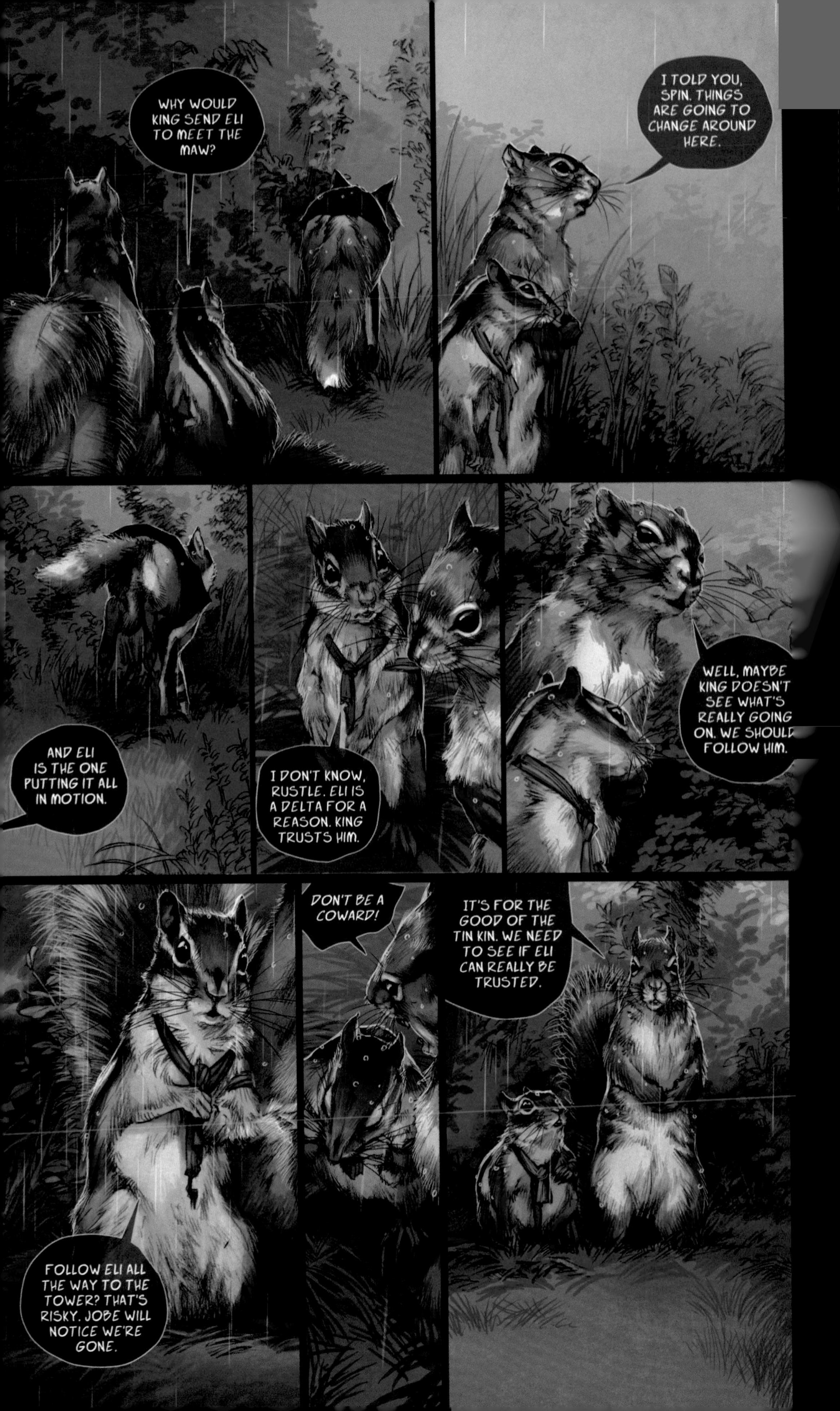
WHY WOULD KING SEND ELI TO MEET THE MAW?
I TOLD YOU, SPIN. THINGS ARE GOING TO CHANGE AROUND HERE.
AND ELI IS THE ONE PUTTING IT ALL IN MOTION.
I DON'T KNOW, RUSTLE. ELI IS A DELTA FOR A REASON. KING TRUSTS HIM.
WELL, MAYBE KING DOESN'T SEE WHAT'S REALLY GOING ON. WE SHOULD FOLLOW HIM.
FOLLOW ELI ALL THE WAY TO THE TOWER? THAT'S RISKY. JOBE WILL NOTICE WE'RE GONE.
DON'T BE A COWARD!
IT'S FOR THE GOOD OF THE TIN KIN. WE NEED TO SEE IF ELI CAN REALLY BE TRUSTED.

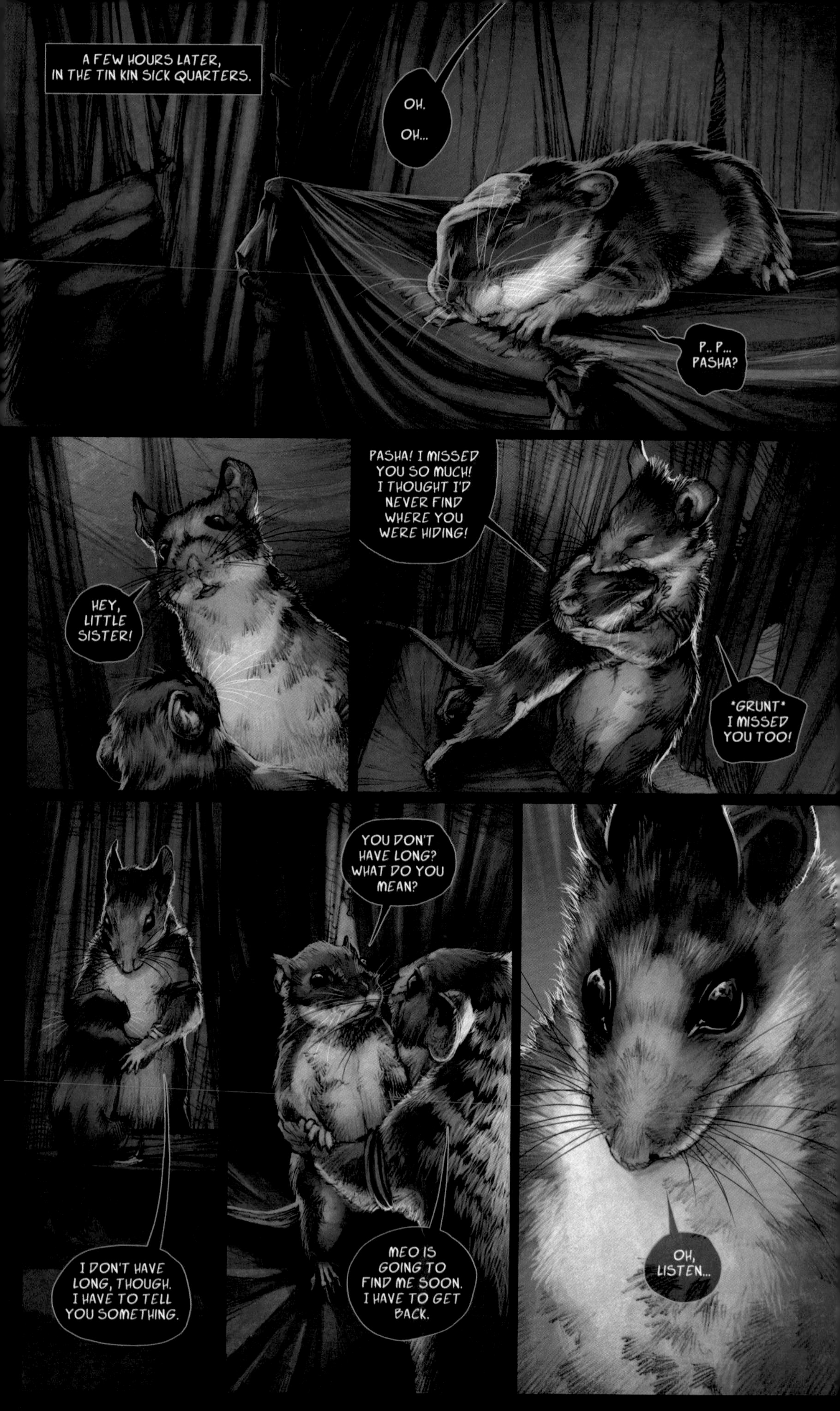
A FEW HOURS LATER, IN THE TIN KIN SICK QUARTERS.
OH.
OH...
P.. P... PASHA?
HEY, LITTLE SISTER!
PASHA! I MISSED YOU SO MUCH! I THOUGHT I'D NEVER FIND WHERE YOU WERE HIDING!
GRUNT I MISSED YOU TOO!
I DON'T HAVE LONG, THOUGH. I HAVE TO TELL YOU SOMETHING.
YOU DON'T HAVE LONG? WHAT DO YOU MEAN?
MEO IS GOING TO FIND ME SOON. I HAVE TO GET BACK.
OH, LISTEN...

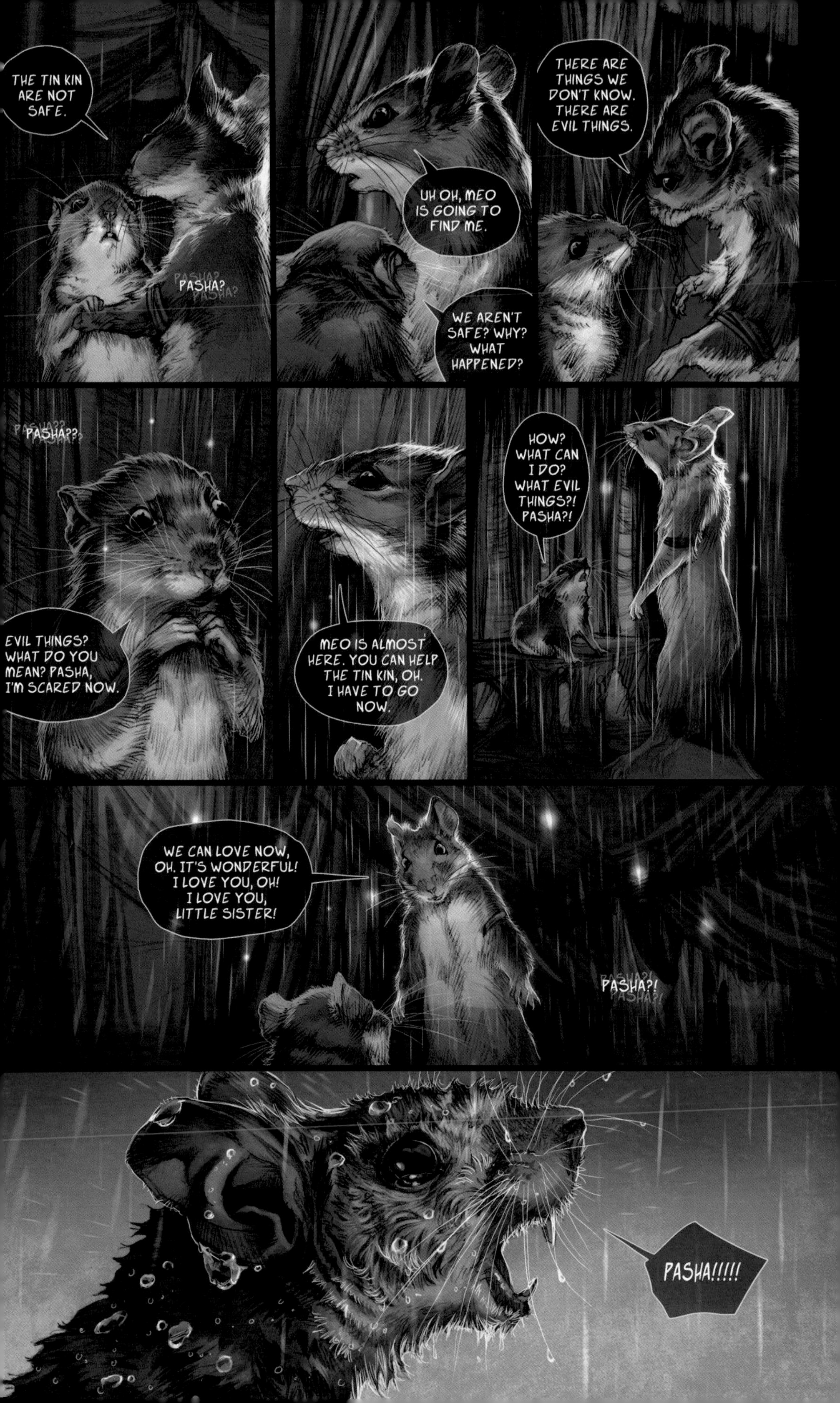

THE TIN KIN ARE NOT SAFE.
PASHA?
UH OH, MEO IS GOING TO FIND ME.
WE AREN'T SAFE? WHY? WHAT HAPPENED?
THERE ARE THINGS WE DON'T KNOW. THERE ARE EVIL THINGS.
PASHA??
EVIL THINGS? WHAT DO YOU MEAN? PASHA, I'M SCARED NOW.
MEO IS ALMOST HERE. YOU CAN HELP THE TIN KIN, OH. I HAVE TO GO NOW.
HOW? WHAT CAN I DO? WHAT EVIL THINGS?! PASHA?!
WE CAN LOVE NOW, OH. IT'S WONDERFUL! I LOVE YOU, OH! I LOVE YOU, LITTLE SISTER!
PASHA?!
PASHA!!!!!

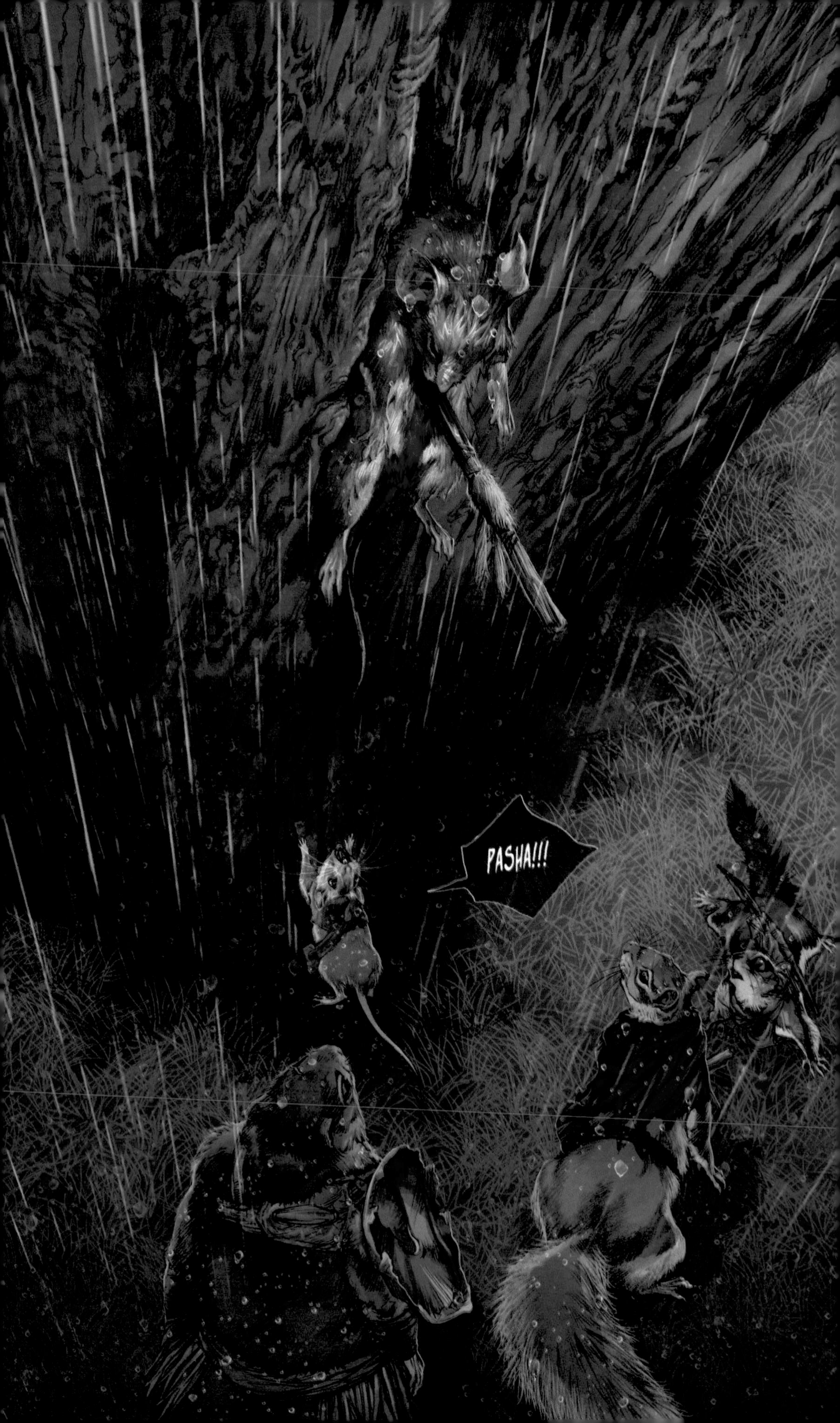
PASHA!!!

Chapter 3: Ghosts

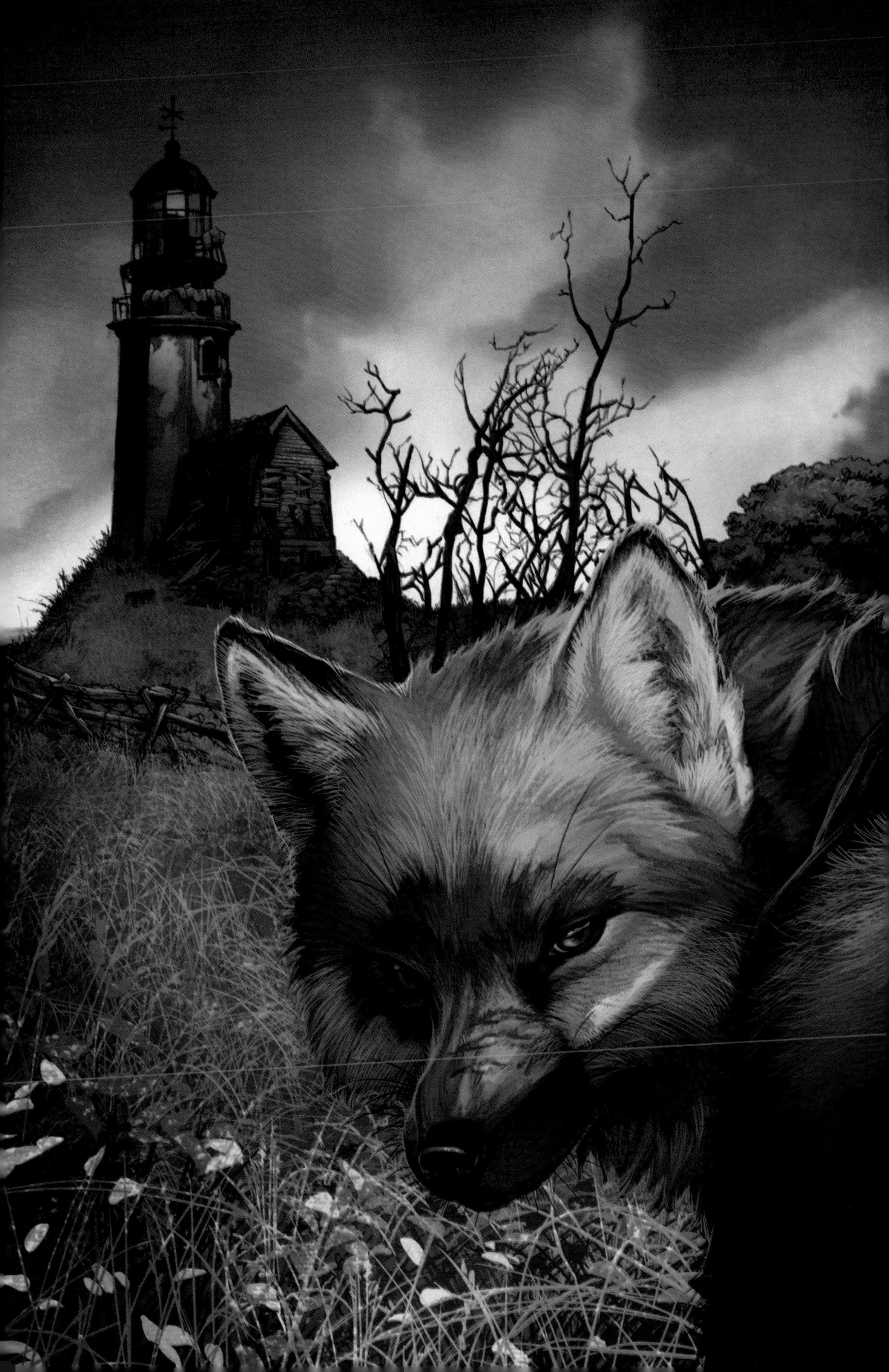

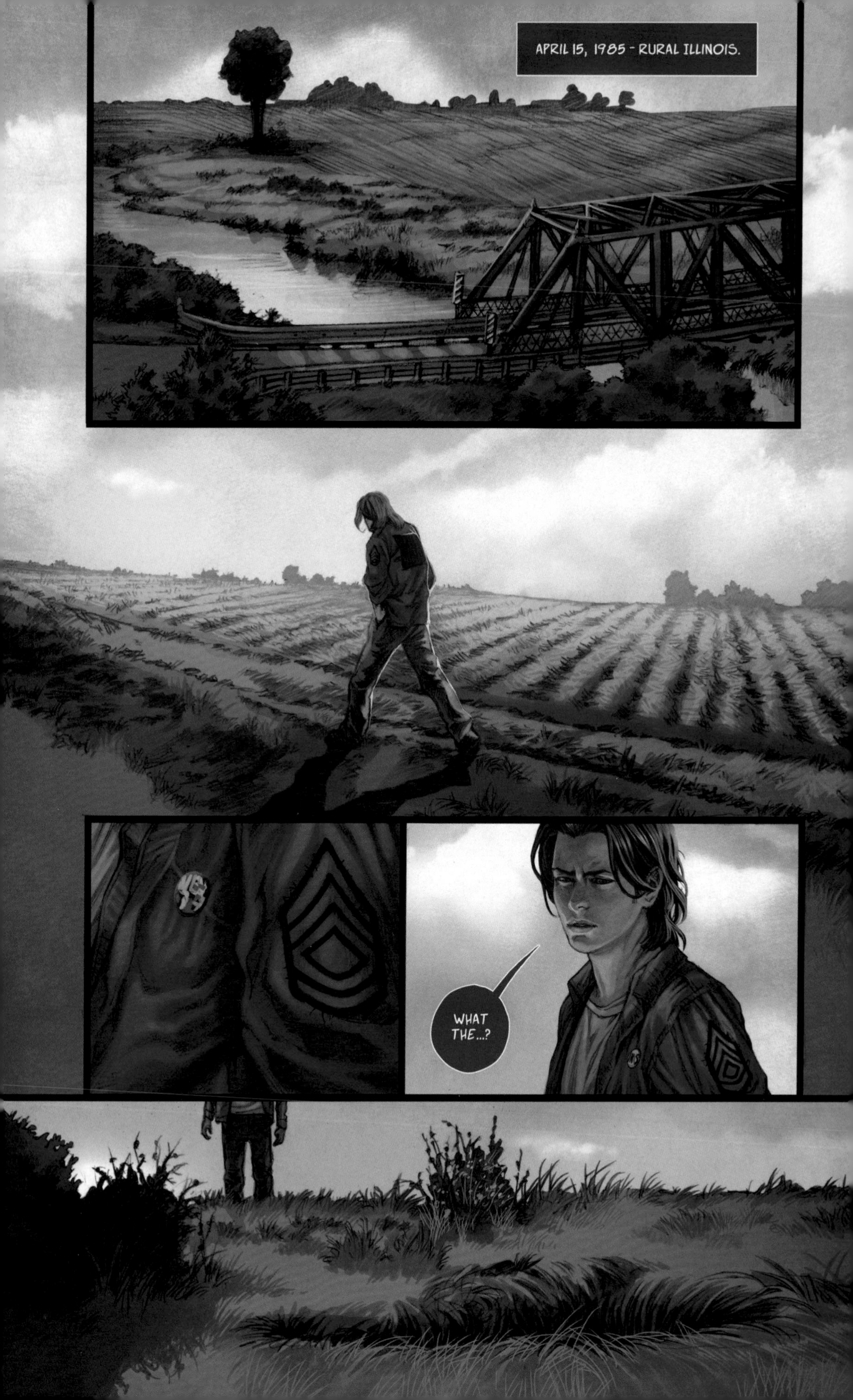
APRIL 15, 1985 - RURAL ILLINOIS.
WHAT THE...?

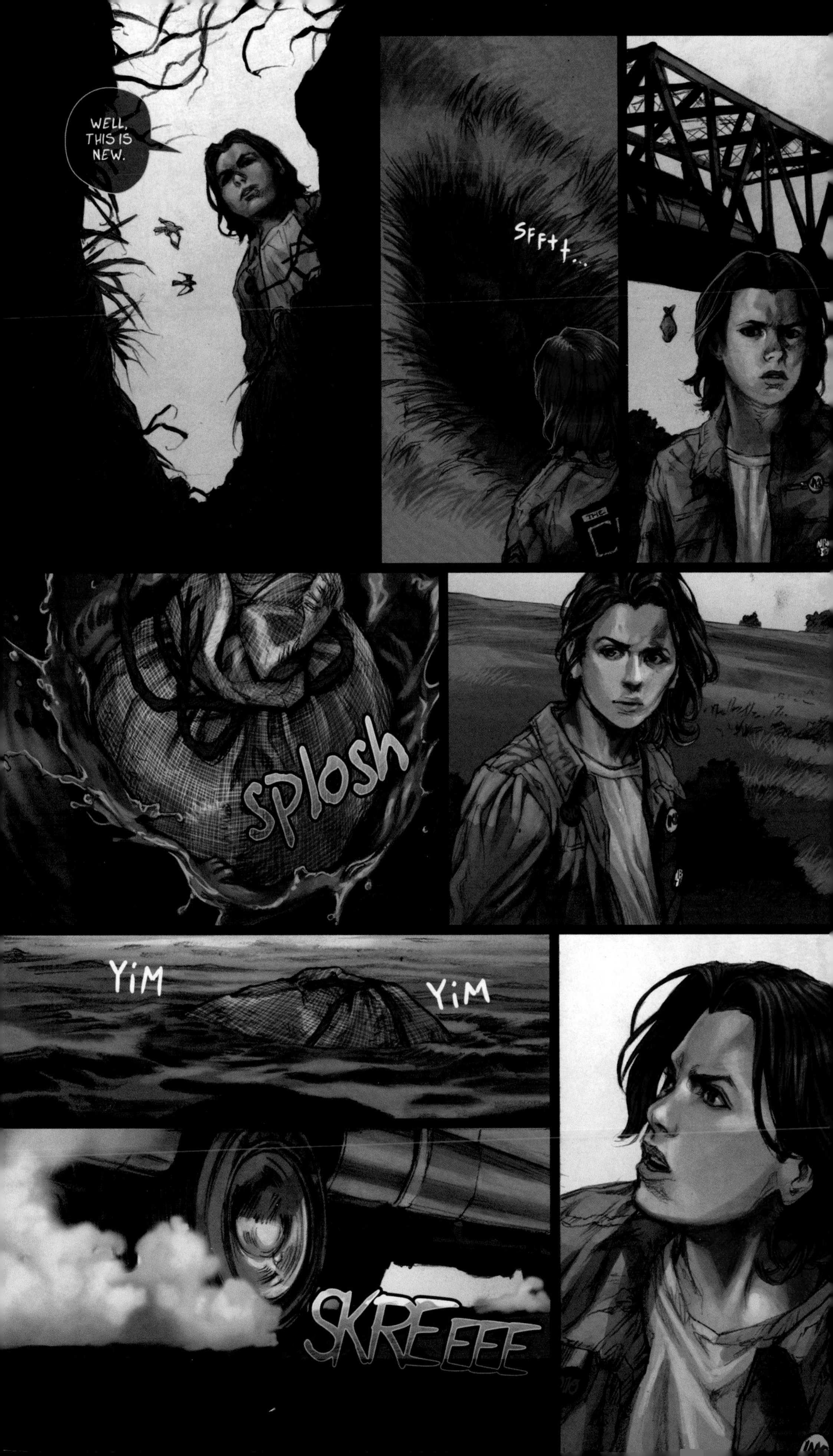
WELL, THIS IS NEW.
SFFtt...
splosh
YiM
YiM
SKREEEE

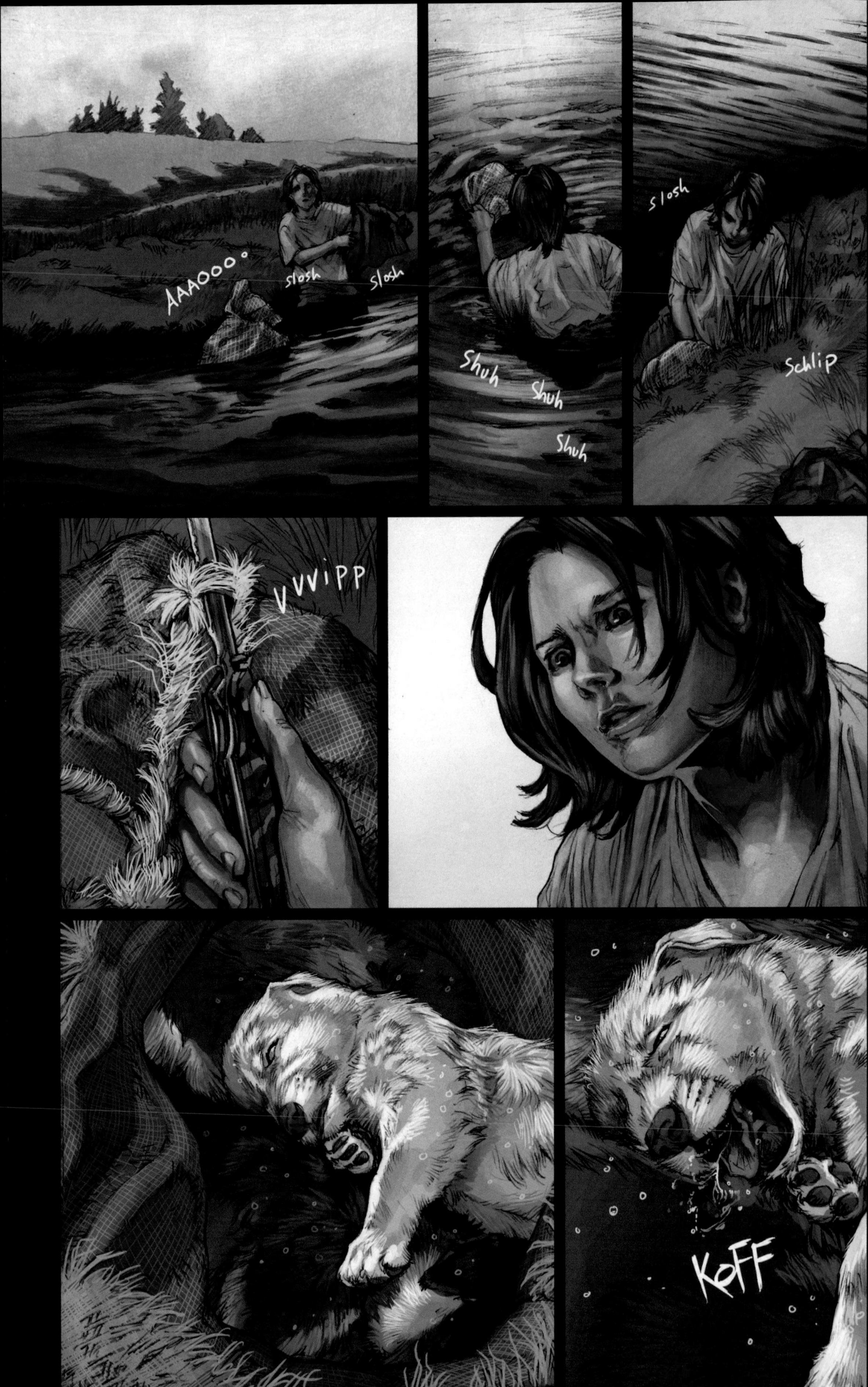
AAAOOOo
slosh
slosh
Shuh
Shuh
Shuh
slosh
Schlip
VVVIPP
KOFF

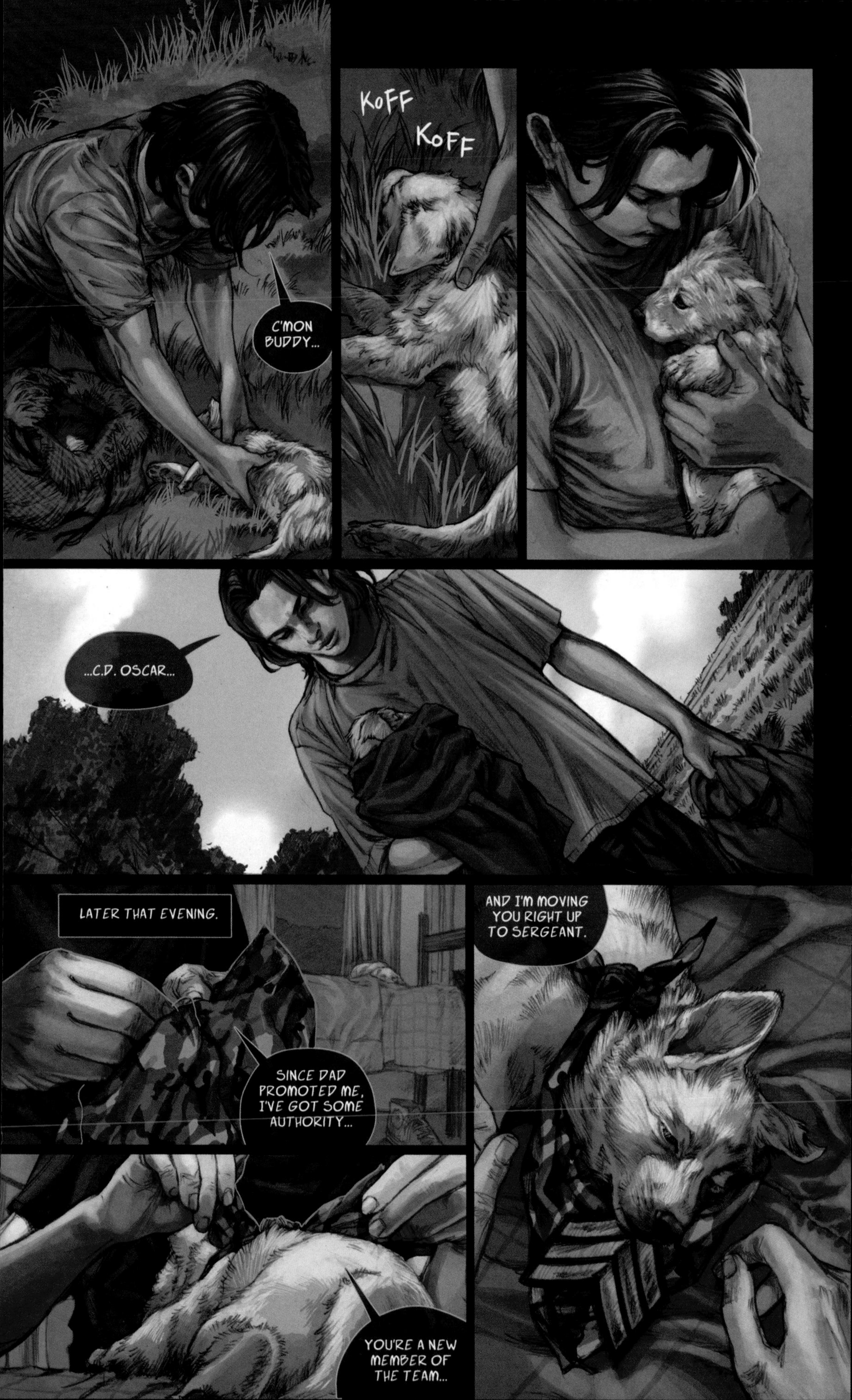
C'MON BUDDY...
KOFF KOFF
...C.D. OSCAR...
LATER THAT EVENING.
SINCE DAD PROMOTED ME, I'VE GOT SOME AUTHORITY...
YOU'RE A NEW MEMBER OF THE TEAM...
AND I'M MOVING YOU RIGHT UP TO SERGEANT.

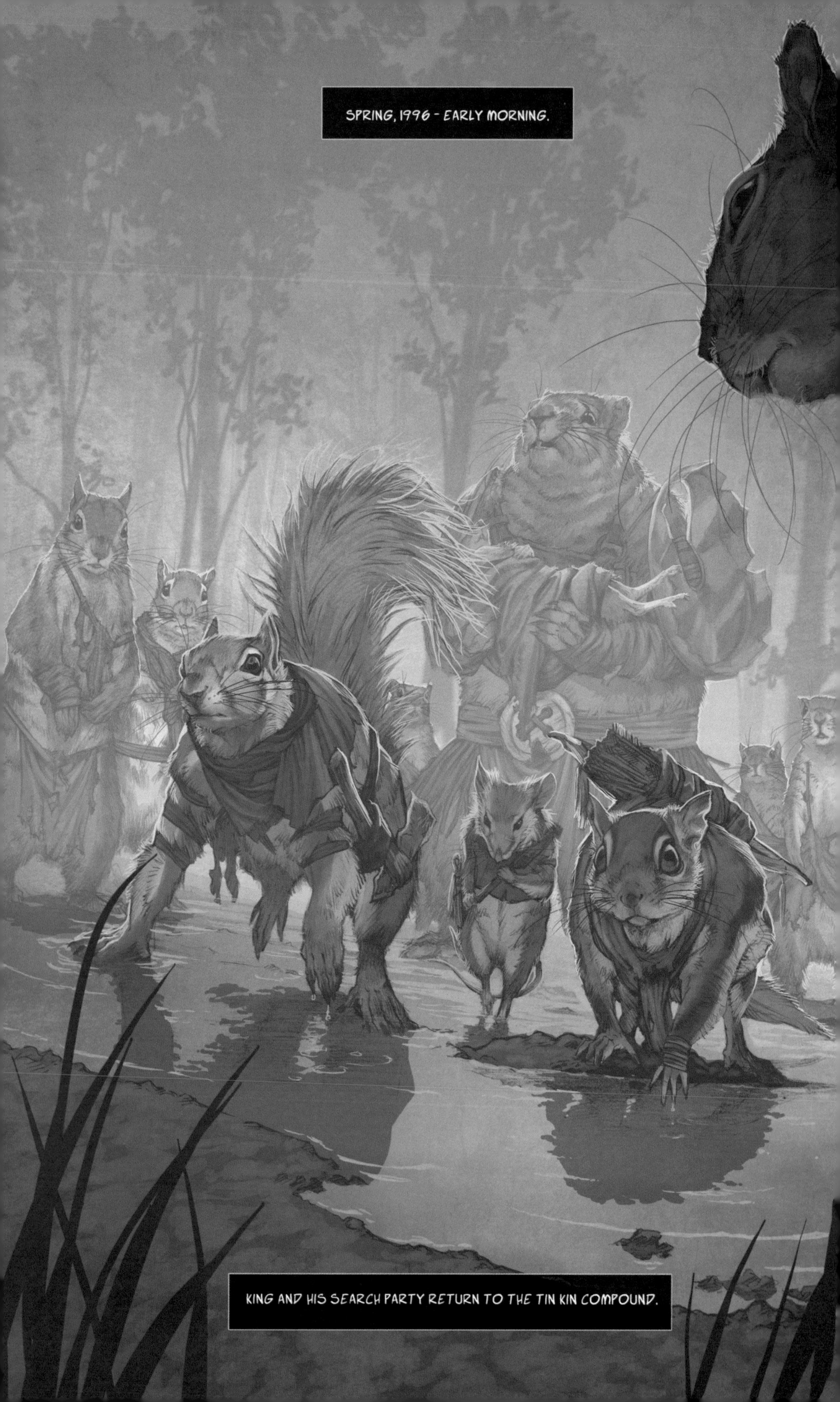
SPRING, 1996 - EARLY MORNING.
KING AND HIS SEARCH PARTY RETURN TO THE TIN KIN COMPOUND.

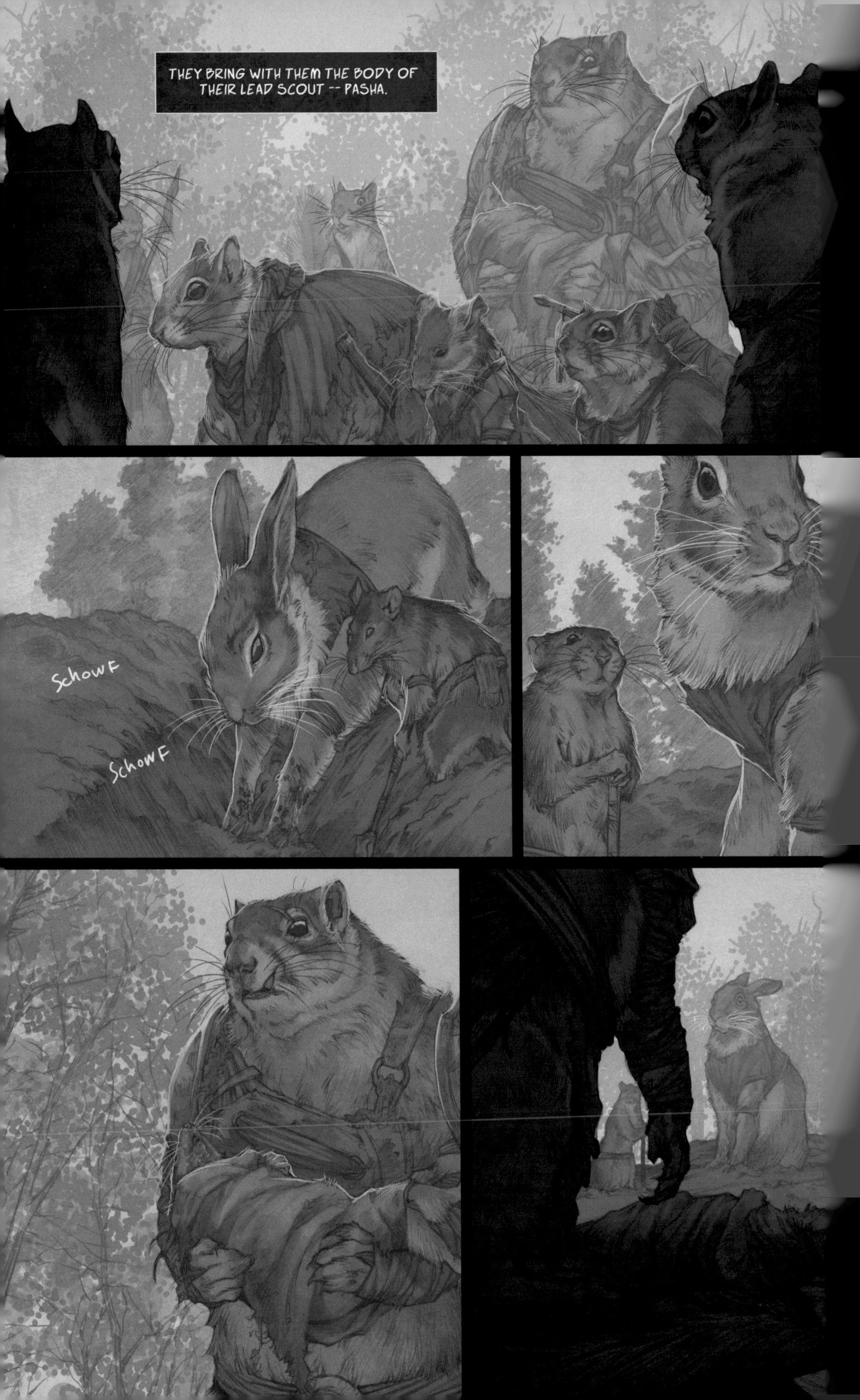
THEY BRING WITH THEM THE BODY OF THEIR LEAD SCOUT -- PASHA.
SCHOWF
SCHOWF

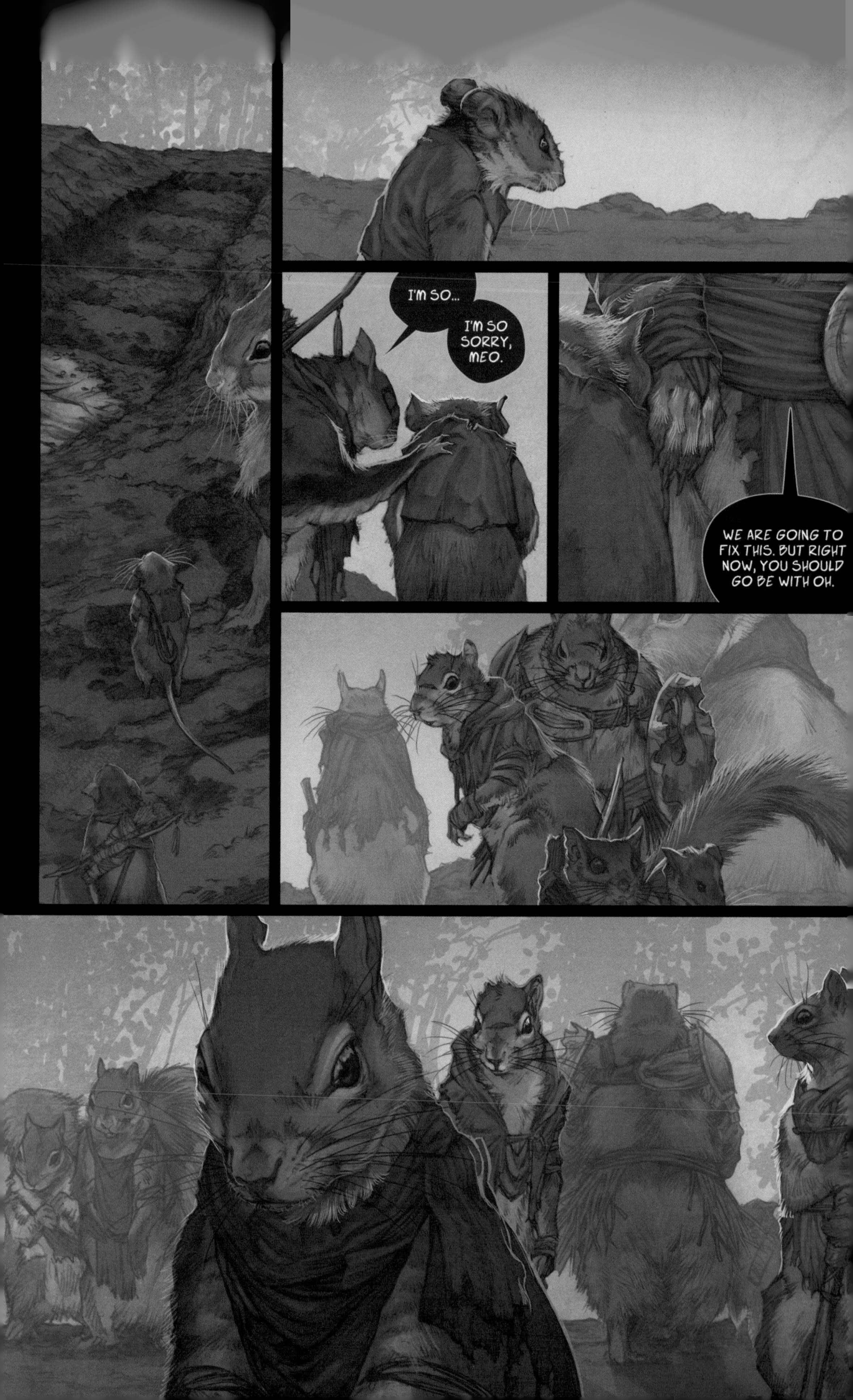
I'M SO...
I'M SO SORRY, MEO.
WE ARE GOING TO FIX THIS. BUT RIGHT NOW, YOU SHOULD GO BE WITH OH.

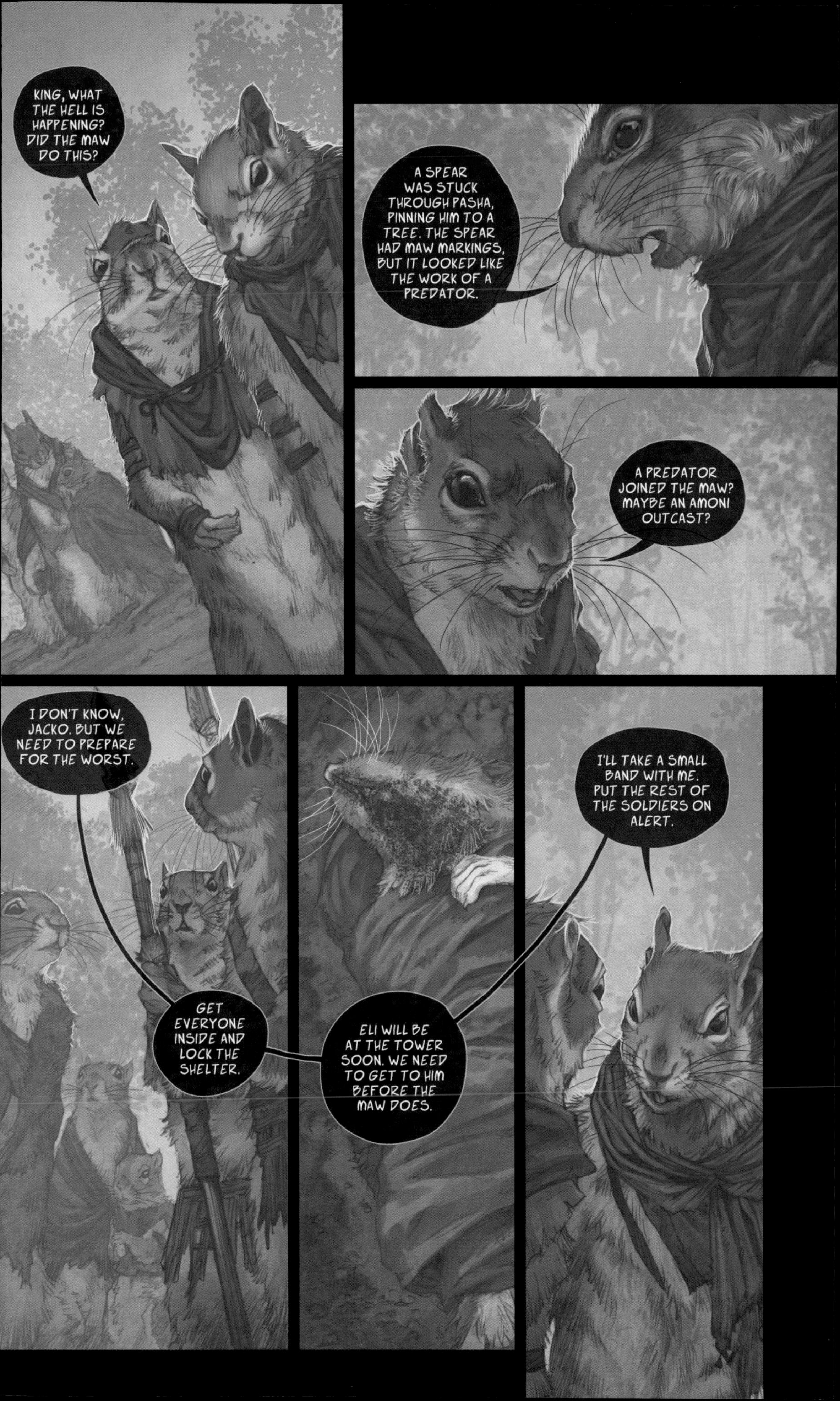
KING, WHAT THE HELL IS HAPPENING? DID THE MAW DO THIS?
A SPEAR WAS STUCK THROUGH PASHA, PINNING HIM TO A TREE. THE SPEAR HAD MAW MARKINGS, BUT IT LOOKED LIKE THE WORK OF A PREDATOR.
A PREDATOR JOINED THE MAW? MAYBE AN AMONI OUTCAST?
I DON'T KNOW, JACKO. BUT WE NEED TO PREPARE FOR THE WORST.
GET EVERYONE INSIDE AND LOCK THE SHELTER.
ELI WILL BE AT THE TOWER SOON. WE NEED TO GET TO HIM BEFORE THE MAW DOES.
I'LL TAKE A SMALL BAND WITH ME. PUT THE REST OF THE SOLDIERS ON ALERT.

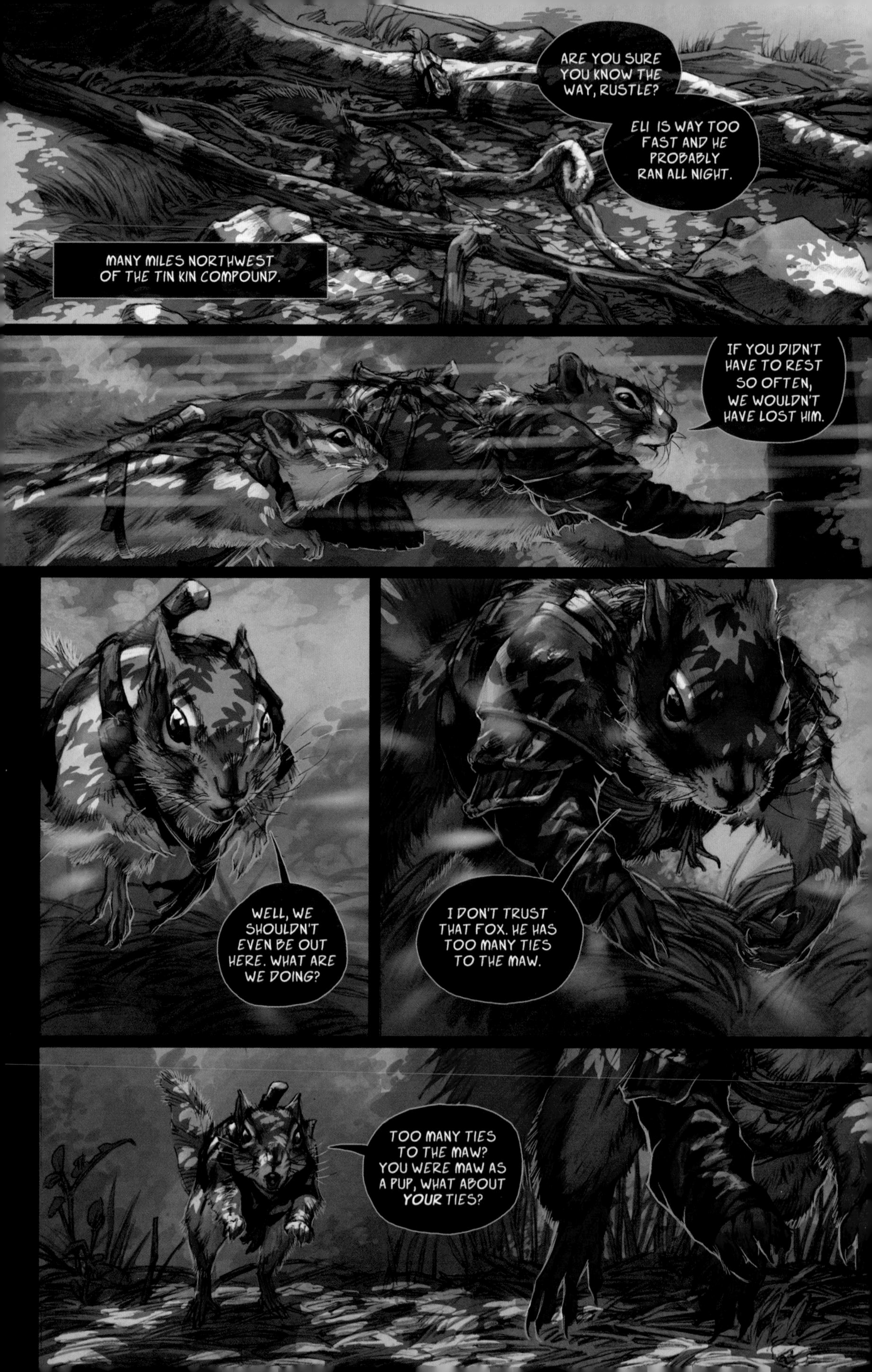
ARE YOU SURE YOU KNOW THE WAY, RUSTLE?
ELI IS WAY TOO FAST AND HE PROBABLY RAN ALL NIGHT.
MANY MILES NORTHWEST OF THE TIN KIN COMPOUND.
IF YOU DIDN'T HAVE TO REST SO OFTEN, WE WOULDN'T HAVE LOST HIM.
WELL, WE SHOULDN'T EVEN BE OUT HERE. WHAT ARE WE DOING?
I DON'T TRUST THAT FOX. HE HAS TOO MANY TIES TO THE MAW.
TOO MANY TIES TO THE MAW? YOU WERE MAW AS A PUP, WHAT ABOUT YOUR TIES?

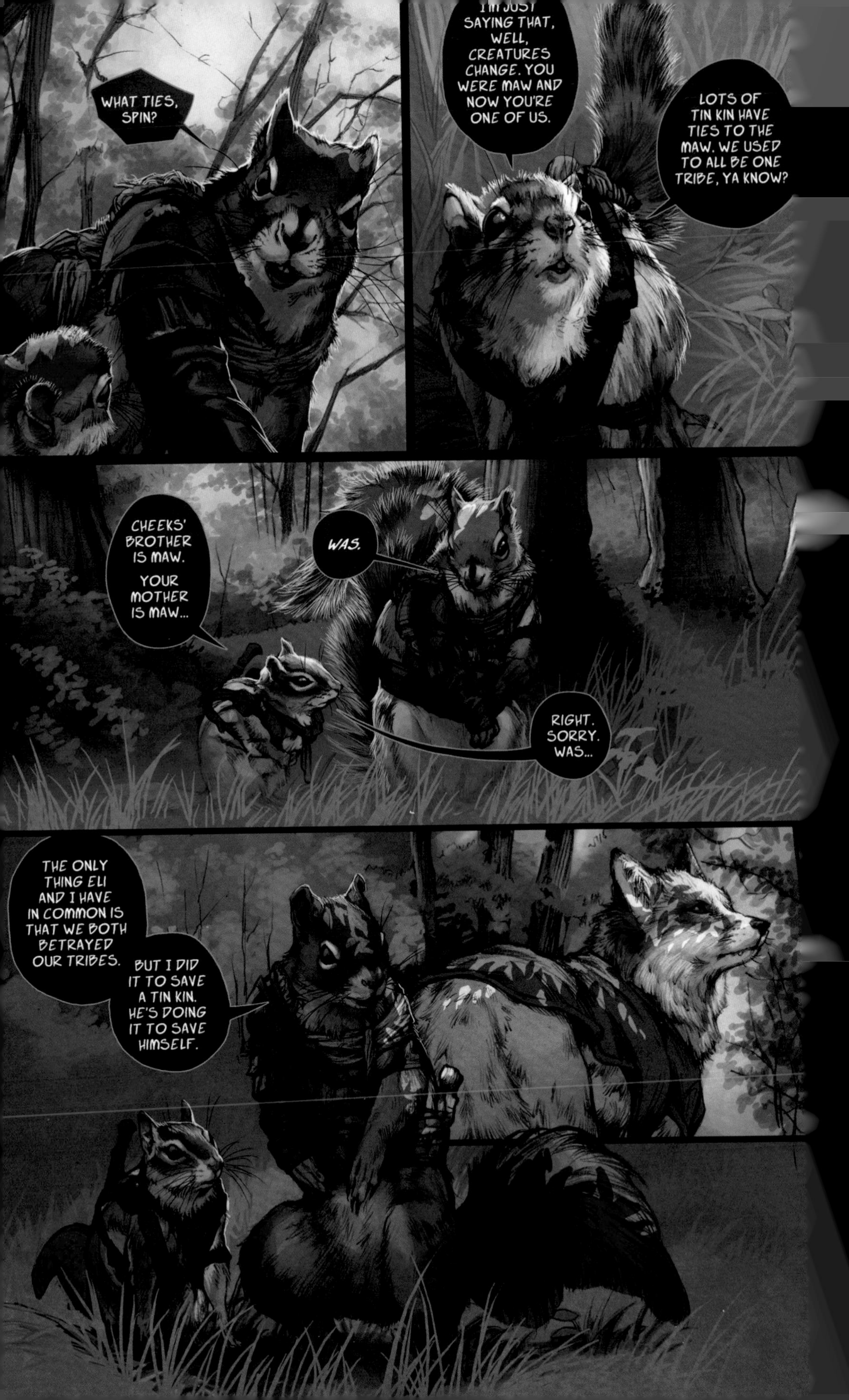
WHAT TIES, SPIN?
I'M JUST SAYING THAT, WELL, CREATURES CHANGE. YOU WERE MAW AND NOW YOU'RE ONE OF US.
LOTS OF TIN KIN HAVE TIES TO THE MAW. WE USED TO ALL BE ONE TRIBE, YA KNOW?
CHEEKS' BROTHER IS MAW.
YOUR MOTHER IS MAW...
WAS.
RIGHT. SORRY. WAS...
THE ONLY THING ELI AND I HAVE IN COMMON IS THAT WE BOTH BETRAYED OUR TRIBES.
BUT I DID IT TO SAVE A TIN KIN. HE'S DOING IT TO SAVE HIMSELF.

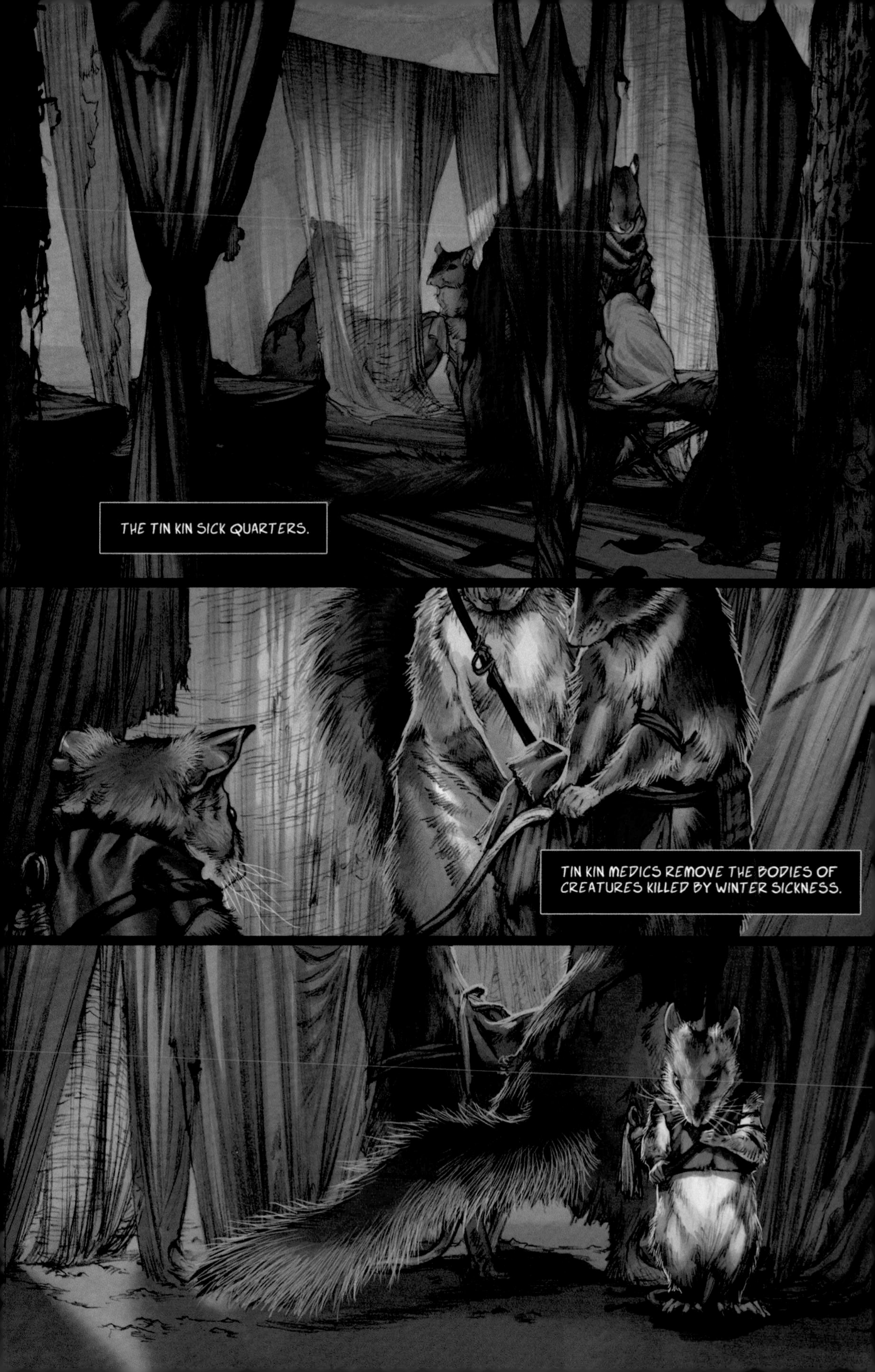
THE TIN KIN SICK QUARTERS.
TIN KIN MEDICS REMOVE THE BODIES OF CREATURES KILLED BY WINTER SICKNESS.

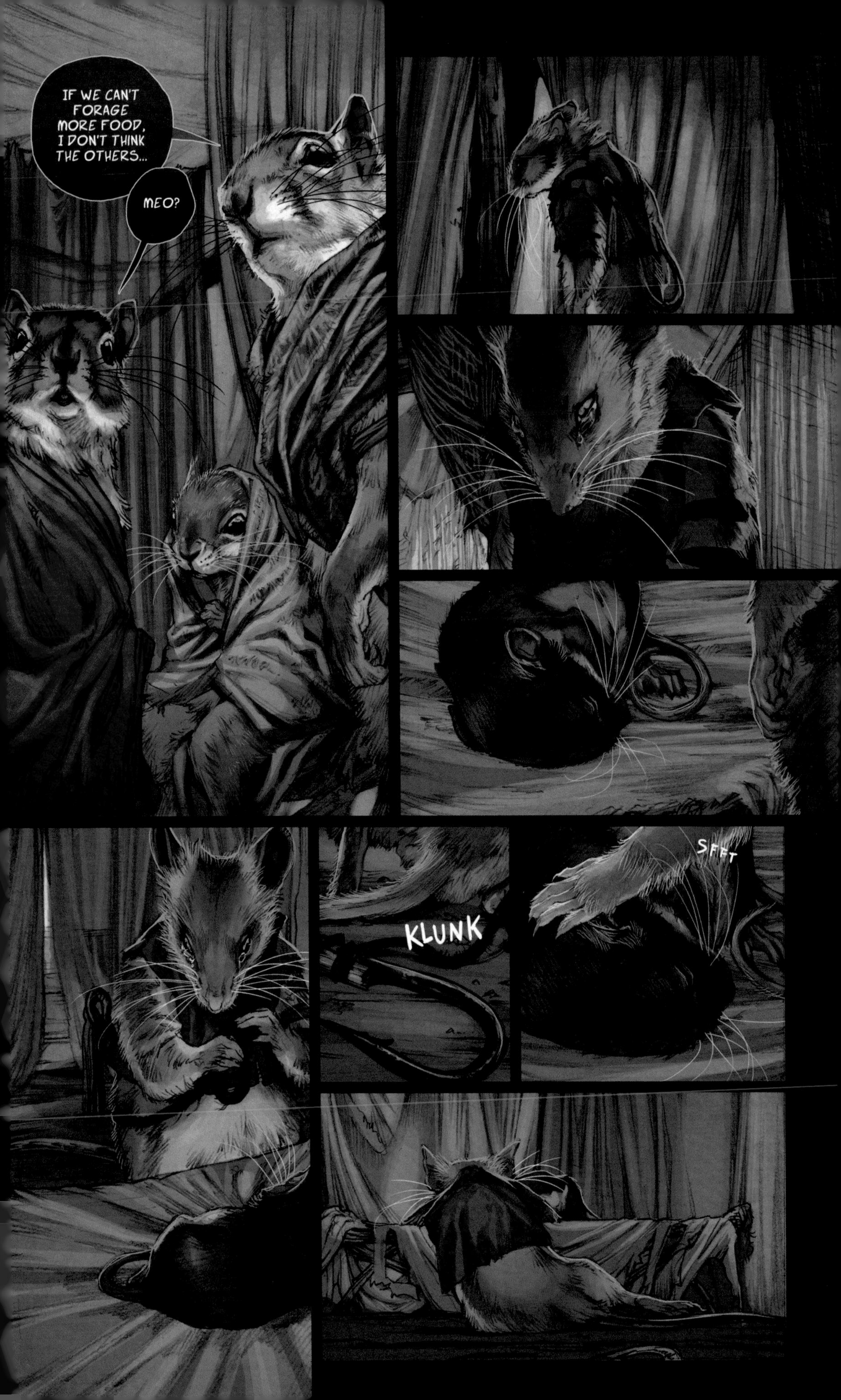
IF WE CAN'T FORAGE MORE FOOD, I DON'T THINK THE OTHERS...
MEO?
KLUNK
SFFT

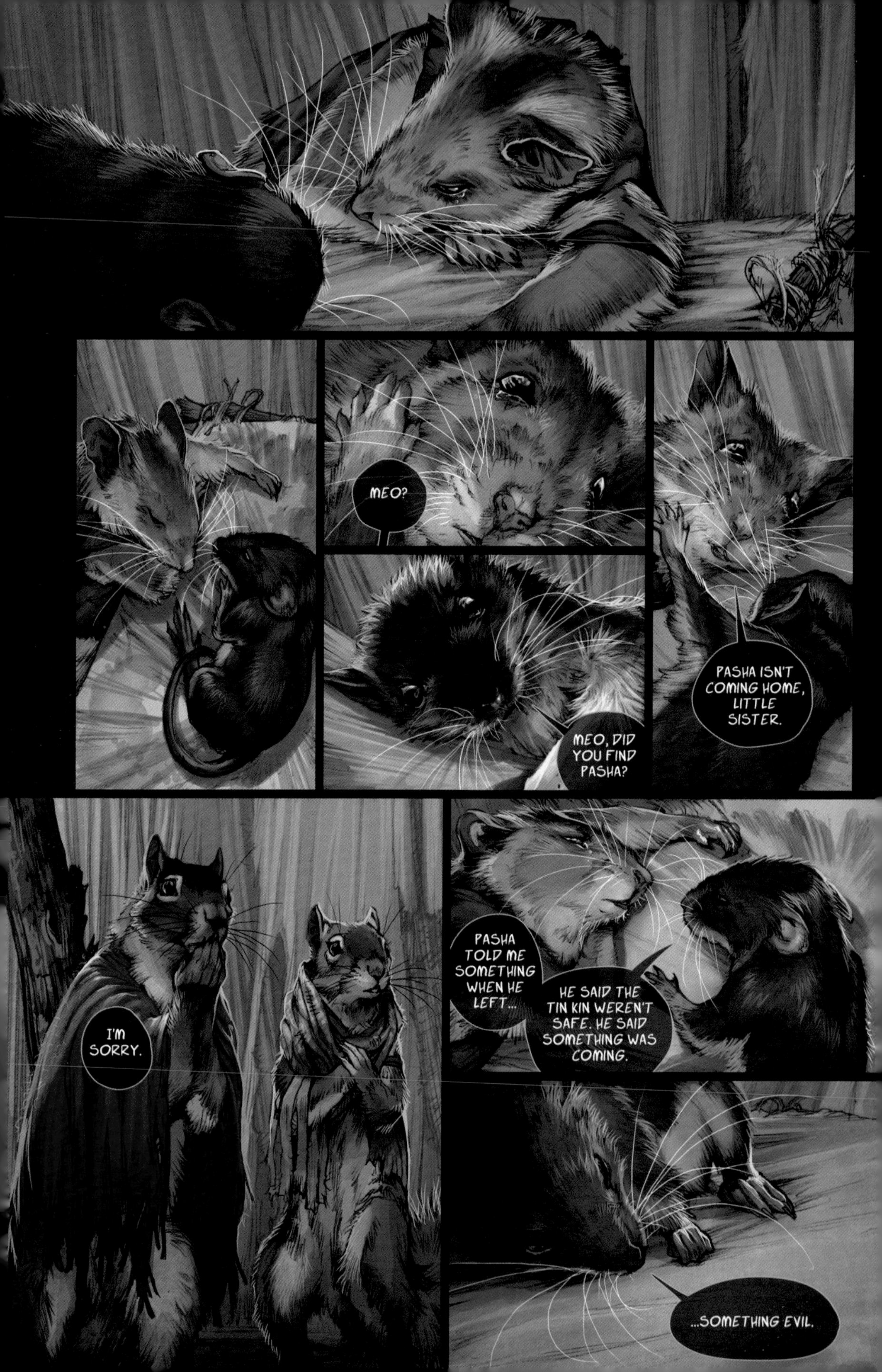
MEO?
MEO, DID YOU FIND PASHA?
PASHA ISN'T COMING HOME, LITTLE SISTER.
I'M SORRY.
PASHA TOLD ME SOMETHING WHEN HE LEFT...
HE SAID THE TIN KIN WEREN'T SAFE. HE SAID SOMETHING WAS COMING.
...SOMETHING EVIL.

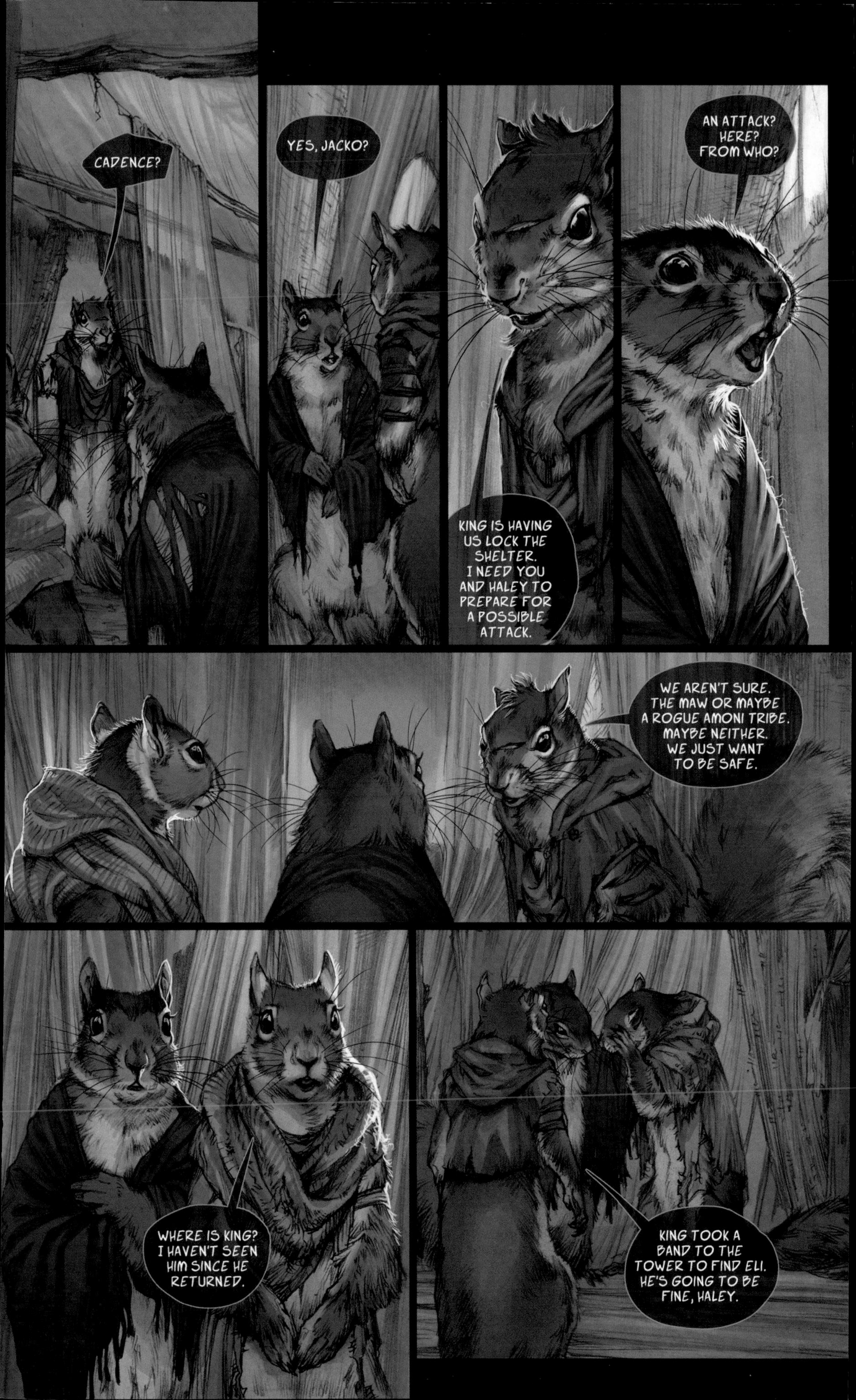
CADENCE?
YES, JACKO?
KING IS HAVING US LOCK THE SHELTER. I NEED YOU AND HALEY TO PREPARE FOR A POSSIBLE ATTACK.
AN ATTACK? HERE? FROM WHO?
WE AREN'T SURE. THE MAW OR MAYBE A ROGUE AMONI TRIBE. MAYBE NEITHER. WE JUST WANT TO BE SAFE.
WHERE IS KING? I HAVEN'T SEEN HIM SINCE HE RETURNED.
KING TOOK A BAND TO THE TOWER TO FIND ELI. HE'S GOING TO BE FINE, HALEY.

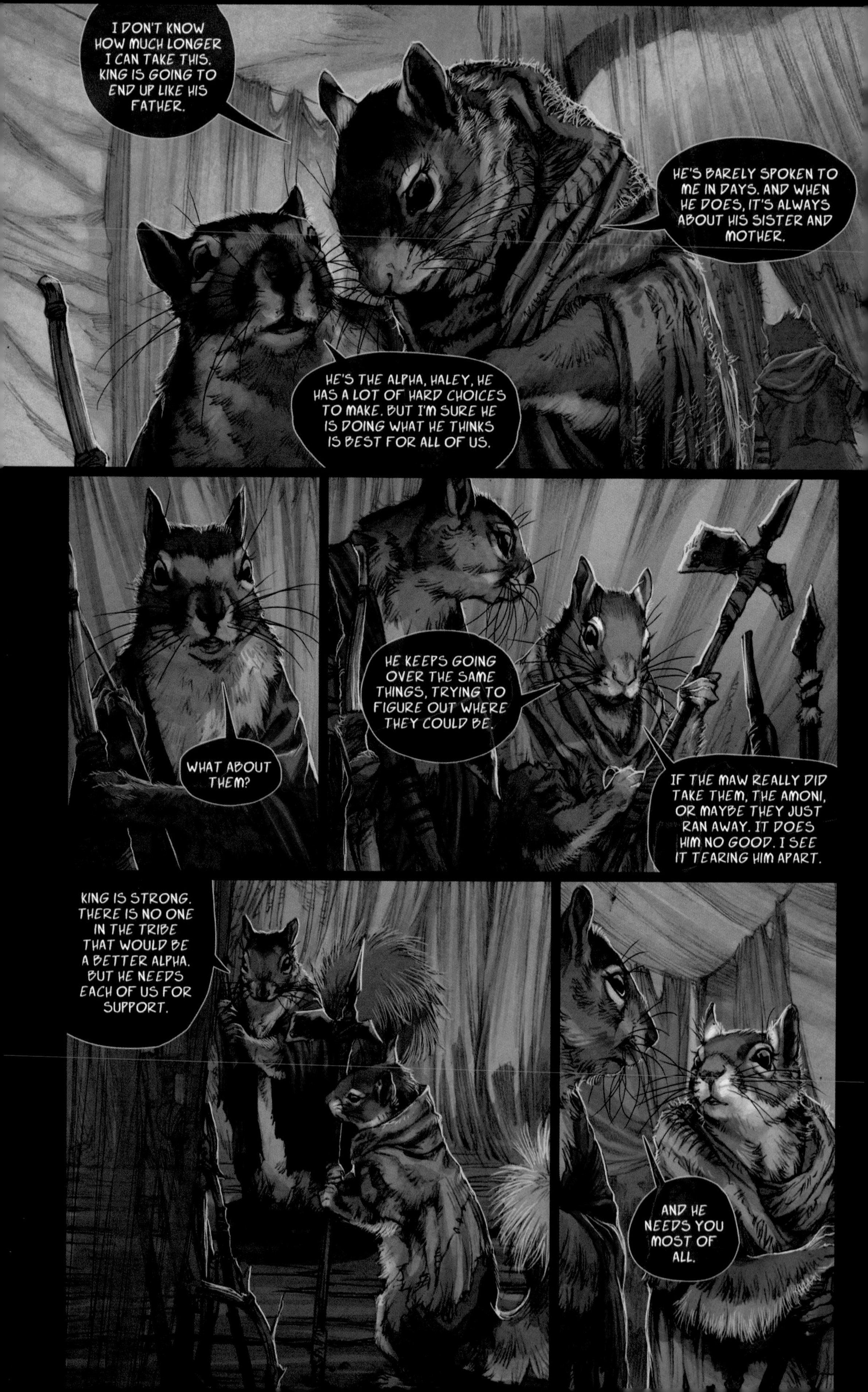
I DON'T KNOW HOW MUCH LONGER I CAN TAKE THIS. KING IS GOING TO END UP LIKE HIS FATHER.
HE'S BARELY SPOKEN TO ME IN DAYS. AND WHEN HE DOES, IT'S ALWAYS ABOUT HIS SISTER AND MOTHER.
HE'S THE ALPHA, HALEY, HE HAS A LOT OF HARD CHOICES TO MAKE. BUT I'M SURE HE IS DOING WHAT HE THINKS IS BEST FOR ALL OF US.
WHAT ABOUT THEM?
HE KEEPS GOING OVER THE SAME THINGS, TRYING TO FIGURE OUT WHERE THEY COULD BE.
IF THE MAW REALLY DID TAKE THEM, THE AMONI, OR MAYBE THEY JUST RAN AWAY. IT DOES HIM NO GOOD. I SEE IT TEARING HIM APART.
KING IS STRONG. THERE IS NO ONE IN THE TRIBE THAT WOULD BE A BETTER ALPHA. BUT HE NEEDS EACH OF US FOR SUPPORT.
AND HE NEEDS YOU MOST OF ALL.

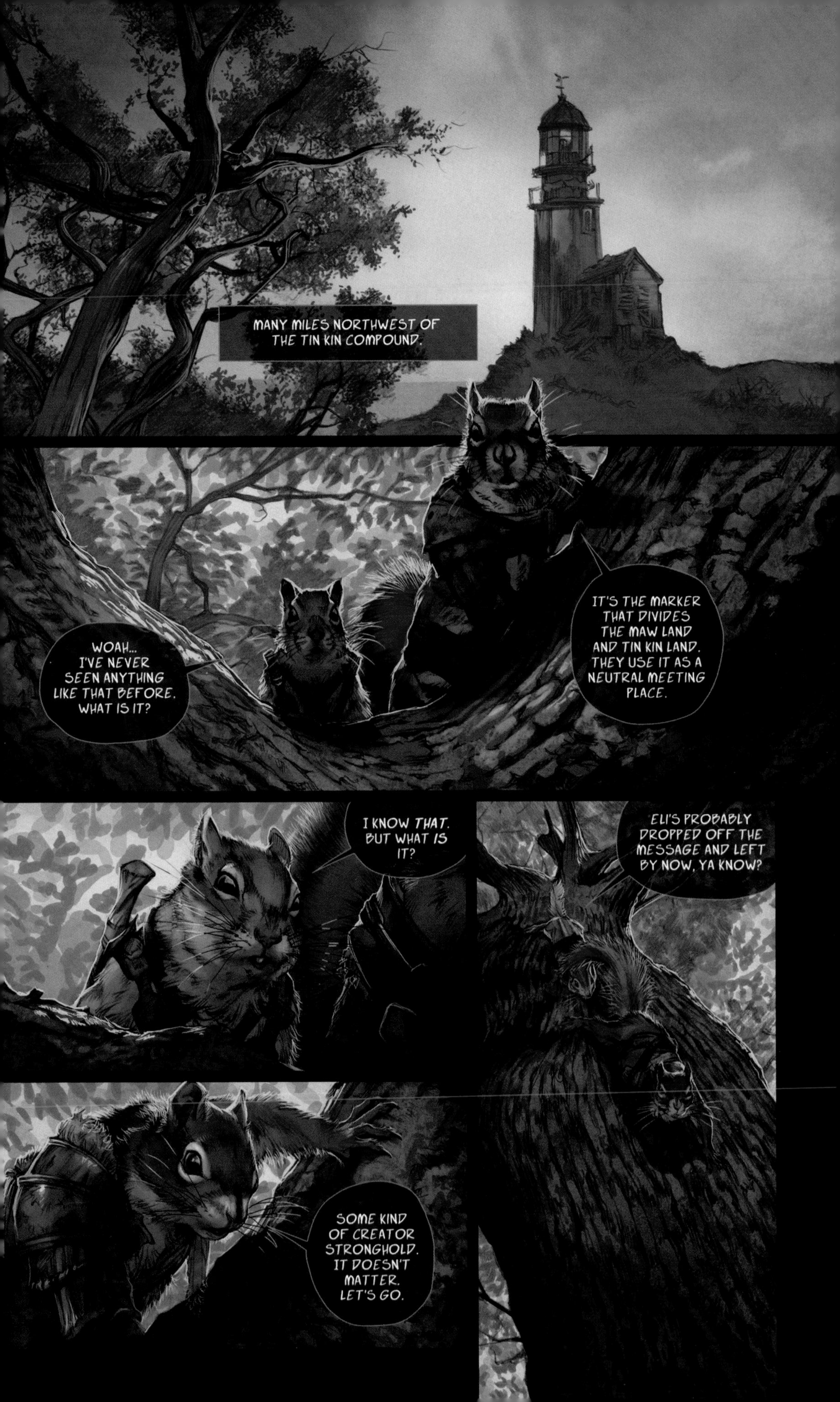
MANY MILES NORTHWEST OF THE TIN KIN COMPOUND.
WOAH... I'VE NEVER SEEN ANYTHING LIKE THAT BEFORE. WHAT IS IT?
IT'S THE MARKER THAT DIVIDES THE MAW LAND AND TIN KIN LAND. THEY USE IT AS A NEUTRAL MEETING PLACE.
I KNOW THAT. BUT WHAT IS IT?
SOME KIND OF CREATOR STRONGHOLD. IT DOESN'T MATTER. LET'S GO.
ELI'S PROBABLY DROPPED OFF THE MESSAGE AND LEFT BY NOW, YA KNOW?

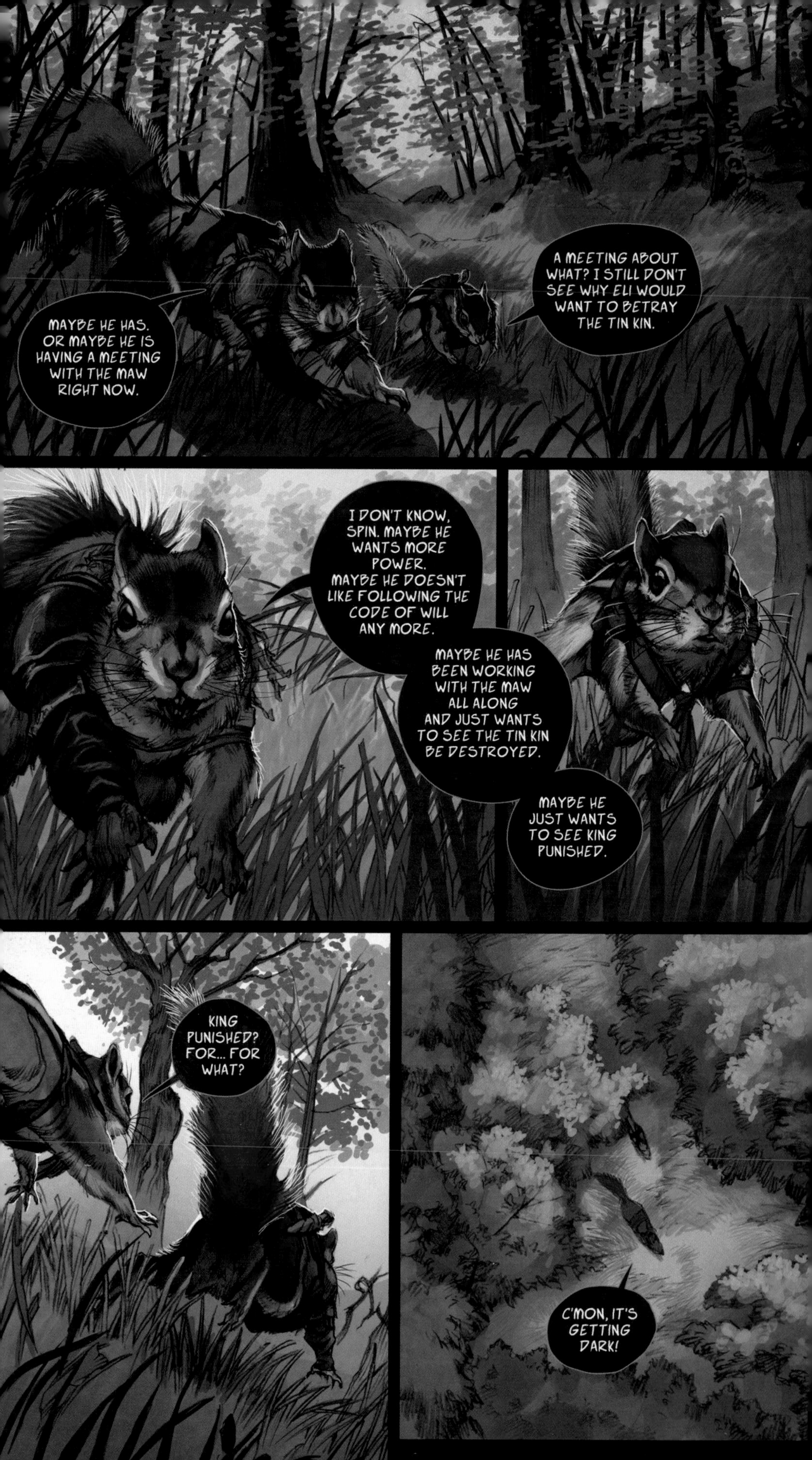
MAYBE HE HAS. OR MAYBE HE IS HAVING A MEETING WITH THE MAW RIGHT NOW.
A MEETING ABOUT WHAT? I STILL DON'T SEE WHY ELI WOULD WANT TO BETRAY THE TIN KIN.
I DON'T KNOW, SPIN. MAYBE HE WANTS MORE POWER. MAYBE HE DOESN'T LIKE FOLLOWING THE CODE OF WILL ANY MORE.
MAYBE HE HAS BEEN WORKING WITH THE MAW ALL ALONG AND JUST WANTS TO SEE THE TIN KIN BE DESTROYED.
MAYBE HE JUST WANTS TO SEE KING PUNISHED.
KING PUNISHED? FOR... FOR WHAT?
C'MON, IT'S GETTING DARK!

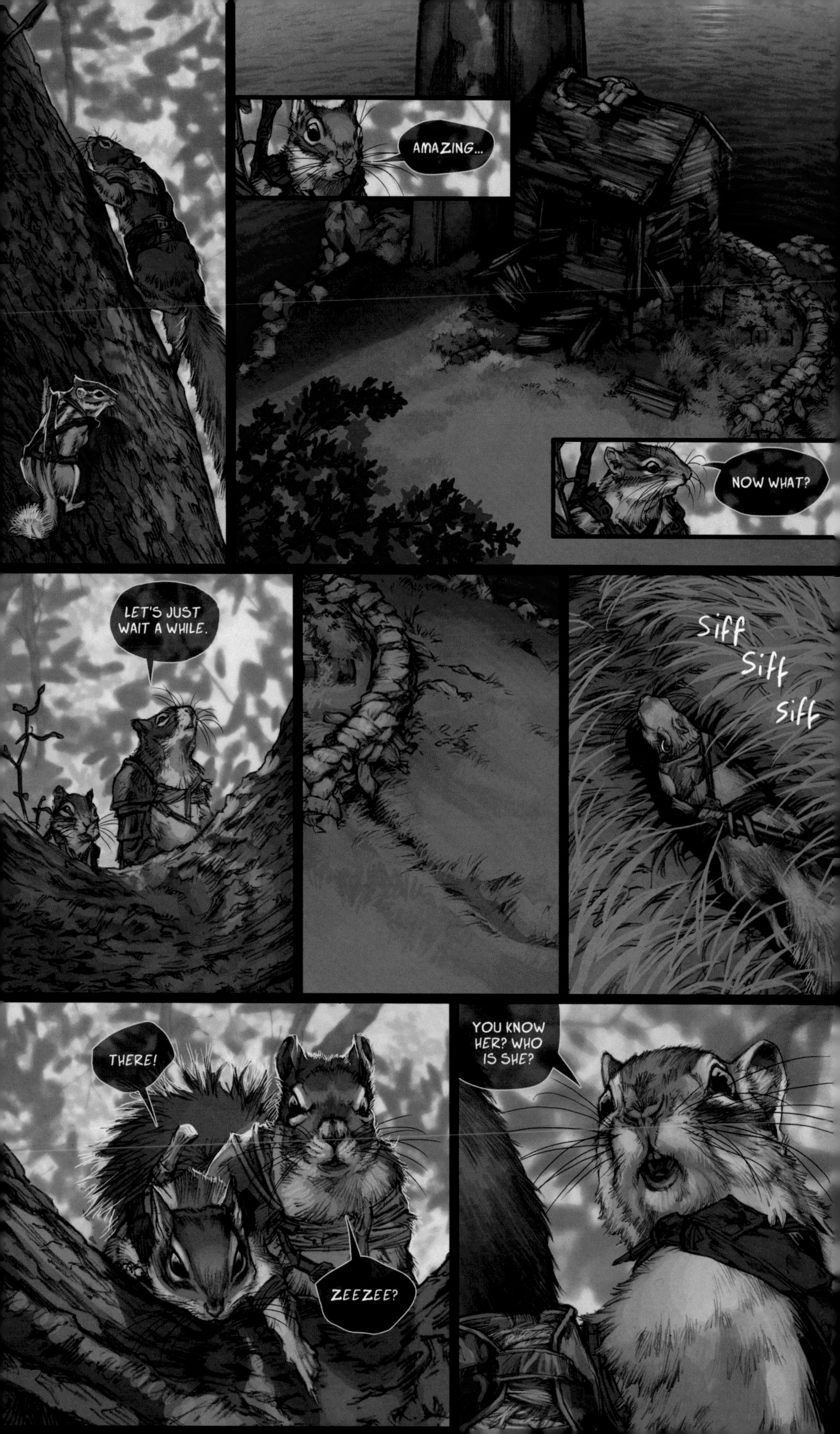
AMAZING...
NOW WHAT?
LET'S JUST WAIT A WHILE.
Siff
Siff
Siff
THERE!
ZEEZEE?
YOU KNOW HER? WHO IS SHE?

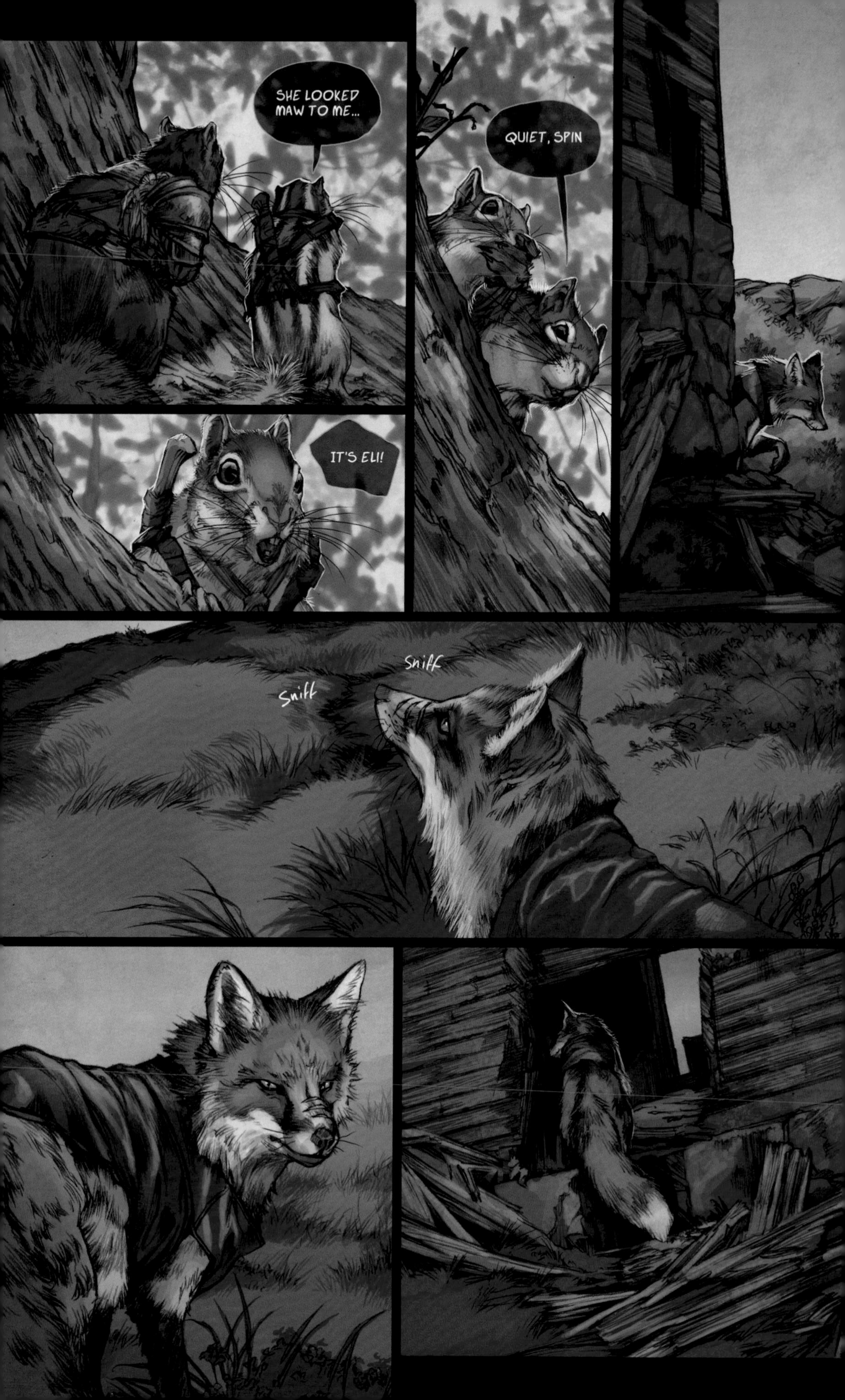
SHE LOOKED MAW TO ME...
QUIET, SPIN
IT'S ELI!
Sniff
Sniff

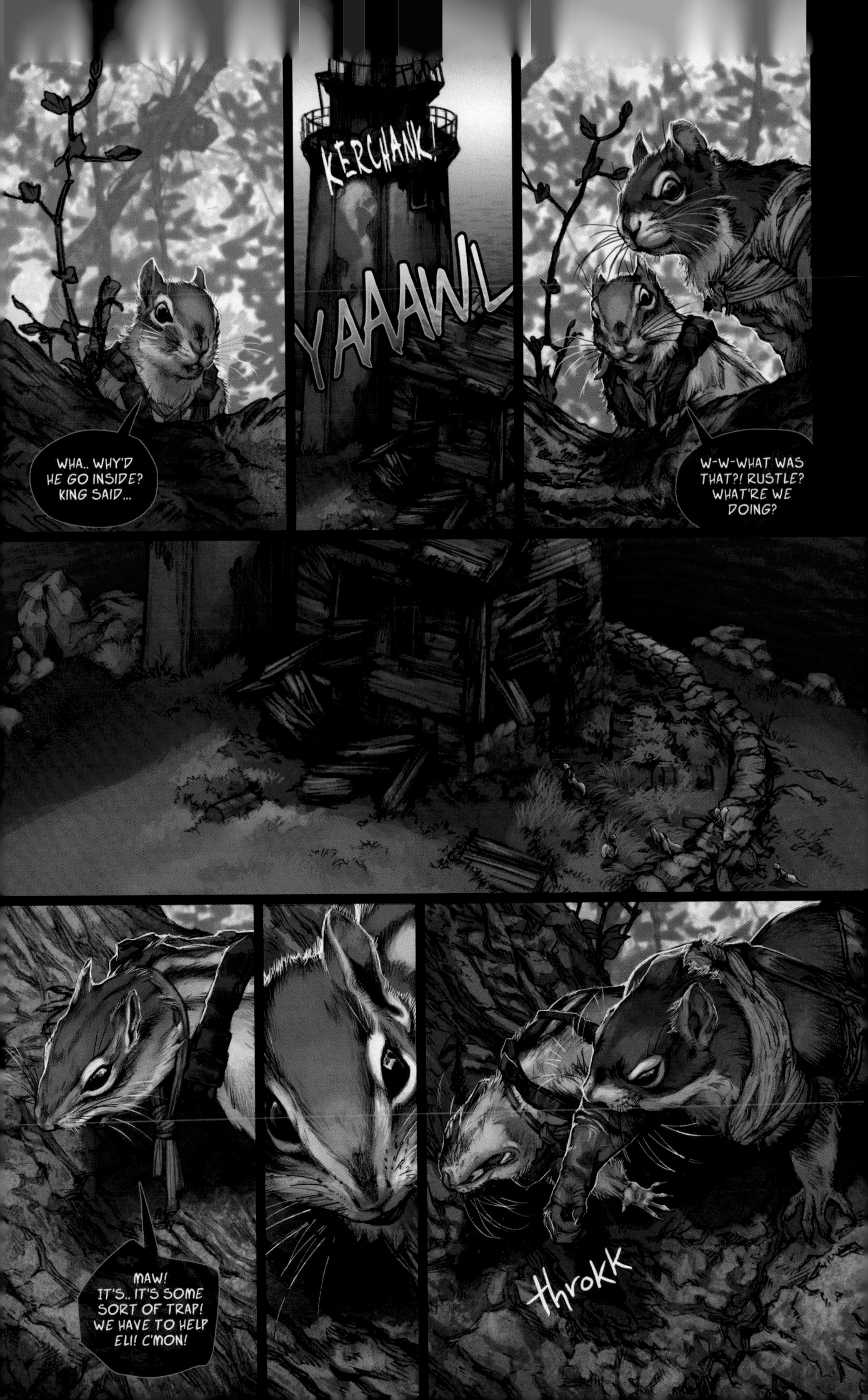
WHA.. WHY'D HE GO INSIDE? KING SAID...
KERCHANK!
YAAAWL
W-W-WHAT WAS THAT?! RUSTLE? WHAT'RE WE DOING?
MAW! IT'S.. IT'S SOME SORT OF TRAP! WE HAVE TO HELP ELI! C'MON!
throkk

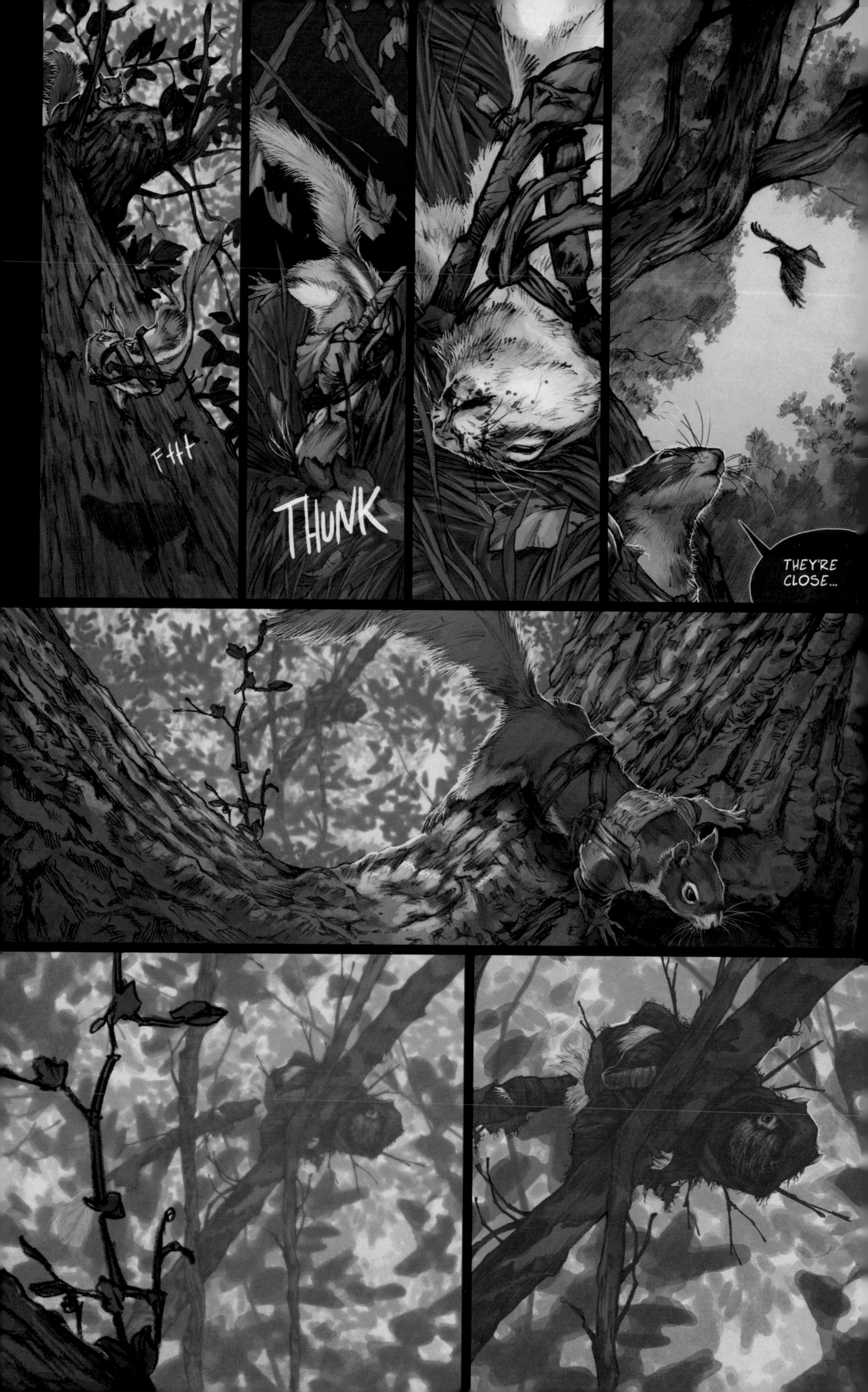
FTTT
THUNK
THEY'RE CLOSE...

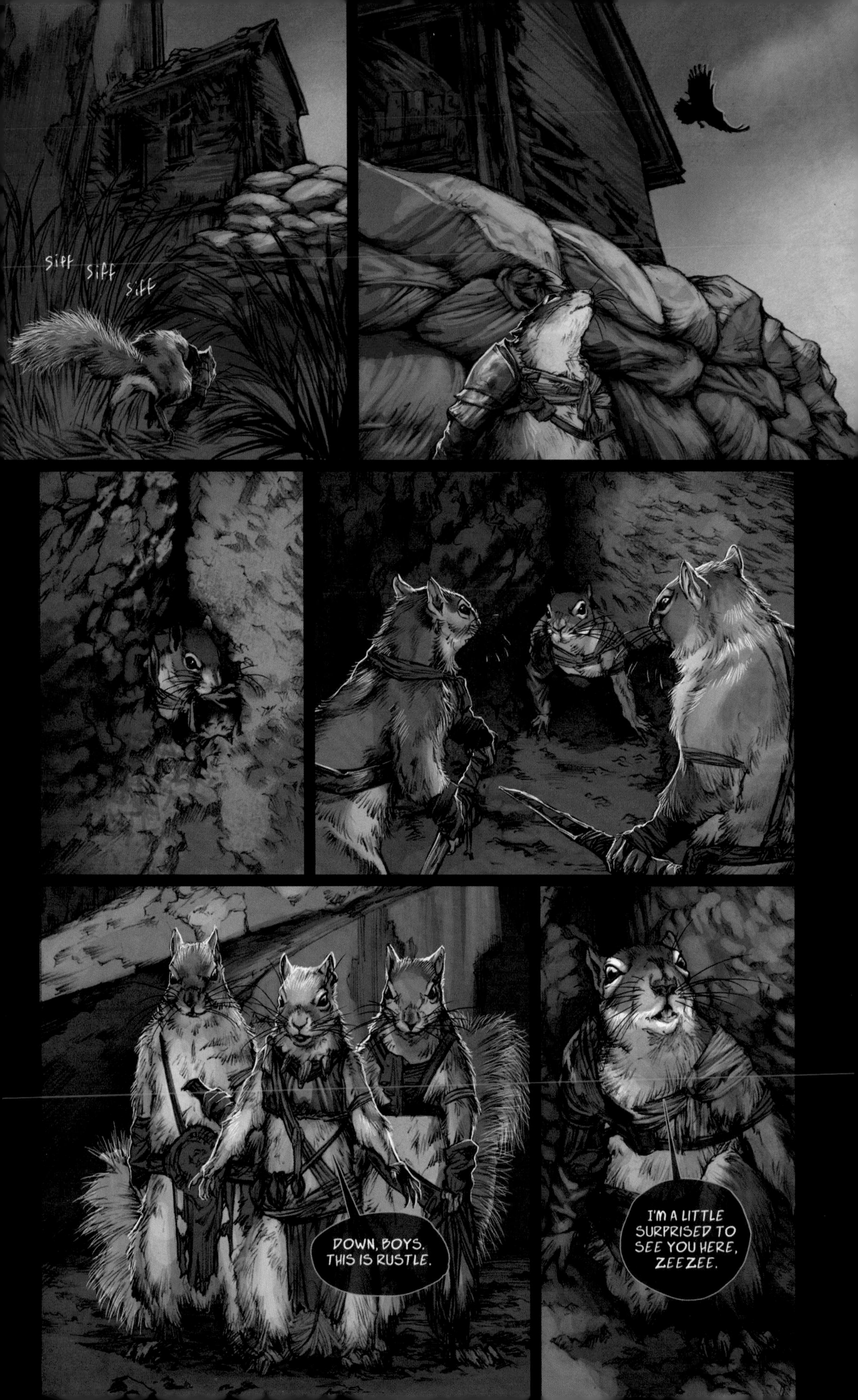
SIFF SIFF SIFF
DOWN, BOYS. THIS IS RUSTLE.
I'M A LITTLE SURPRISED TO SEE YOU HERE, ZEEZEE.

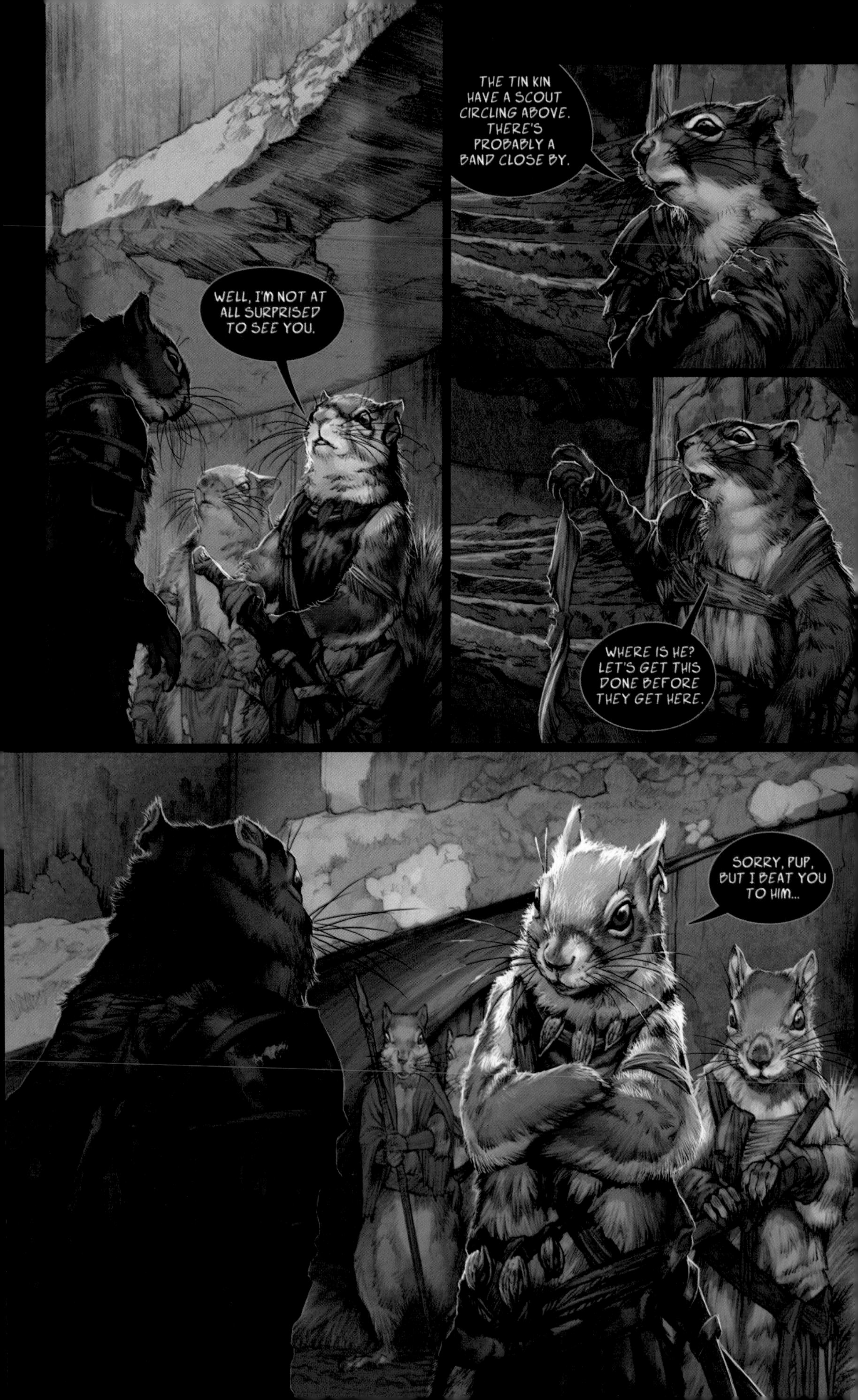
WELL, I'M NOT AT ALL SURPRISED TO SEE YOU.
THE TIN KIN HAVE A SCOUT CIRCLING ABOVE. THERE'S PROBABLY A BAND CLOSE BY.
WHERE IS HE? LET'S GET THIS DONE BEFORE THEY GET HERE.
SORRY, PUP, BUT I BEAT YOU TO HIM...

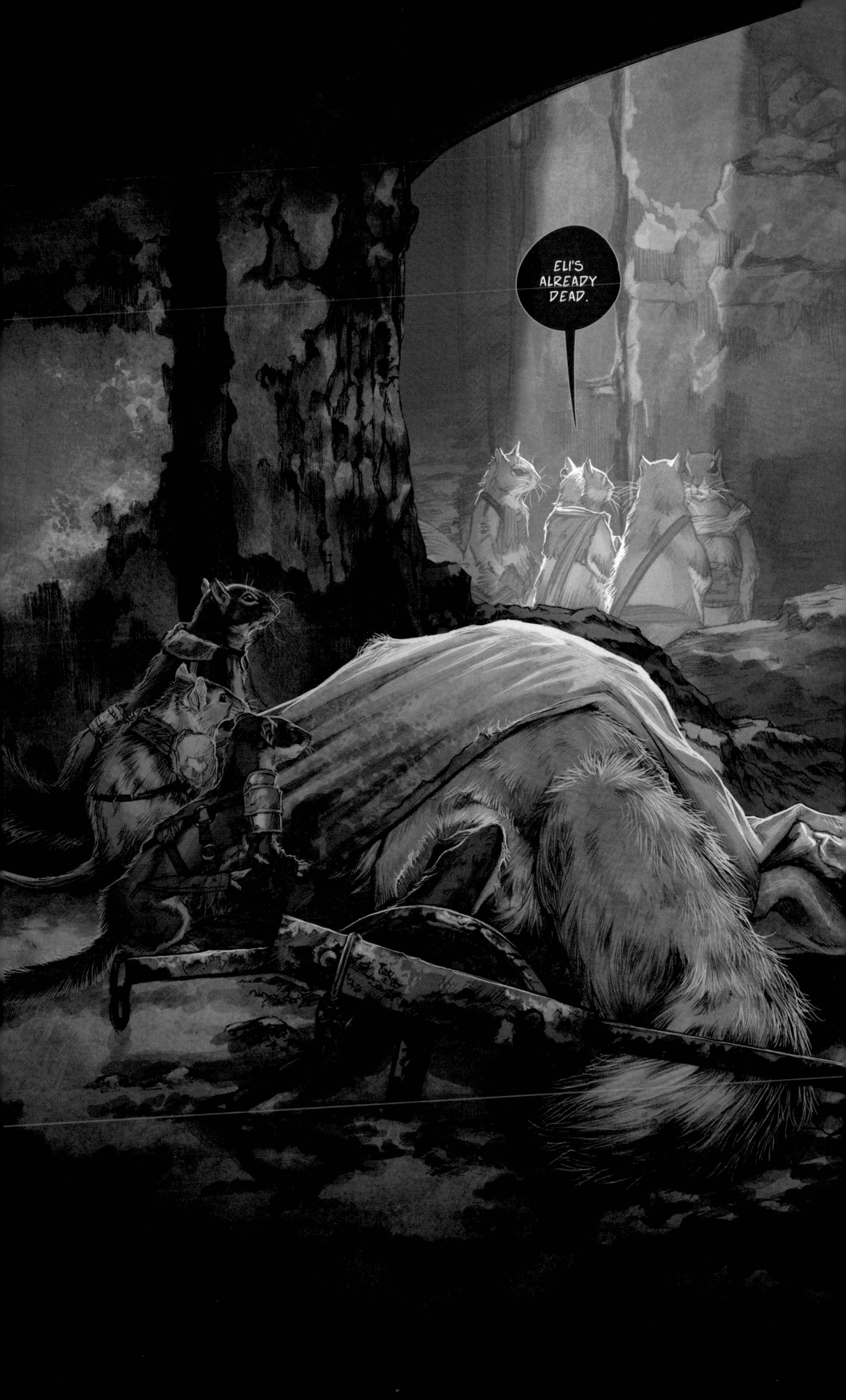
ELI'S ALREADY DEAD.

Chapter 4: Brothers in Harm

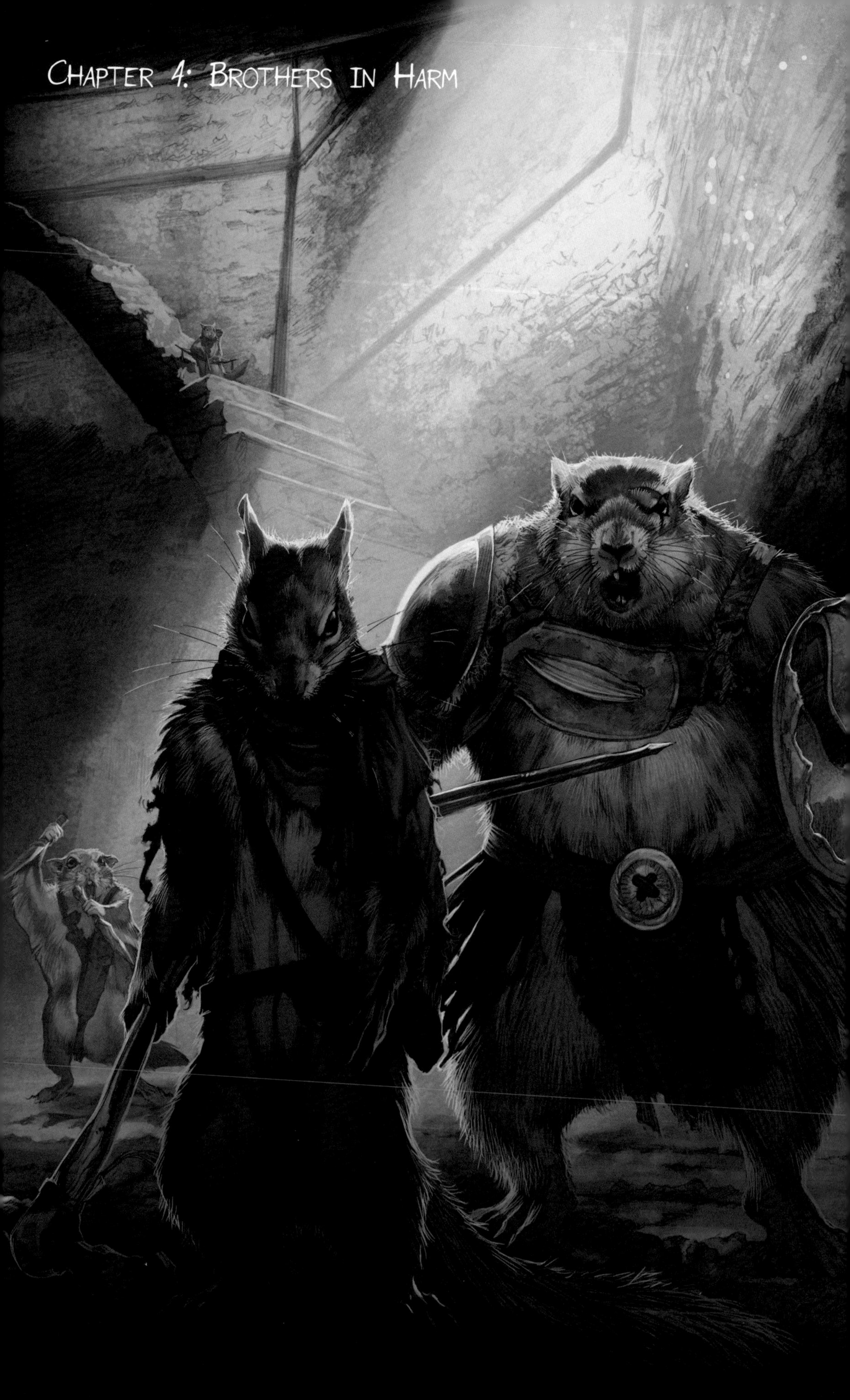

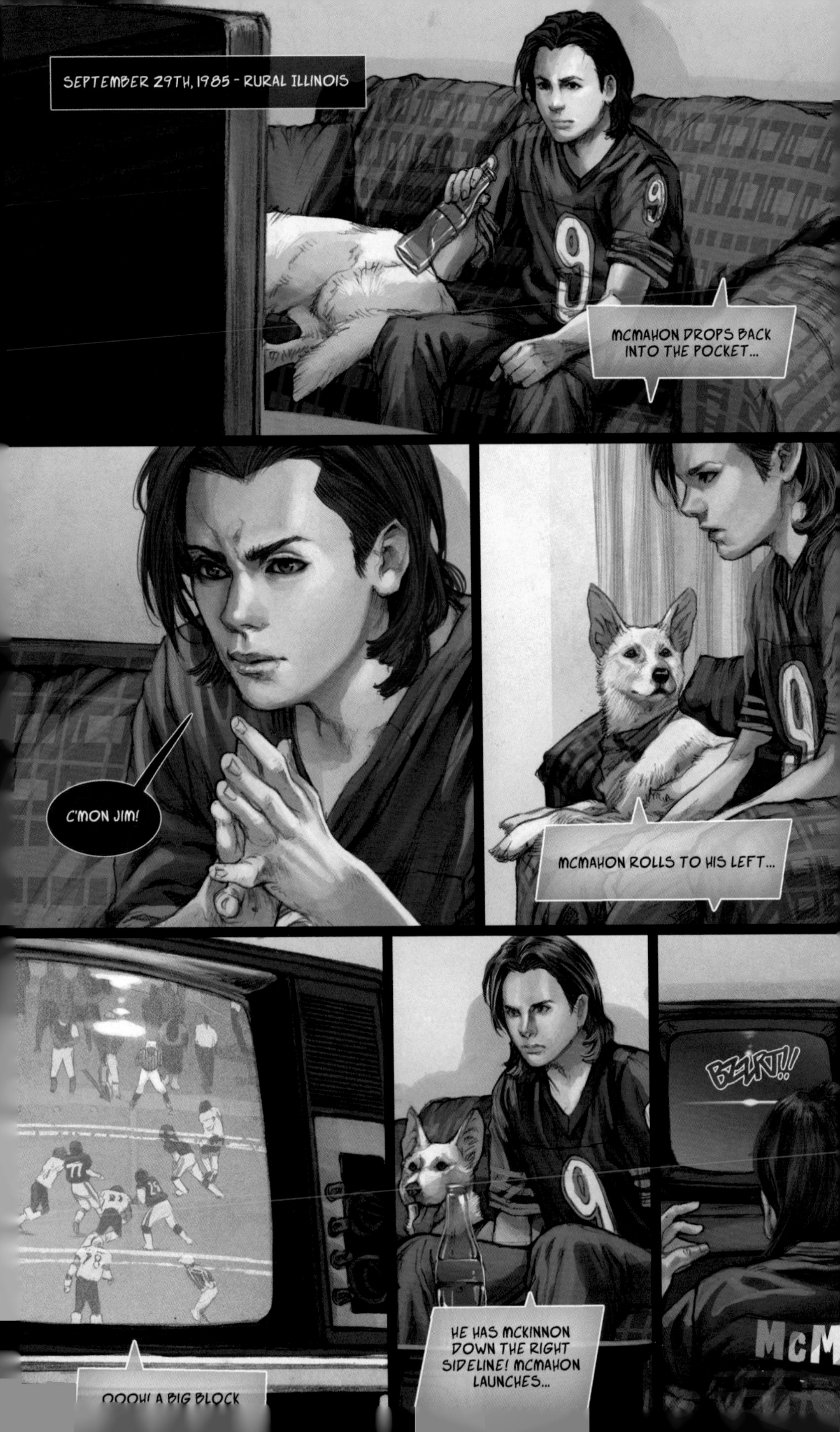
SEPTEMBER 29TH, 1985 - RURAL ILLINOIS
MCMAHON DROPS BACK INTO THE POCKET...
C'MON JIM!
MCMAHON ROLLS TO HIS LEFT...
OOOH! A BIG BLOCK
HE HAS MCKINNON DOWN THE RIGHT SIDELINE! MCMAHON LAUNCHES...
BZZRT!!
McM

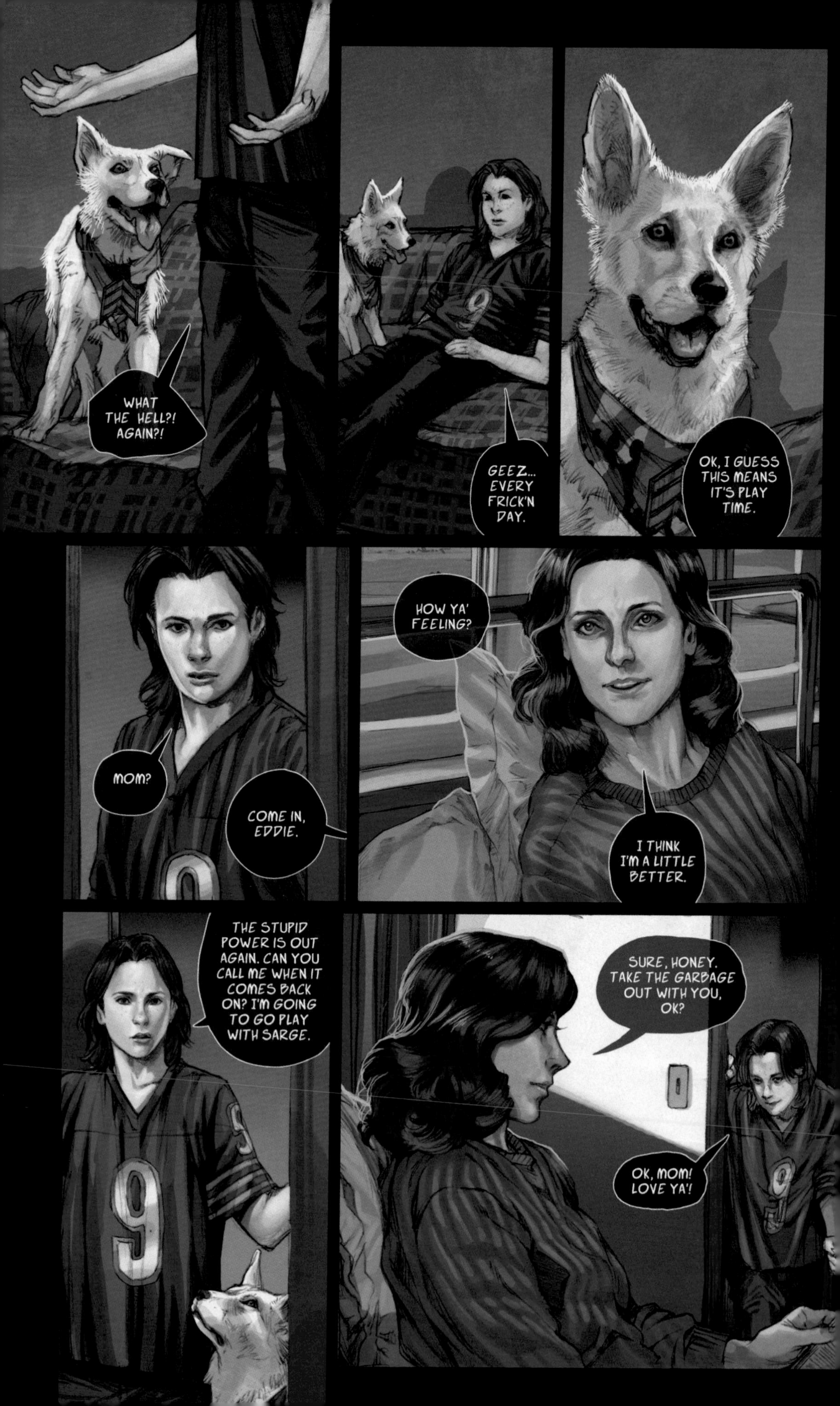

WHAT THE HELL?! AGAIN?!
GEEZ... EVERY FRICK'N DAY.
OK, I GUESS THIS MEANS IT'S PLAY TIME.
MOM?
COME IN, EDDIE.
HOW YA' FEELING?
I THINK I'M A LITTLE BETTER.
THE STUPID POWER IS OUT AGAIN. CAN YOU CALL ME WHEN IT COMES BACK ON? I'M GOING TO GO PLAY WITH SARGE.
SURE, HONEY. TAKE THE GARBAGE OUT WITH YOU, OK?
OK, MOM! LOVE YA'!

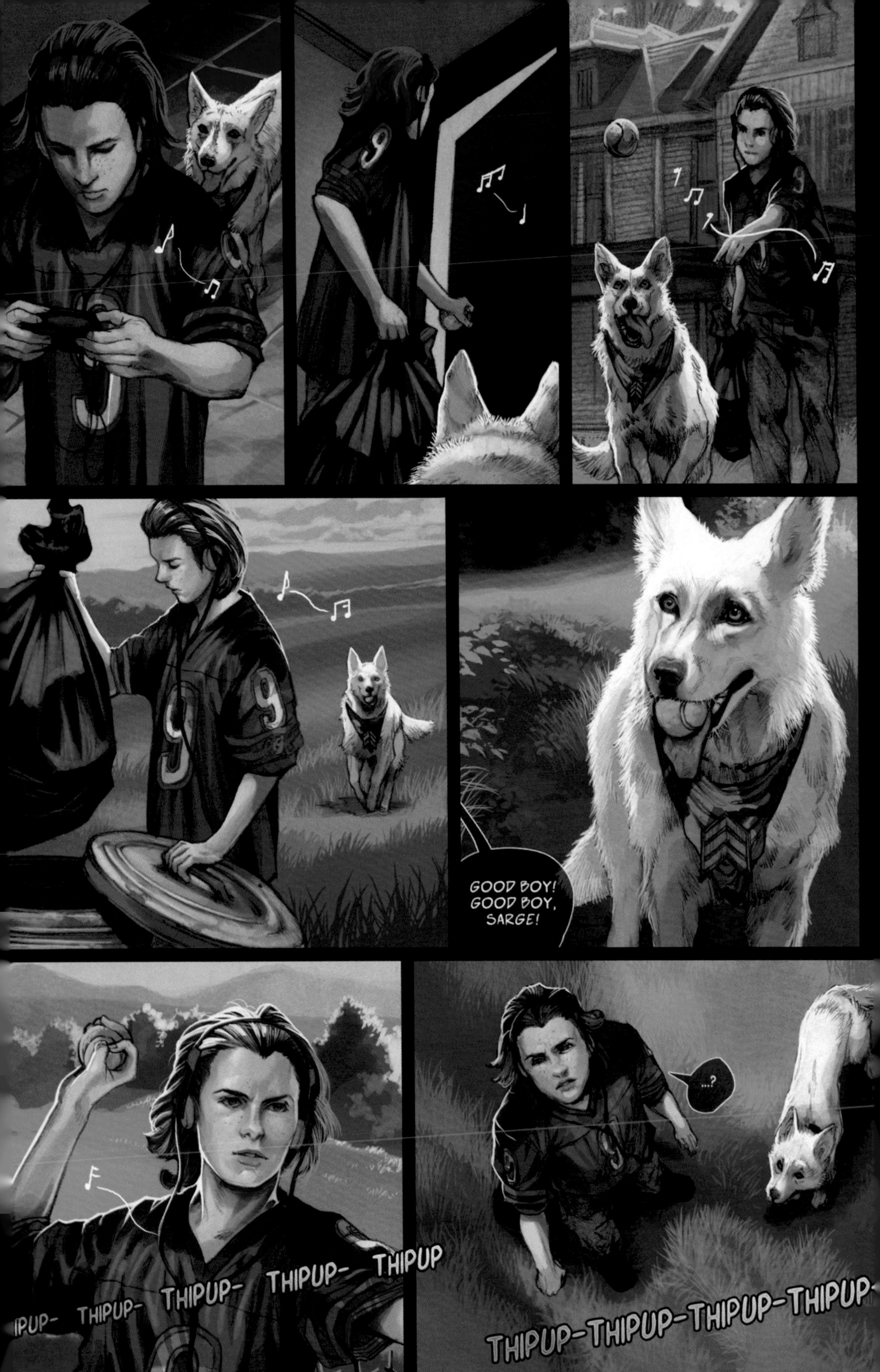
GOOD BOY! GOOD BOY, SARGE!
...?
IPUP- THIPUP- THIPUP- THIPUP- THIPUP
THIPUP-THIPUP-THIPUP-THIPUP-

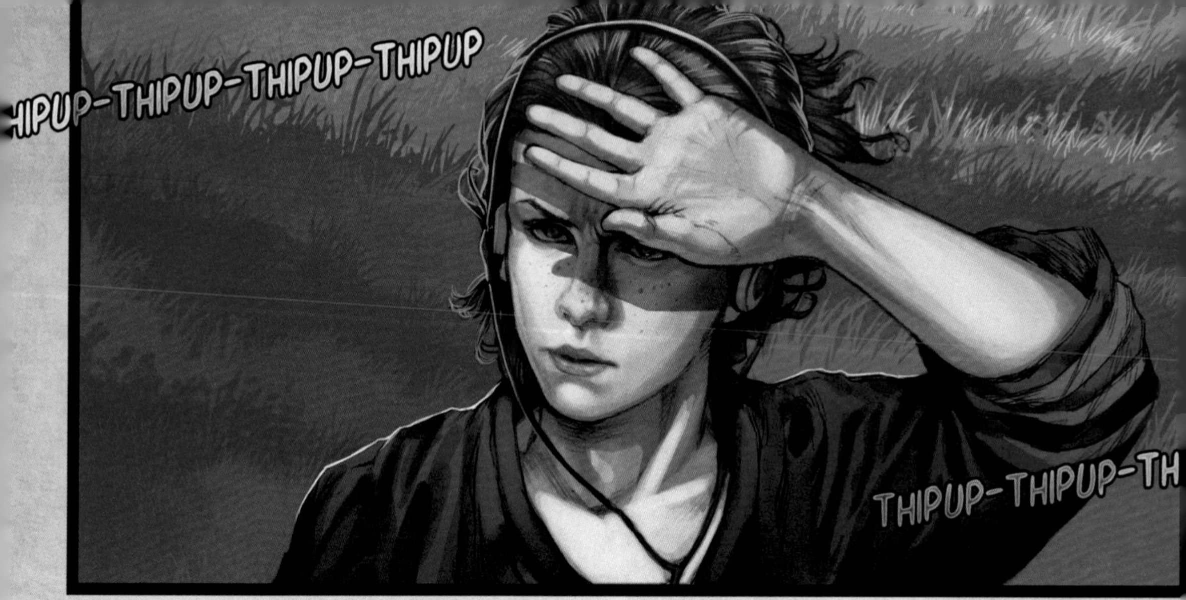
HIPUP-THIPUP-THIPUP-THIPUP
THIPUP-THIPUP-TH

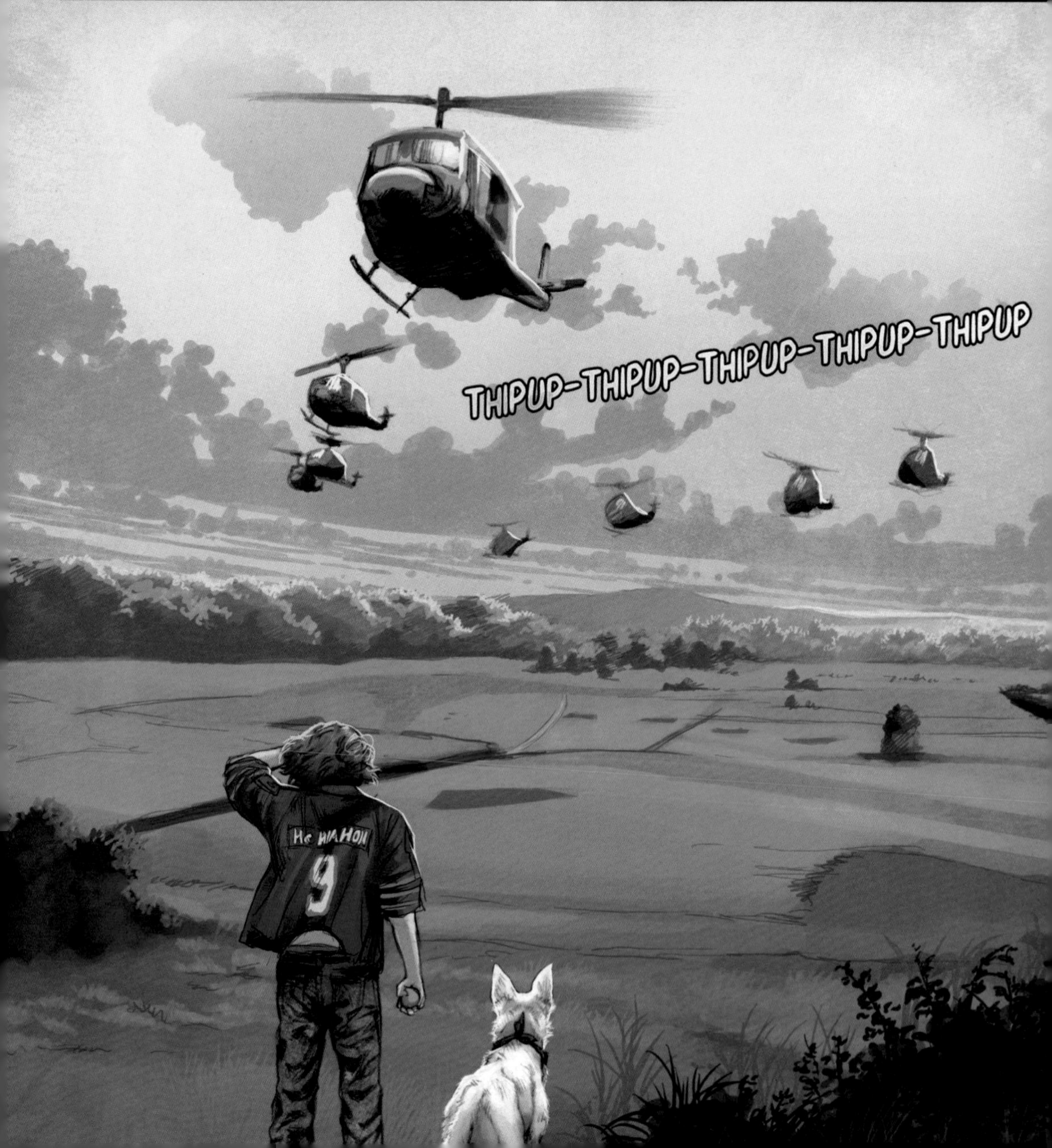
THIPUP-THIPUP-THIPUP-THIPUP-THIPUP

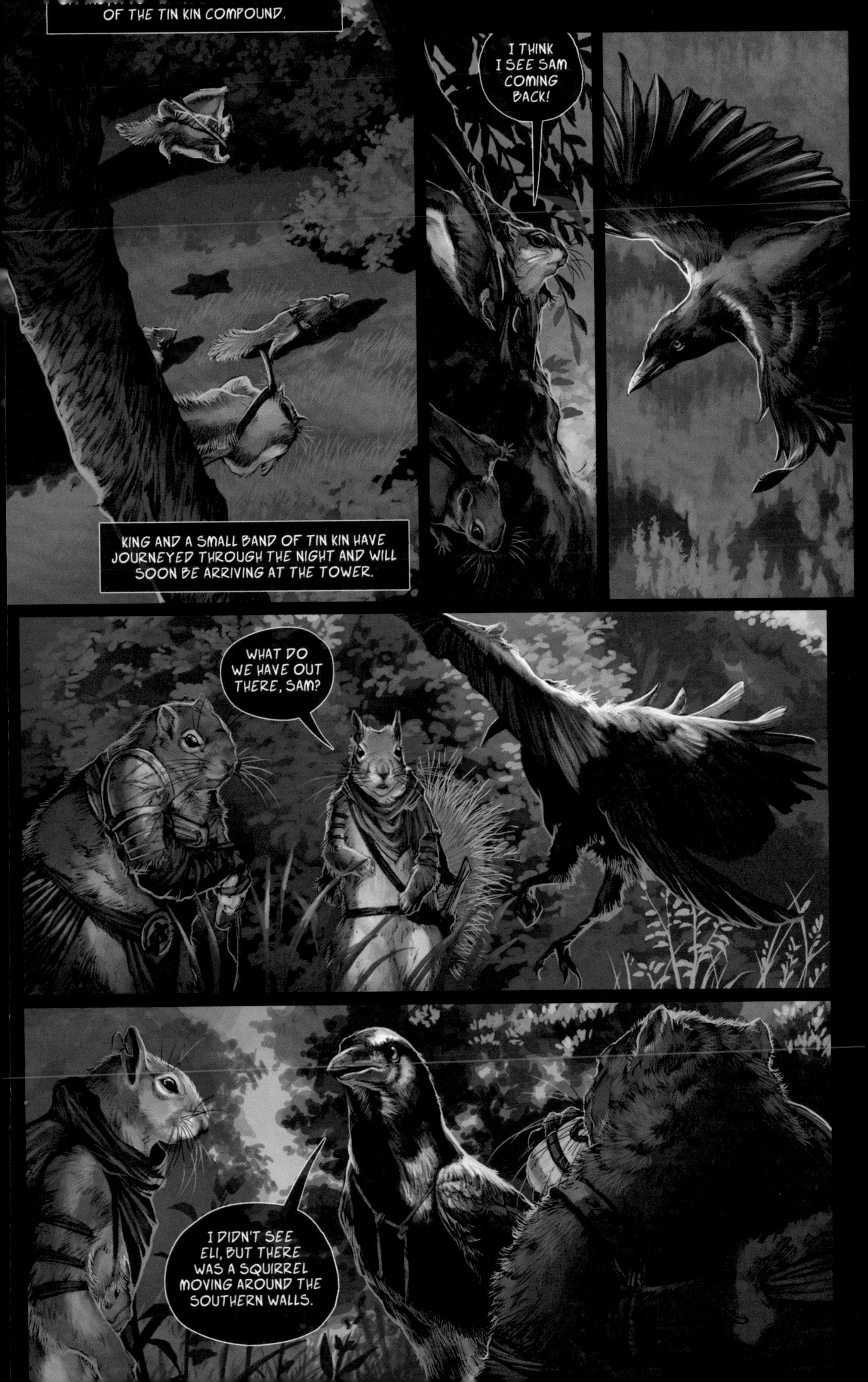
OF THE TIN KIN COMPOUND.
KING AND A SMALL BAND OF TIN KIN HAVE JOURNEYED THROUGH THE NIGHT AND WILL SOON BE ARRIVING AT THE TOWER.
I THINK I SEE SAM COMING BACK!
WHAT DO WE HAVE OUT THERE, SAM?
I DIDN'T SEE ELI, BUT THERE WAS A SQUIRREL MOVING AROUND THE SOUTHERN WALLS.

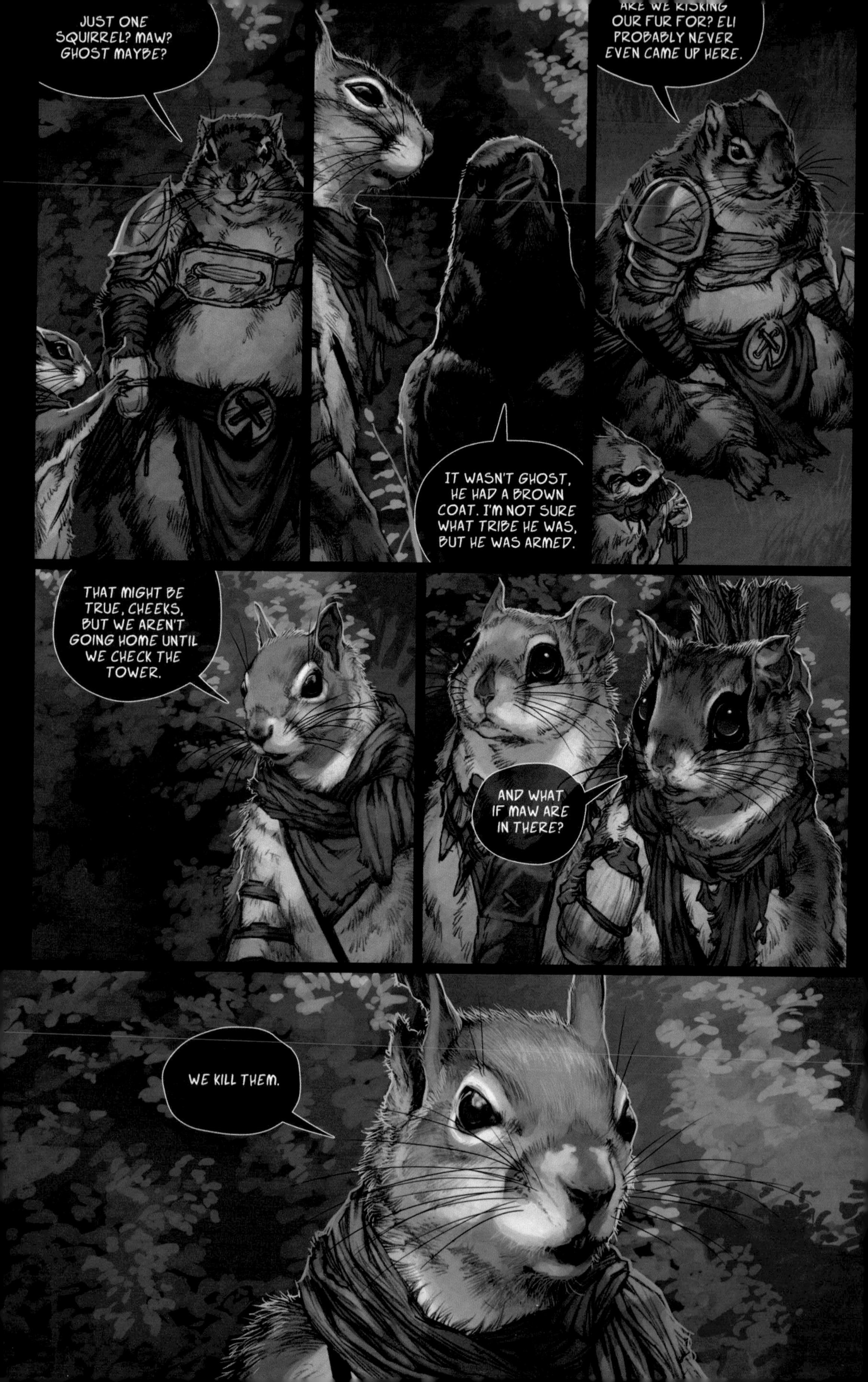

JUST ONE SQUIRREL? MAW? GHOST MAYBE?
ARE WE RISKING OUR FUR FOR? ELI PROBABLY NEVER EVEN CAME UP HERE.
IT WASN'T GHOST. HE HAD A BROWN COAT. I'M NOT SURE WHAT TRIBE HE WAS, BUT HE WAS ARMED.
THAT MIGHT BE TRUE, CHEEKS, BUT WE AREN'T GOING HOME UNTIL WE CHECK THE TOWER.
AND WHAT IF MAW ARE IN THERE?
WE KILL THEM.

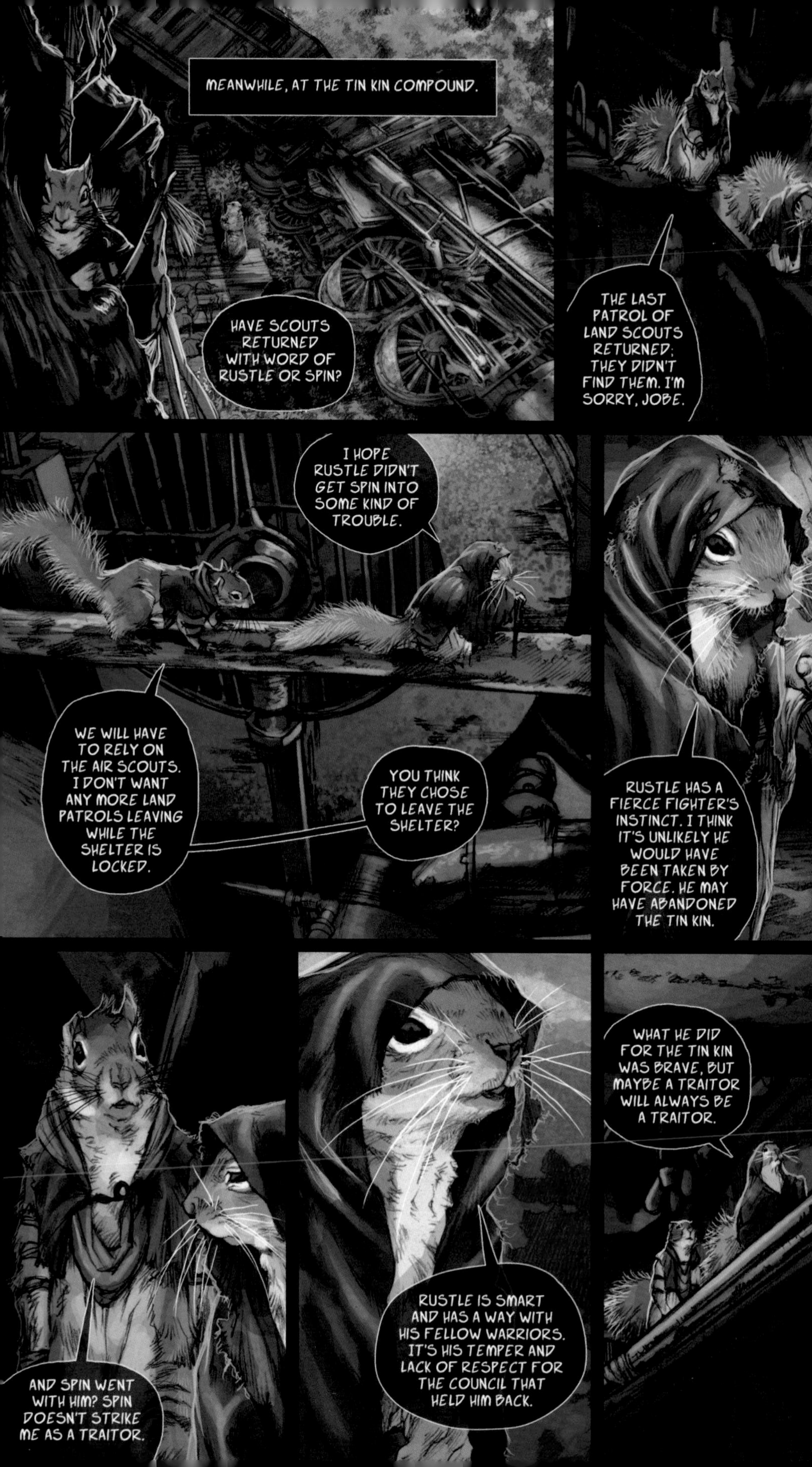
MEANWHILE, AT THE TIN KIN COMPOUND.
HAVE SCOUTS RETURNED WITH WORD OF RUSTLE OR SPIN?
THE LAST PATROL OF LAND SCOUTS RETURNED; THEY DIDN'T FIND THEM. I'M SORRY, JOBE.
I HOPE RUSTLE DIDN'T GET SPIN INTO SOME KIND OF TROUBLE.
WE WILL HAVE TO RELY ON THE AIR SCOUTS. I DON'T WANT ANY MORE LAND PATROLS LEAVING WHILE THE SHELTER IS LOCKED.
YOU THINK THEY CHOSE TO LEAVE THE SHELTER?
RUSTLE HAS A FIERCE FIGHTER'S INSTINCT. I THINK IT'S UNLIKELY HE WOULD HAVE BEEN TAKEN BY FORCE. HE MAY HAVE ABANDONED THE TIN KIN.
AND SPIN WENT WITH HIM? SPIN DOESN'T STRIKE ME AS A TRAITOR.
RUSTLE IS SMART AND HAS A WAY WITH HIS FELLOW WARRIORS. IT'S HIS TEMPER AND LACK OF RESPECT FOR THE COUNCIL THAT HELD HIM BACK.
WHAT HE DID FOR THE TIN KIN WAS BRAVE, BUT MAYBE A TRAITOR WILL ALWAYS BE A TRAITOR.

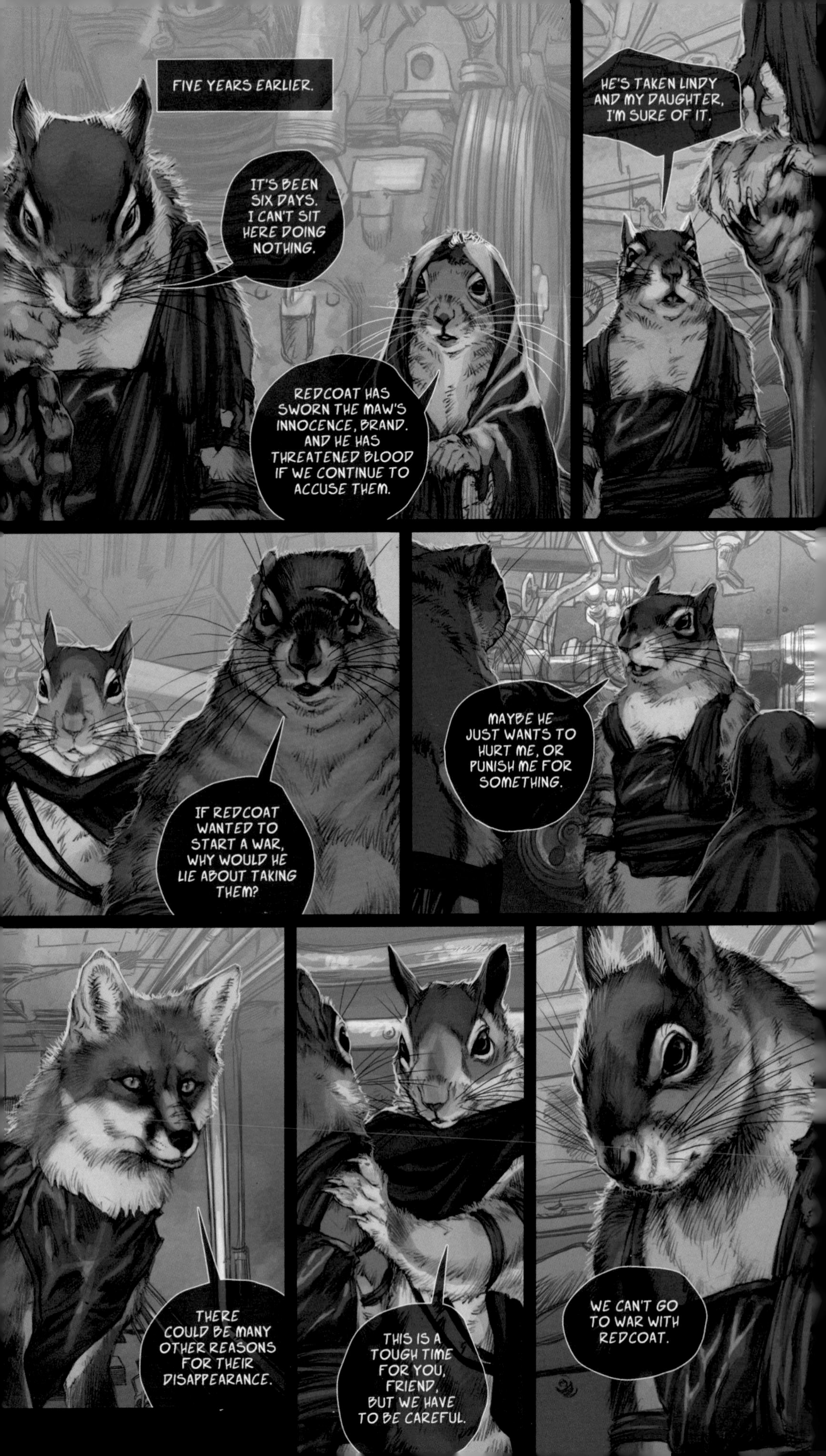
FIVE YEARS EARLIER.
IT'S BEEN SIX DAYS. I CAN'T SIT HERE DOING NOTHING.
REDCOAT HAS SWORN THE MAW'S INNOCENCE, BRAND. AND HE HAS THREATENED BLOOD IF WE CONTINUE TO ACCUSE THEM.
HE'S TAKEN LINDY AND MY DAUGHTER, I'M SURE OF IT.
IF REDCOAT WANTED TO START A WAR, WHY WOULD HE LIE ABOUT TAKING THEM?
MAYBE HE JUST WANTS TO HURT ME, OR PUNISH ME FOR SOMETHING.
THERE COULD BE MANY OTHER REASONS FOR THEIR DISAPPEARANCE.
THIS IS A TOUGH TIME FOR YOU, FRIEND, BUT WE HAVE TO BE CAREFUL.
WE CAN'T GO TO WAR WITH REDCOAT.

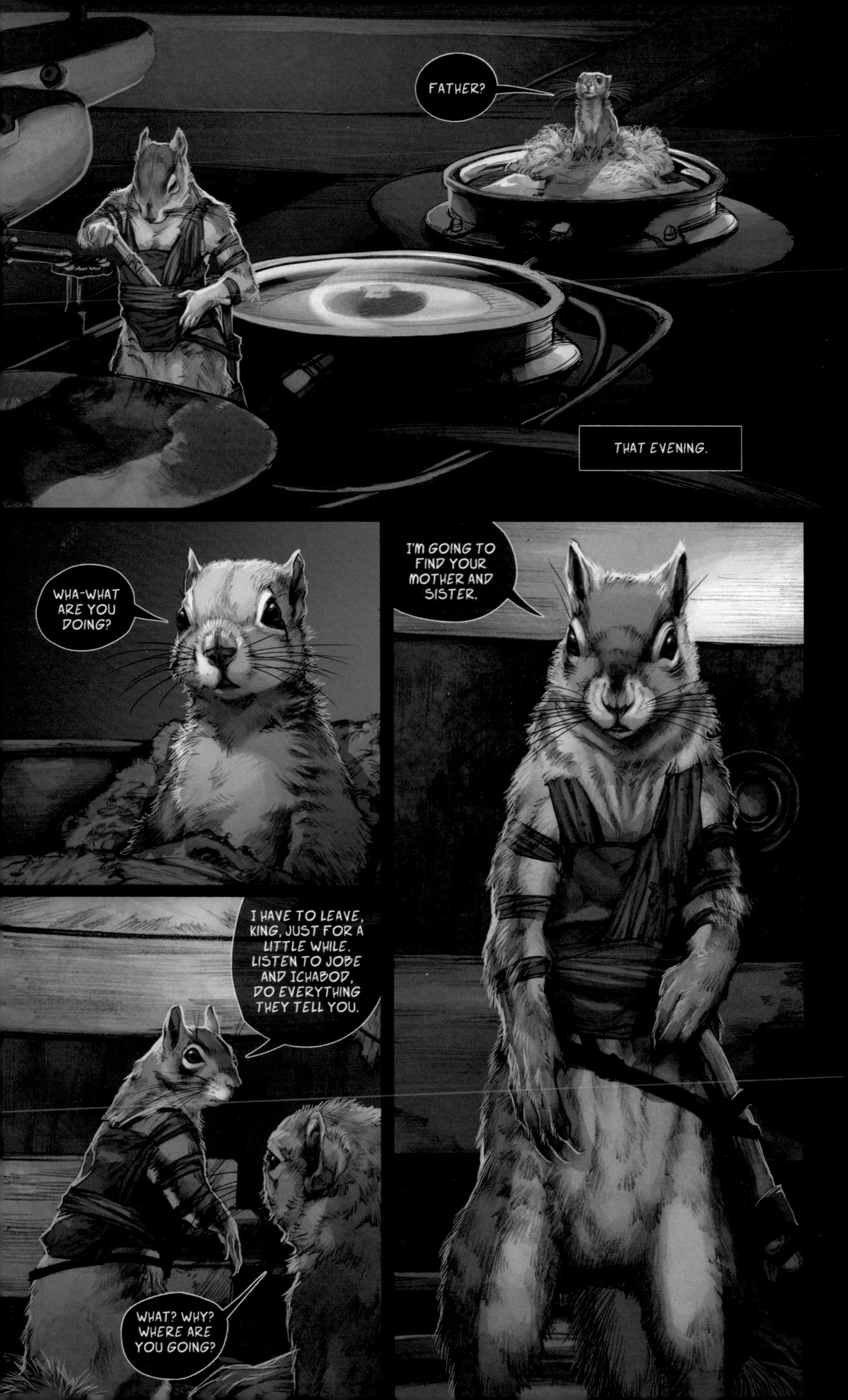
FATHER?
THAT EVENING.
WHA-WHAT ARE YOU DOING?
I'M GOING TO FIND YOUR MOTHER AND SISTER.
I HAVE TO LEAVE, KING, JUST FOR A LITTLE WHILE. LISTEN TO JOBE AND ICHABOD, DO EVERYTHING THEY TELL YOU.
WHAT? WHY? WHERE ARE YOU GOING?

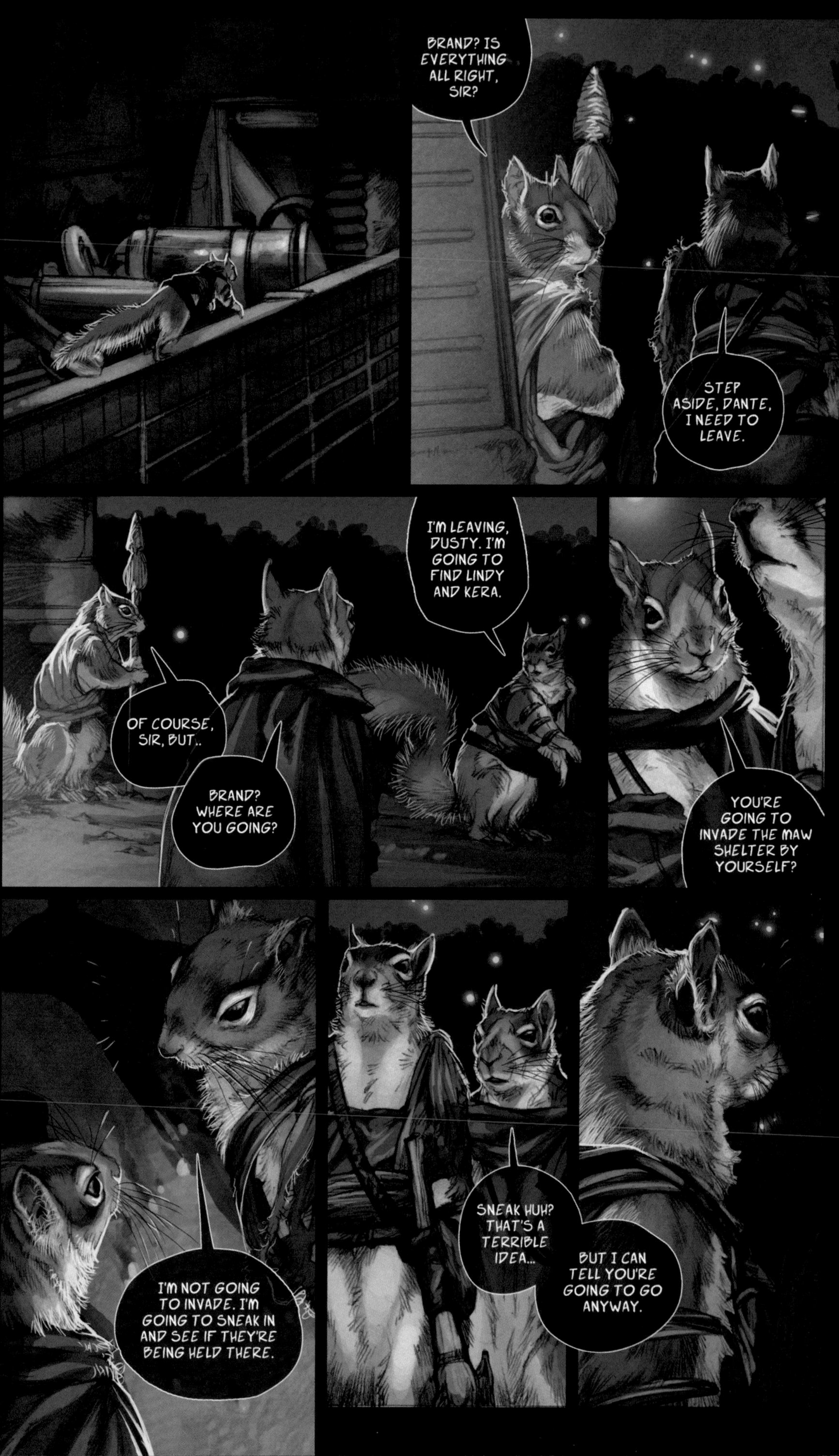
BRAND? IS EVERYTHING ALL RIGHT, SIR?
STEP ASIDE, DANTE, I NEED TO LEAVE.
OF COURSE, SIR, BUT..
BRAND? WHERE ARE YOU GOING?
I'M LEAVING, DUSTY. I'M GOING TO FIND LINDY AND KERA.
YOU'RE GOING TO INVADE THE MAW SHELTER BY YOURSELF?
I'M NOT GOING TO INVADE. I'M GOING TO SNEAK IN AND SEE IF THEY'RE BEING HELD THERE.
SNEAK HUH? THAT'S A TERRIBLE IDEA...
BUT I CAN TELL YOU'RE GOING TO GO ANYWAY.

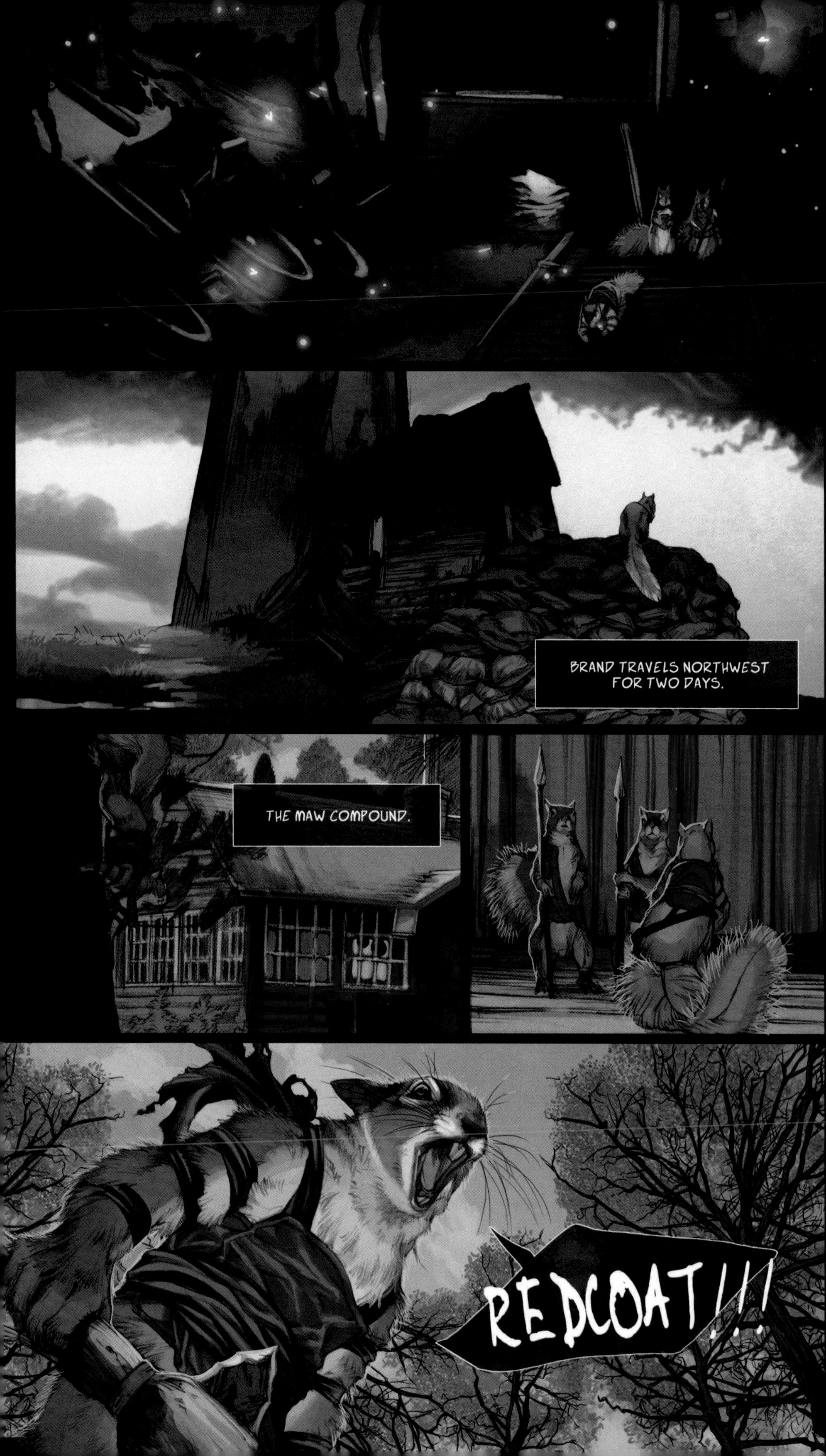
BRAND TRAVELS NORTHWEST FOR TWO DAYS.
THE MAW COMPOUND.
REDCOAT!!!

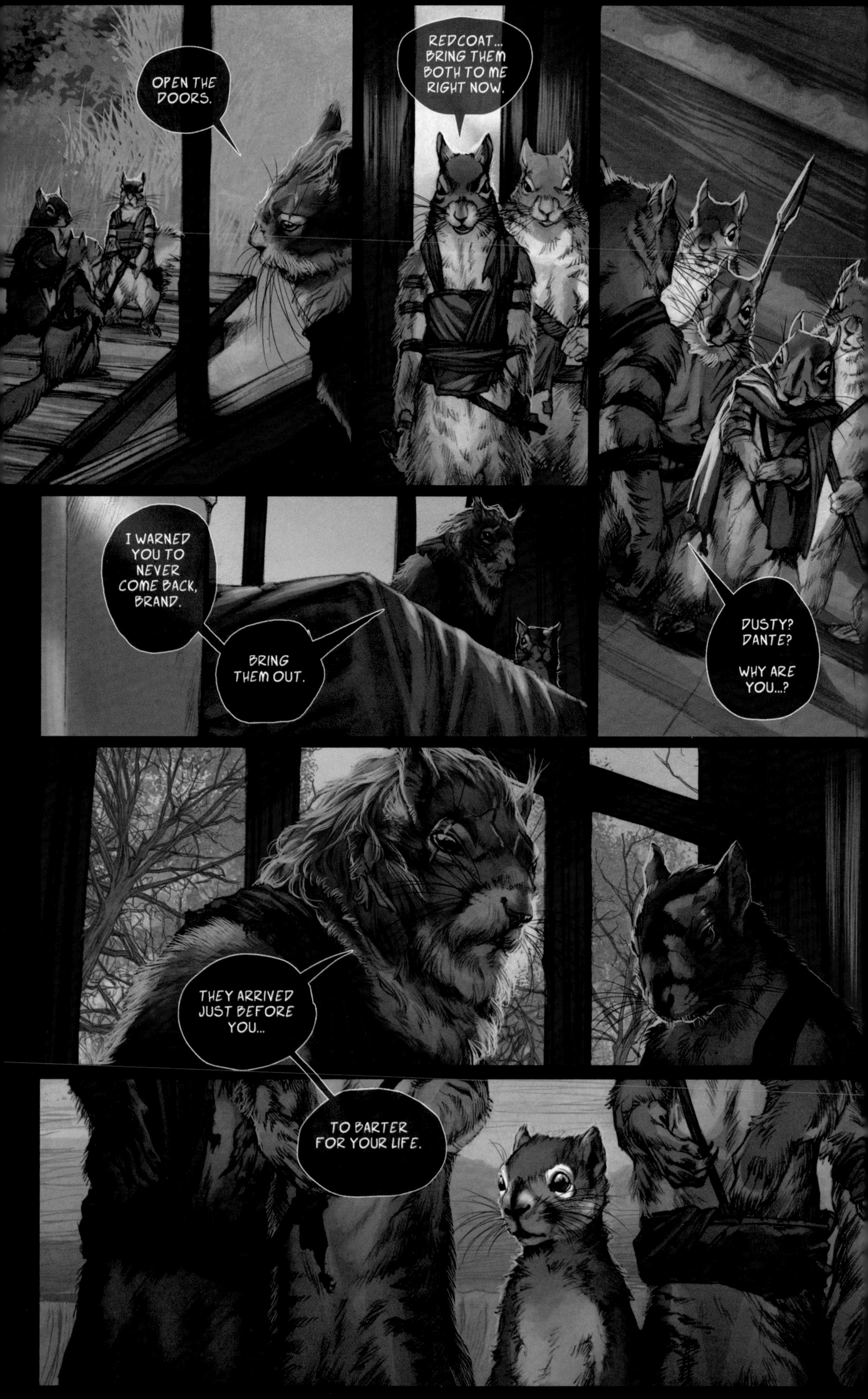
OPEN THE DOORS.
REDCOAT... BRING THEM BOTH TO ME RIGHT NOW.
I WARNED YOU TO NEVER COME BACK, BRAND.
BRING THEM OUT.
DUSTY? DANTE?
WHY ARE YOU...?
THEY ARRIVED JUST BEFORE YOU...
TO BARTER FOR YOUR LIFE.

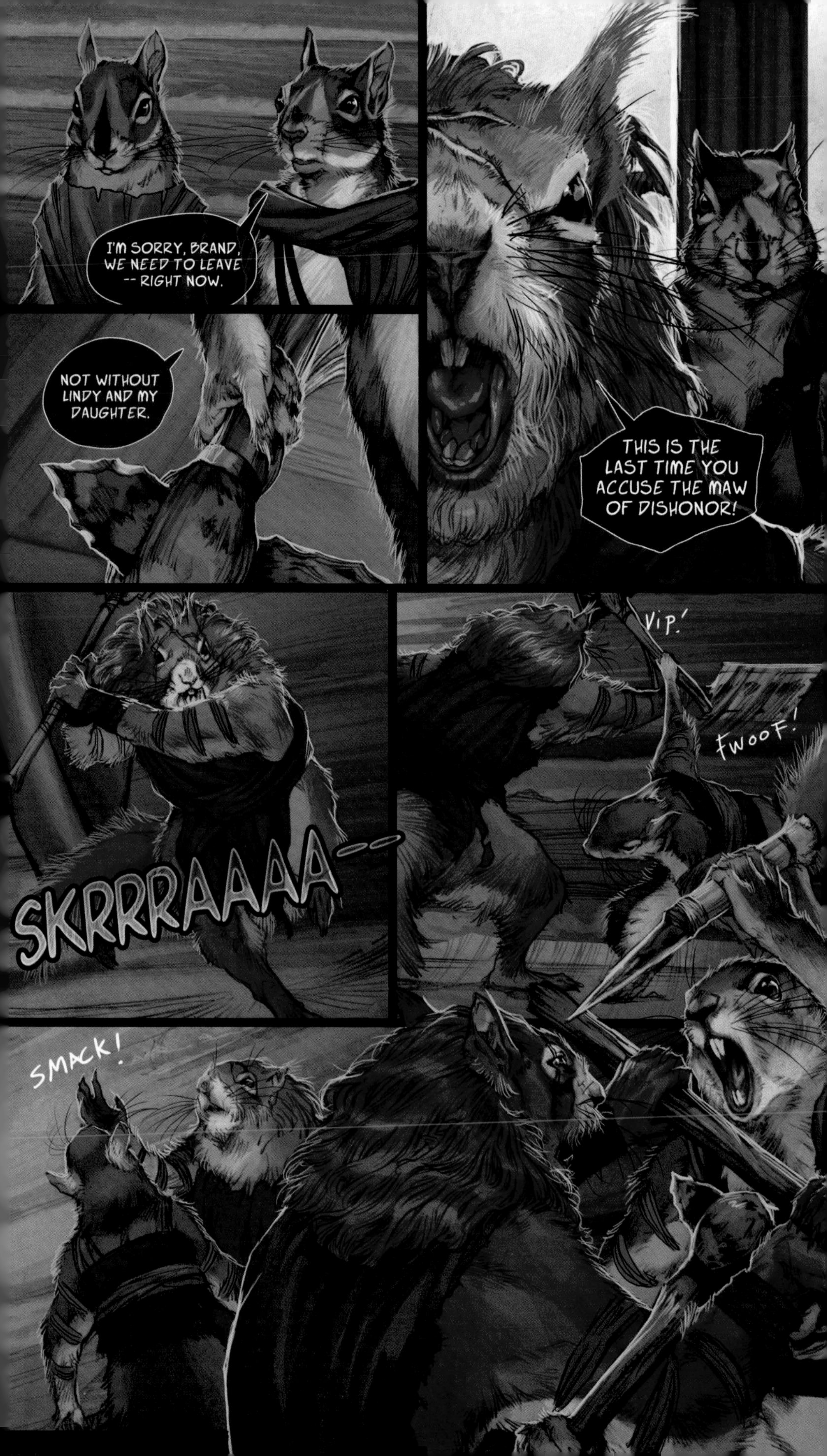
I'M SORRY, BRAND, WE NEED TO LEAVE -- RIGHT NOW.
NOT WITHOUT LINDY AND MY DAUGHTER.
THIS IS THE LAST TIME YOU ACCUSE THE MAW OF DISHONOR!
SKRRRAAAA--
VIP!
FWOOF!
SMACK!

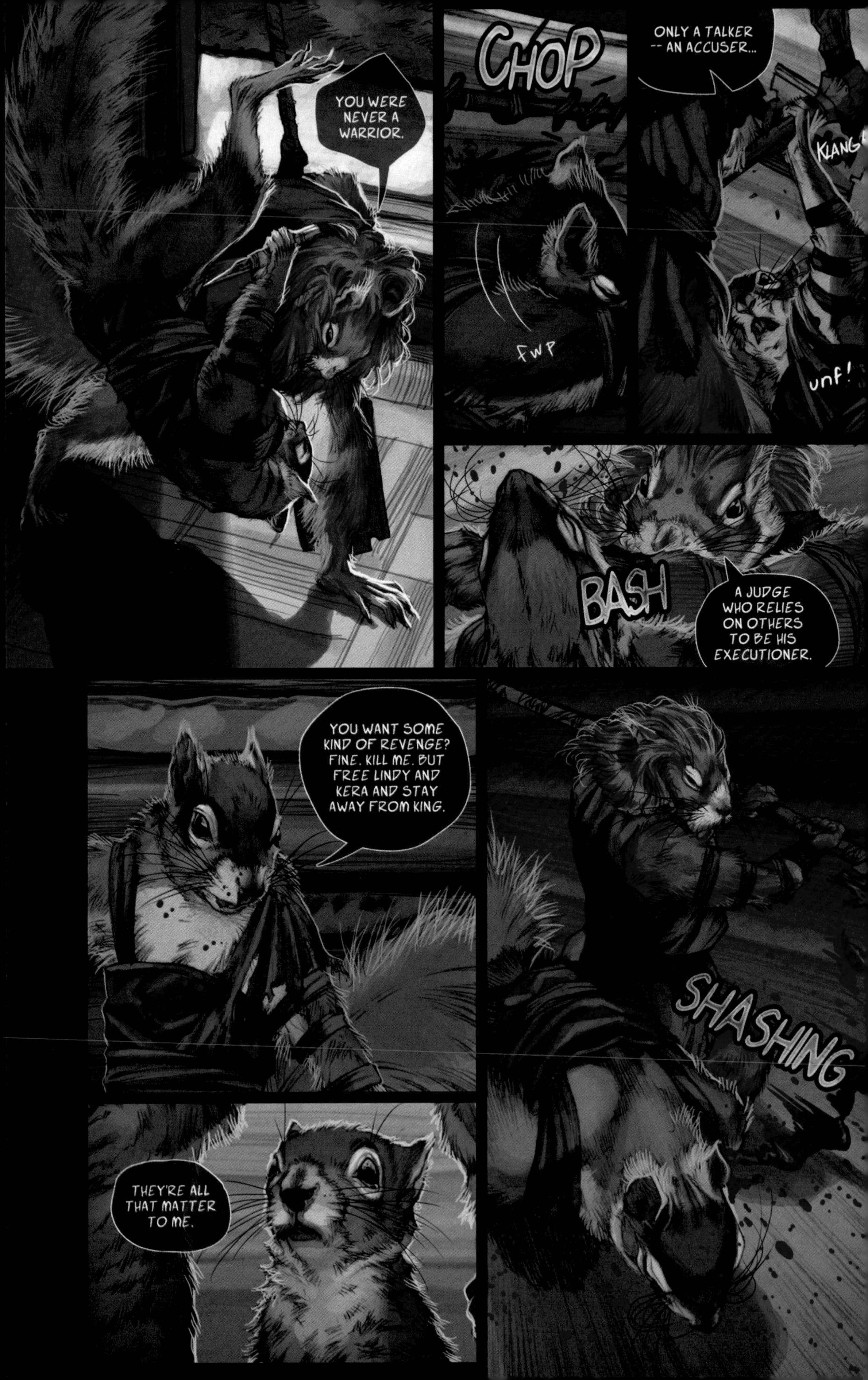
YOU WERE NEVER A WARRIOR.
CHOP
fwp
ONLY A TALKER -- AN ACCUSER...
KLANG!
unf!
BASH
A JUDGE WHO RELIES ON OTHERS TO BE HIS EXECUTIONER.
YOU WANT SOME KIND OF REVENGE? FINE. KILL ME. BUT FREE LINDY AND KERA AND STAY AWAY FROM KING.
THEY'RE ALL THAT MATTER TO ME.
SHASHING

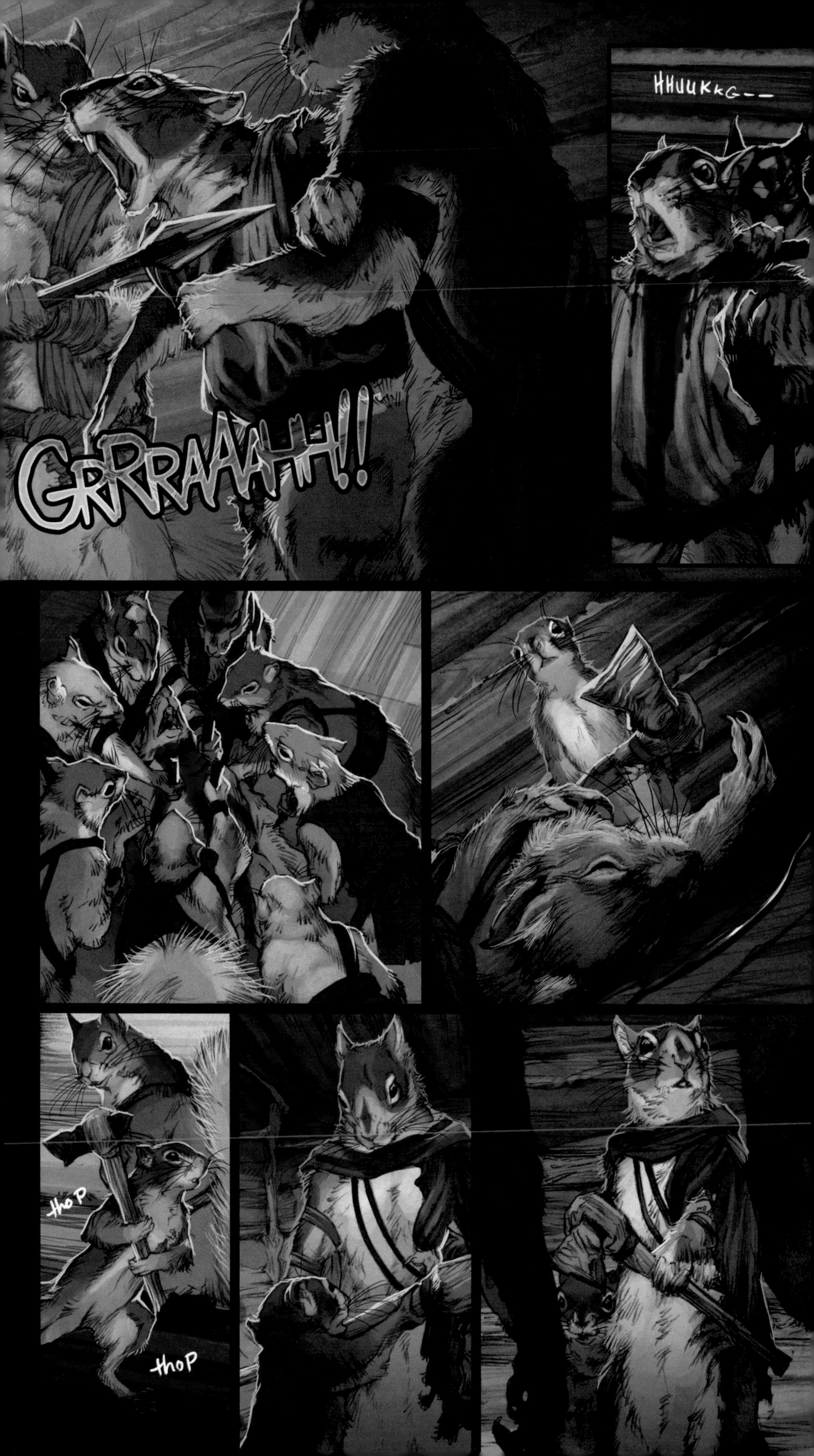
GRRRAAAHH!!
HHUUKKG--
thop
thop

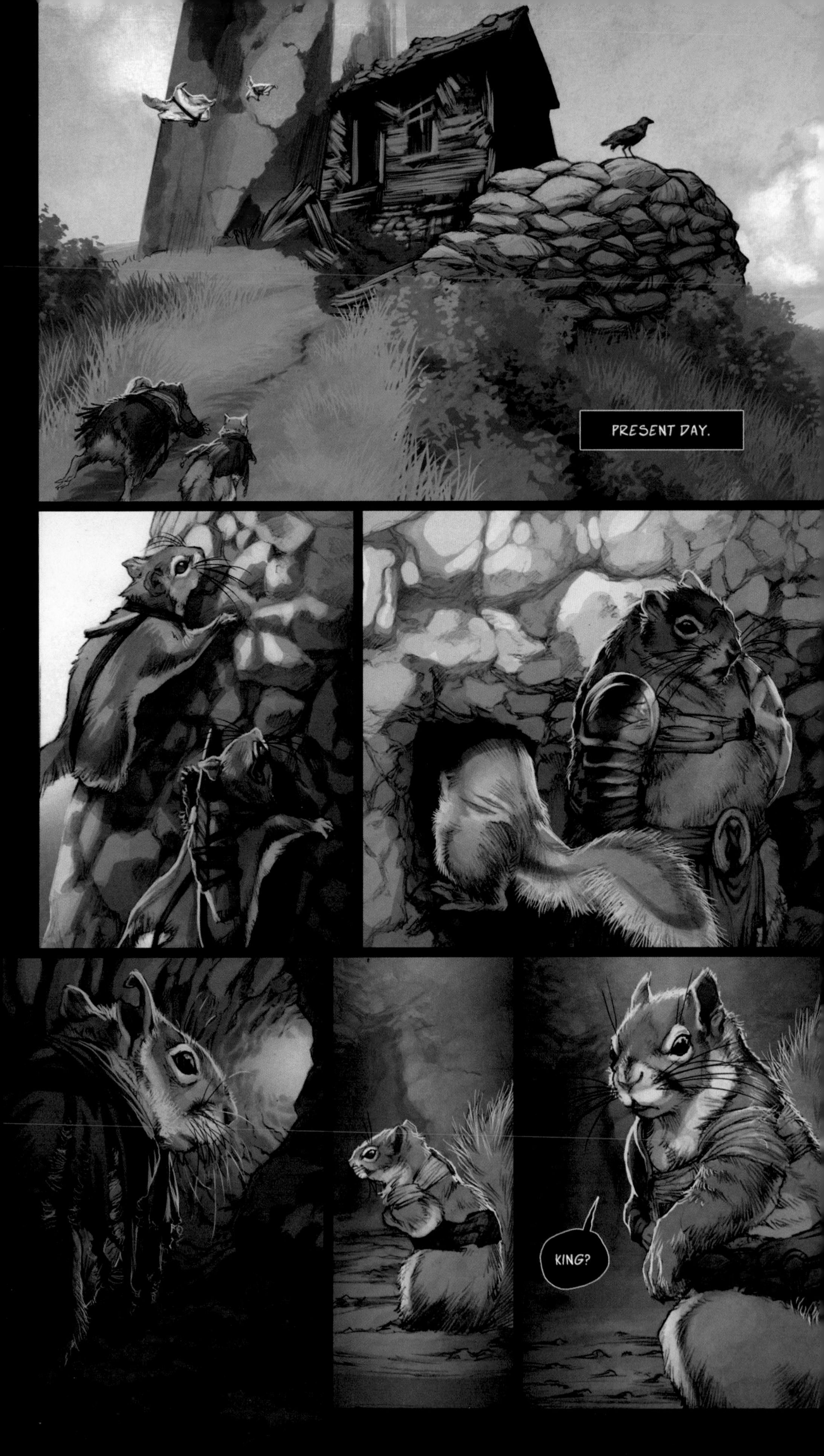
PRESENT DAY.
KING?

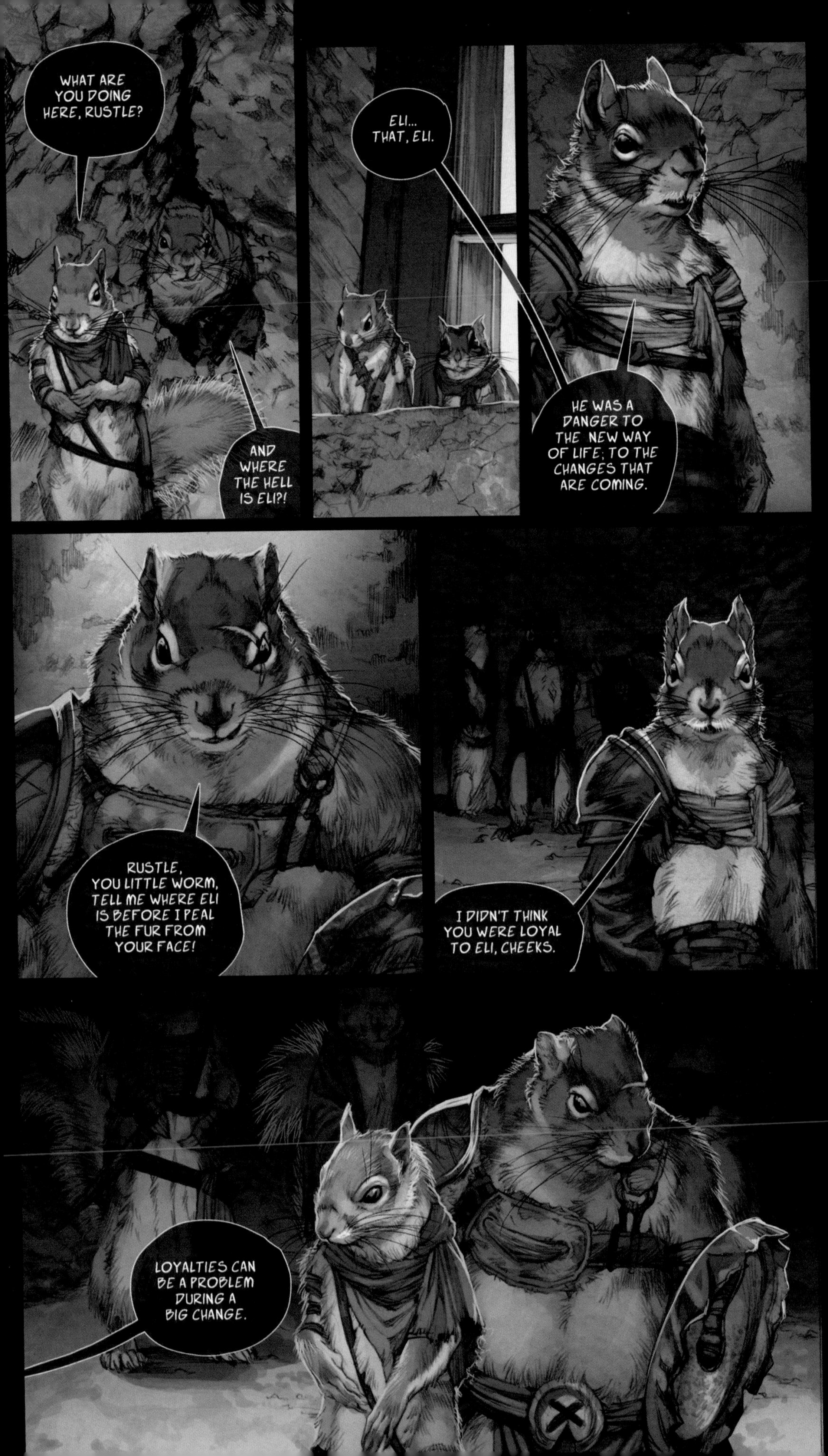
WHAT ARE YOU DOING HERE, RUSTLE?
AND WHERE THE HELL IS ELI?!
ELI... THAT, ELI.
HE WAS A DANGER TO THE NEW WAY OF LIFE; TO THE CHANGES THAT ARE COMING.
RUSTLE, YOU LITTLE WORM, TELL ME WHERE ELI IS BEFORE I PEAL THE FUR FROM YOUR FACE!
I DIDN'T THINK YOU WERE LOYAL TO ELI, CHEEKS.
LOYALTIES CAN BE A PROBLEM DURING A BIG CHANGE.

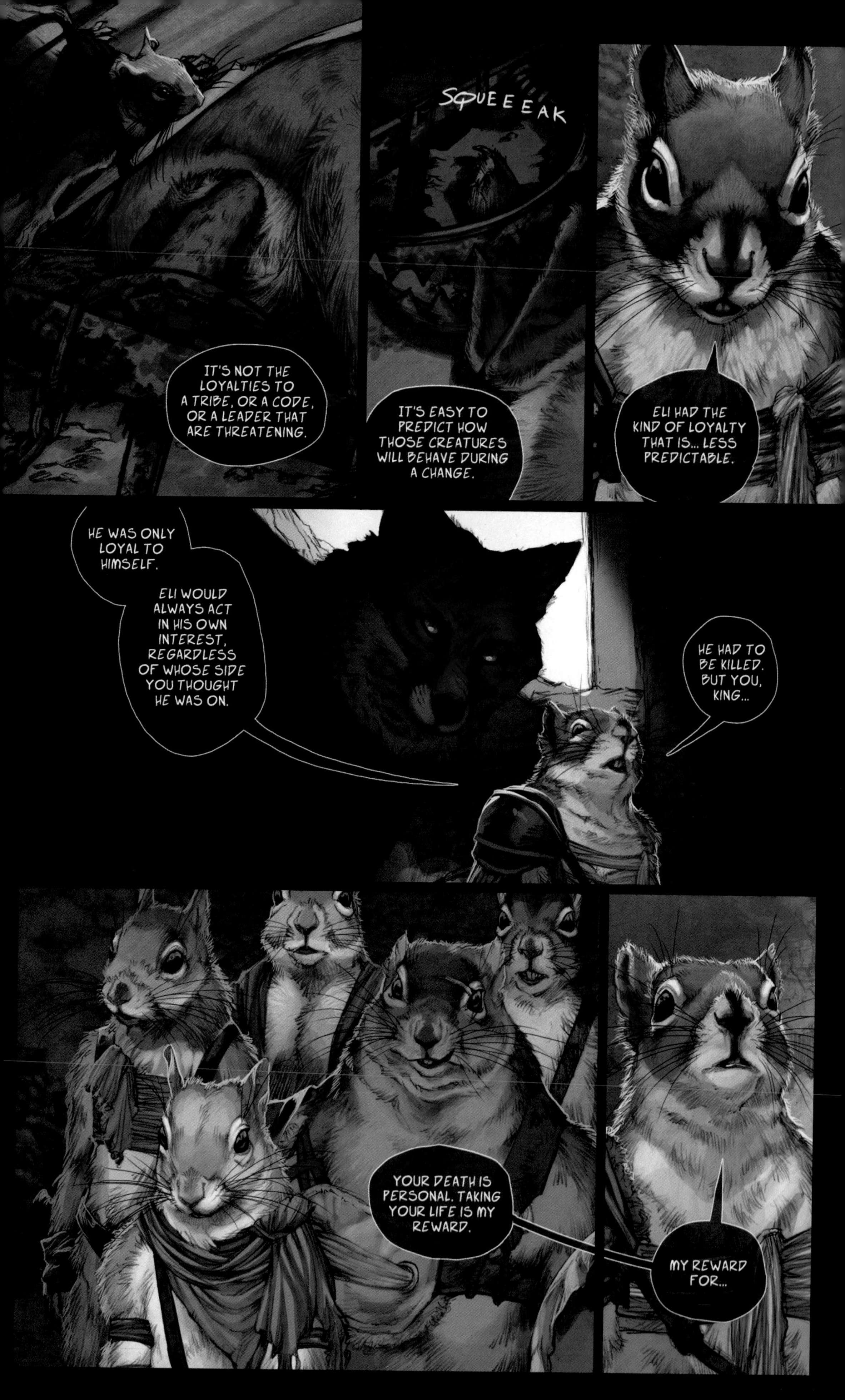
IT'S NOT THE LOYALTIES TO A TRIBE, OR A CODE, OR A LEADER THAT ARE THREATENING.
SQUEEEAK
IT'S EASY TO PREDICT HOW THOSE CREATURES WILL BEHAVE DURING A CHANGE.
ELI HAD THE KIND OF LOYALTY THAT IS... LESS PREDICTABLE.
HE WAS ONLY LOYAL TO HIMSELF.
ELI WOULD ALWAYS ACT IN HIS OWN INTEREST, REGARDLESS OF WHOSE SIDE YOU THOUGHT HE WAS ON.
HE HAD TO BE KILLED. BUT YOU, KING...
YOUR DEATH IS PERSONAL. TAKING YOUR LIFE IS MY REWARD.
MY REWARD FOR...

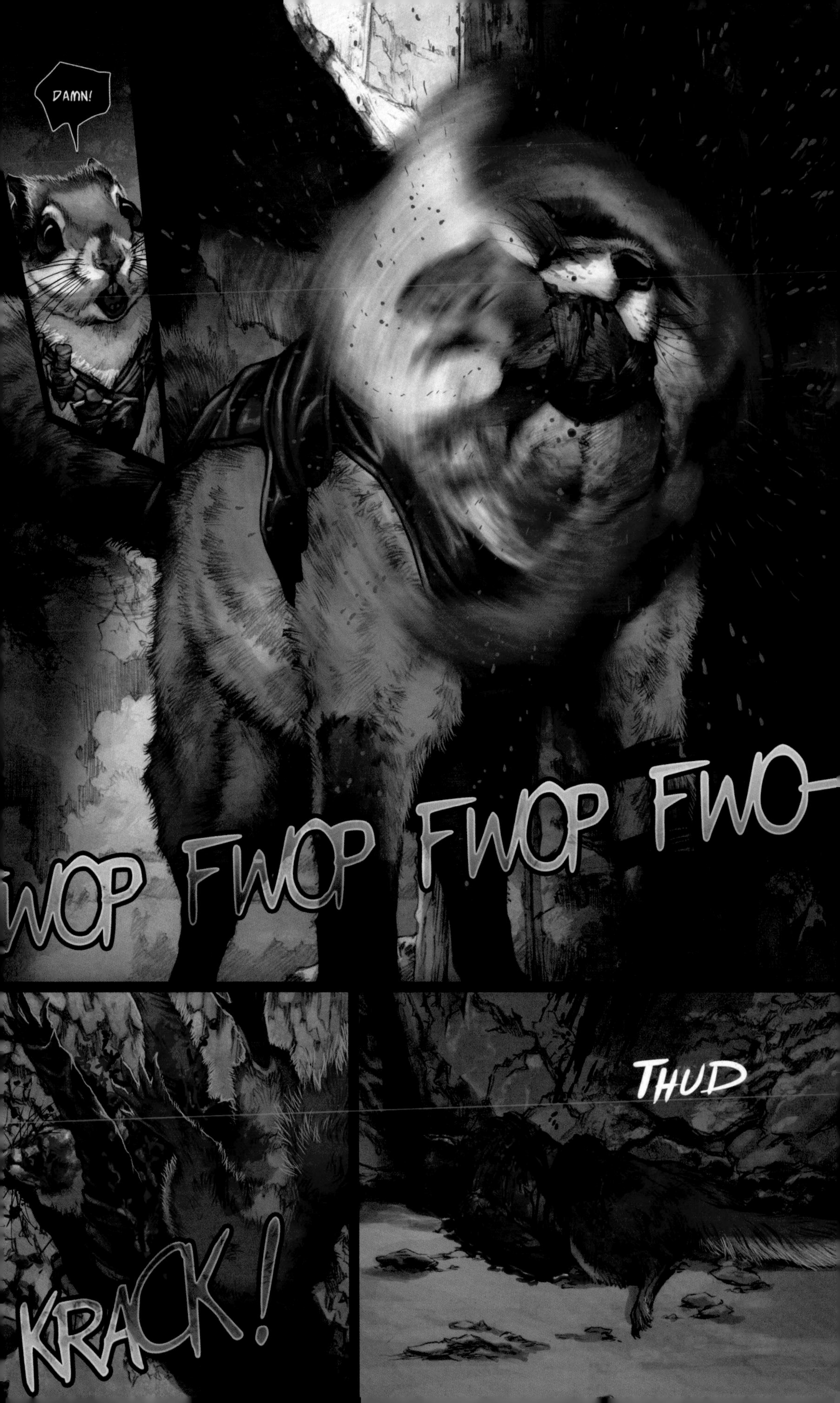
DAMN!
FWOP FWOP FWOP FWO—
KRACK!
THUD

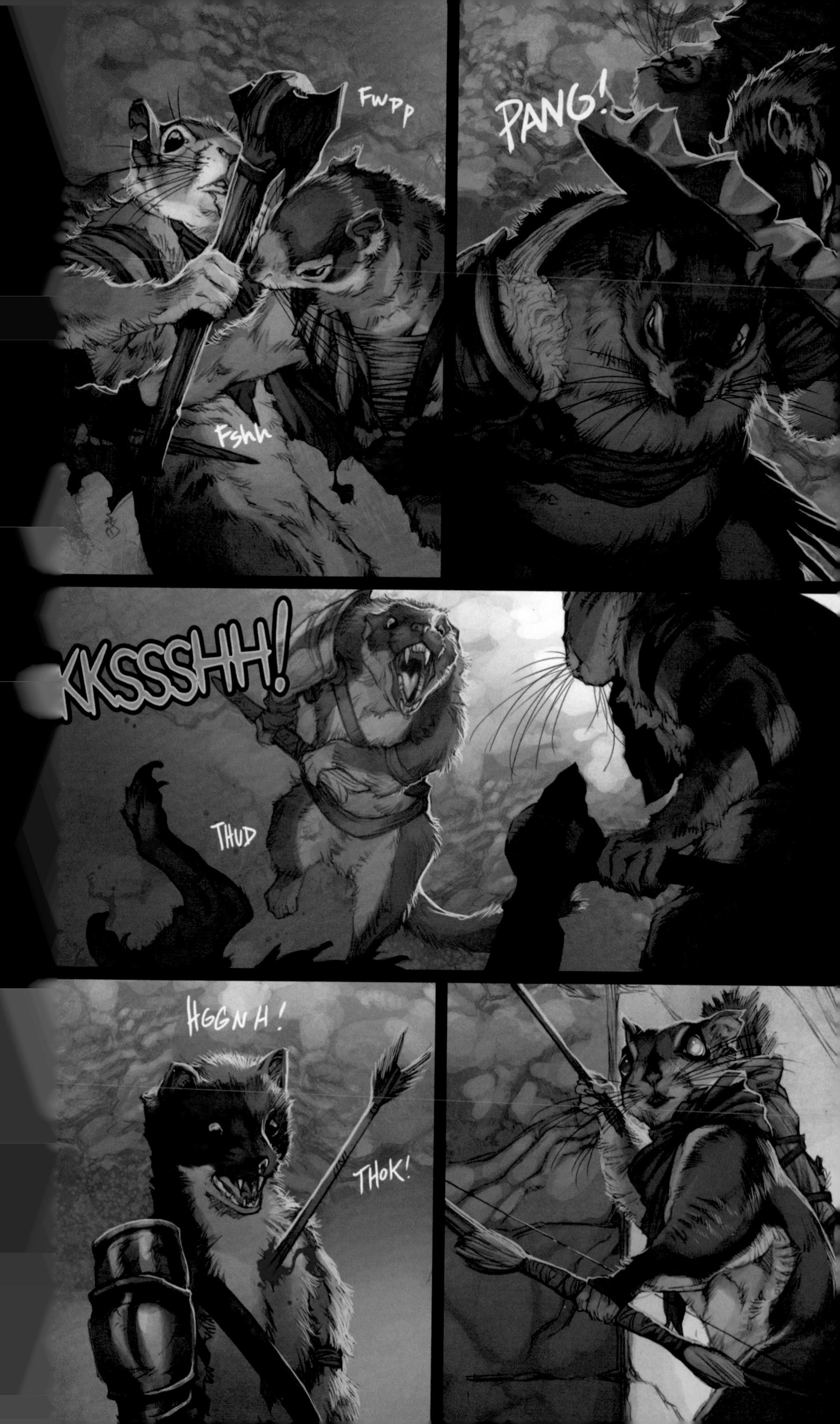

FWPP
FSHH
PANG!
KKSSSHH!
THUD
HGGNH!
THOK!

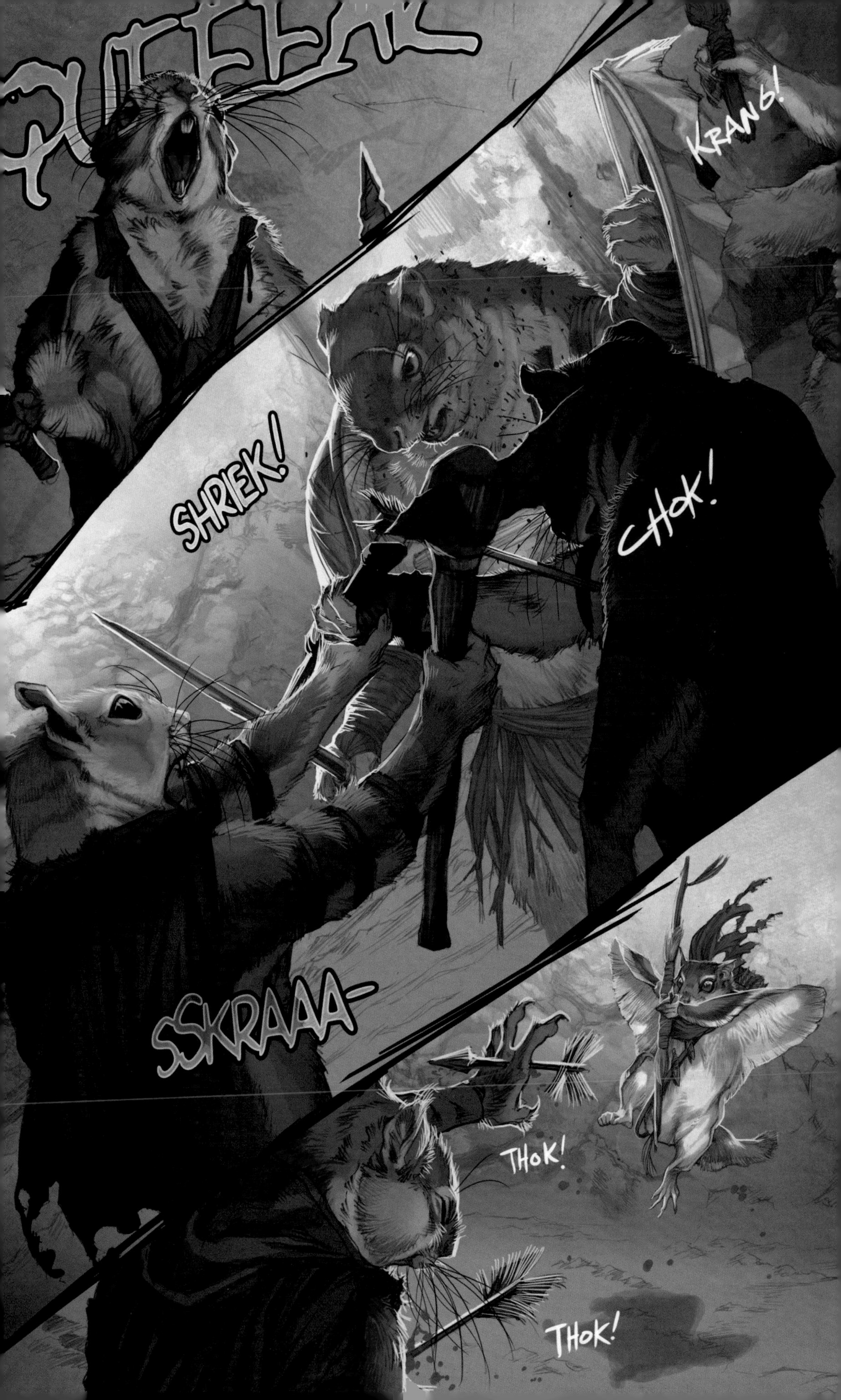

KRANG!
SHRIEK!
CHOK!
SSKRAAA-
THOK!
THOK!

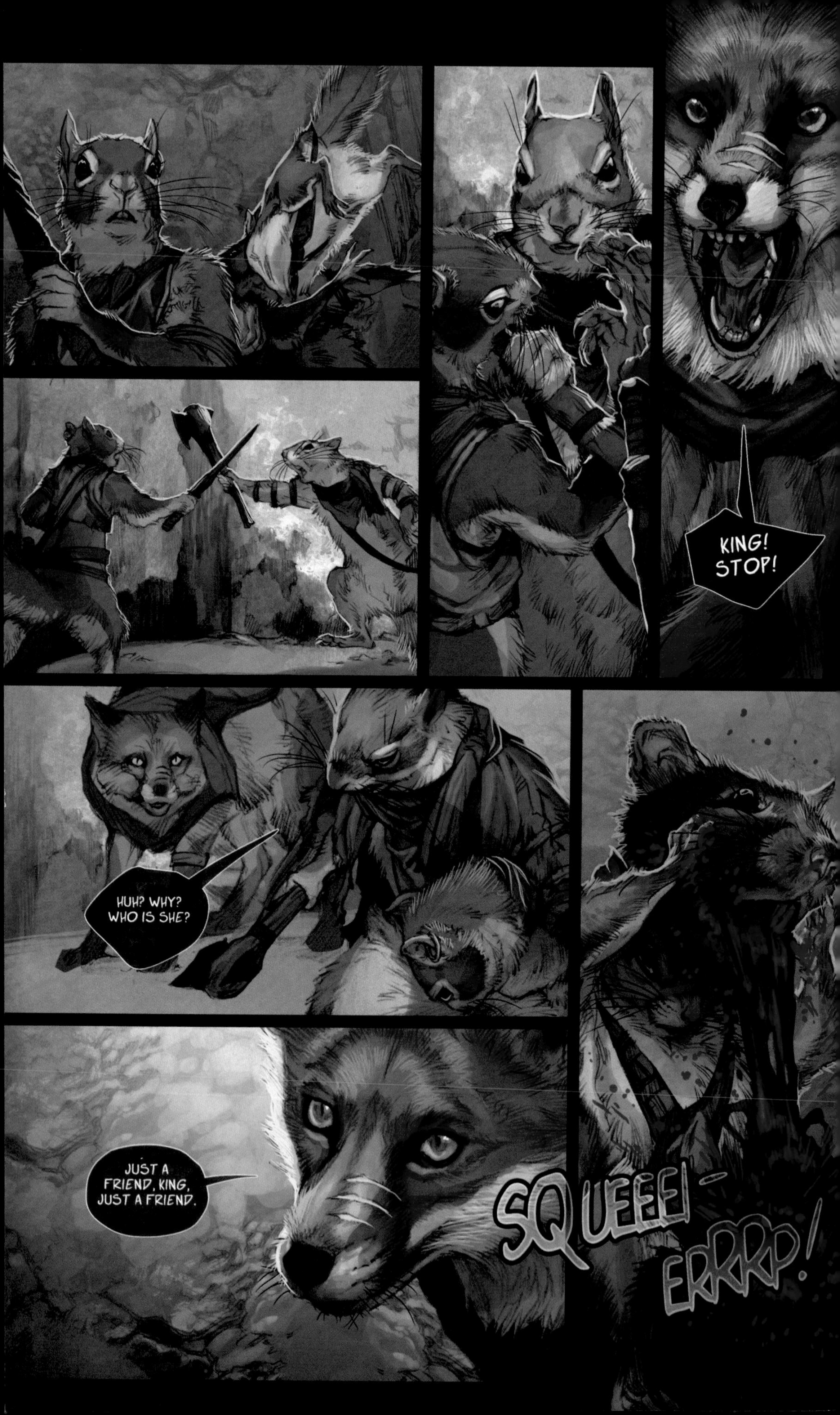
KING! STOP!
HUH? WHY? WHO IS SHE?
JUST A FRIEND, KING, JUST A FRIEND.
SQUEEEI-ERRRP!

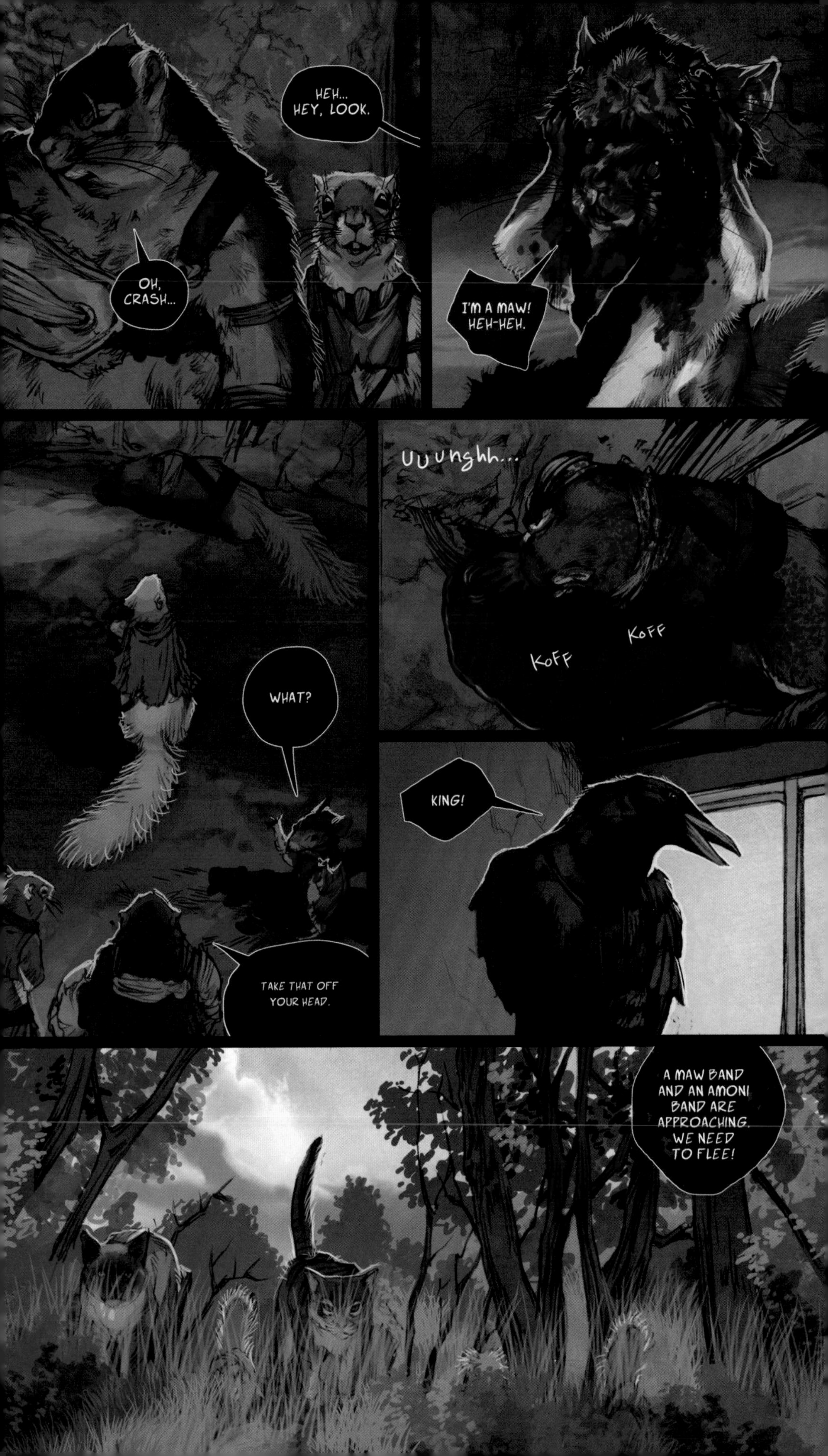
HEH...
HEY, LOOK.
OH,
CRASH...
I'M A MAW!
HEH-HEH.
WHAT?
TAKE THAT OFF
YOUR HEAD.
UUUNGHH...
KOFF
KOFF
KING!
A MAW BAND
AND AN AMONI
BAND ARE
APPROACHING.
WE NEED
TO FLEE!

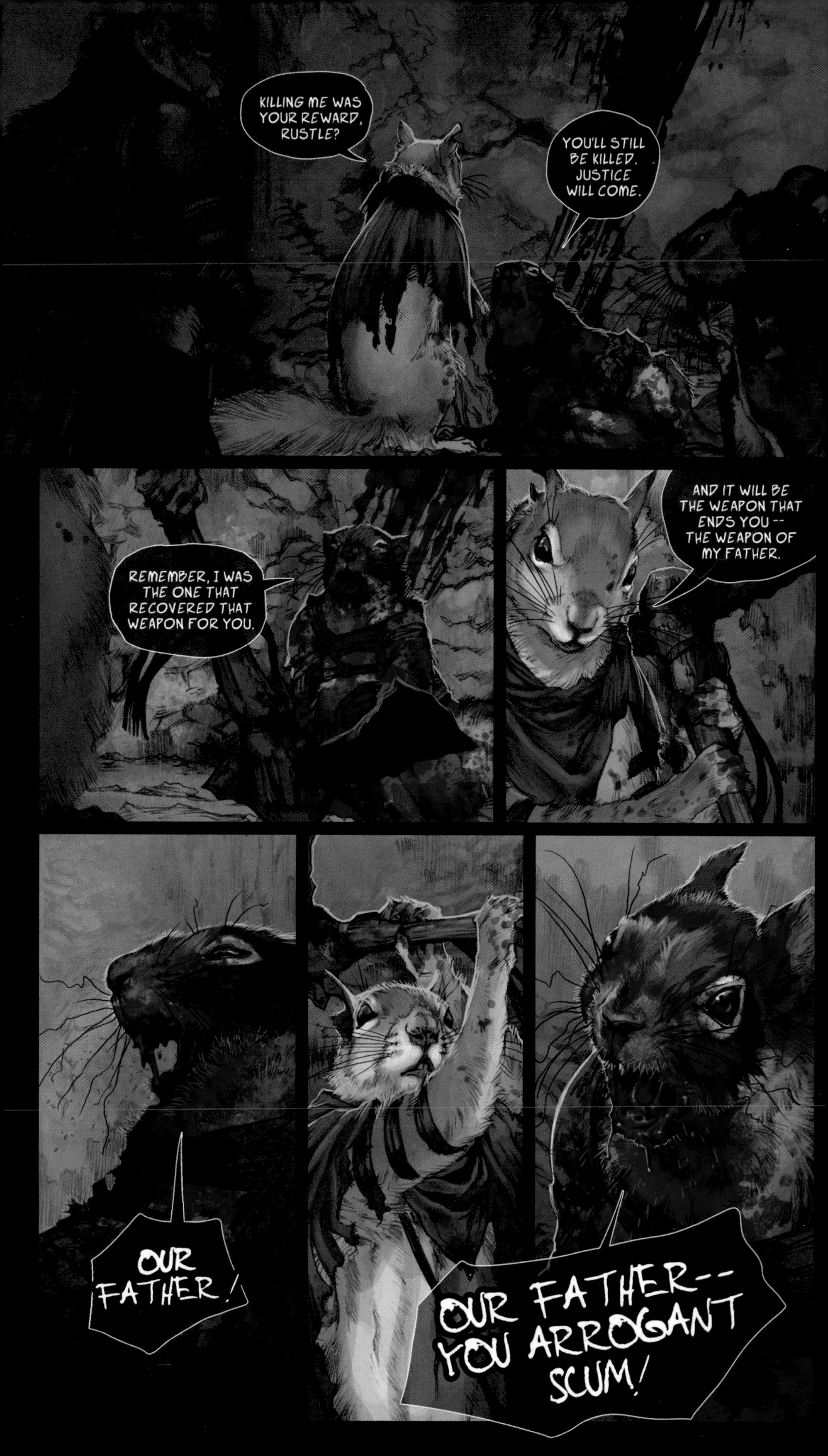
KILLING ME WAS YOUR REWARD, RUSTLE?
YOU'LL STILL BE KILLED. JUSTICE WILL COME.
REMEMBER, I WAS THE ONE THAT RECOVERED THAT WEAPON FOR YOU.
AND IT WILL BE THE WEAPON THAT ENDS YOU -- THE WEAPON OF MY FATHER.
OUR FATHER!
OUR FATHER-- YOU ARROGANT SCUM!

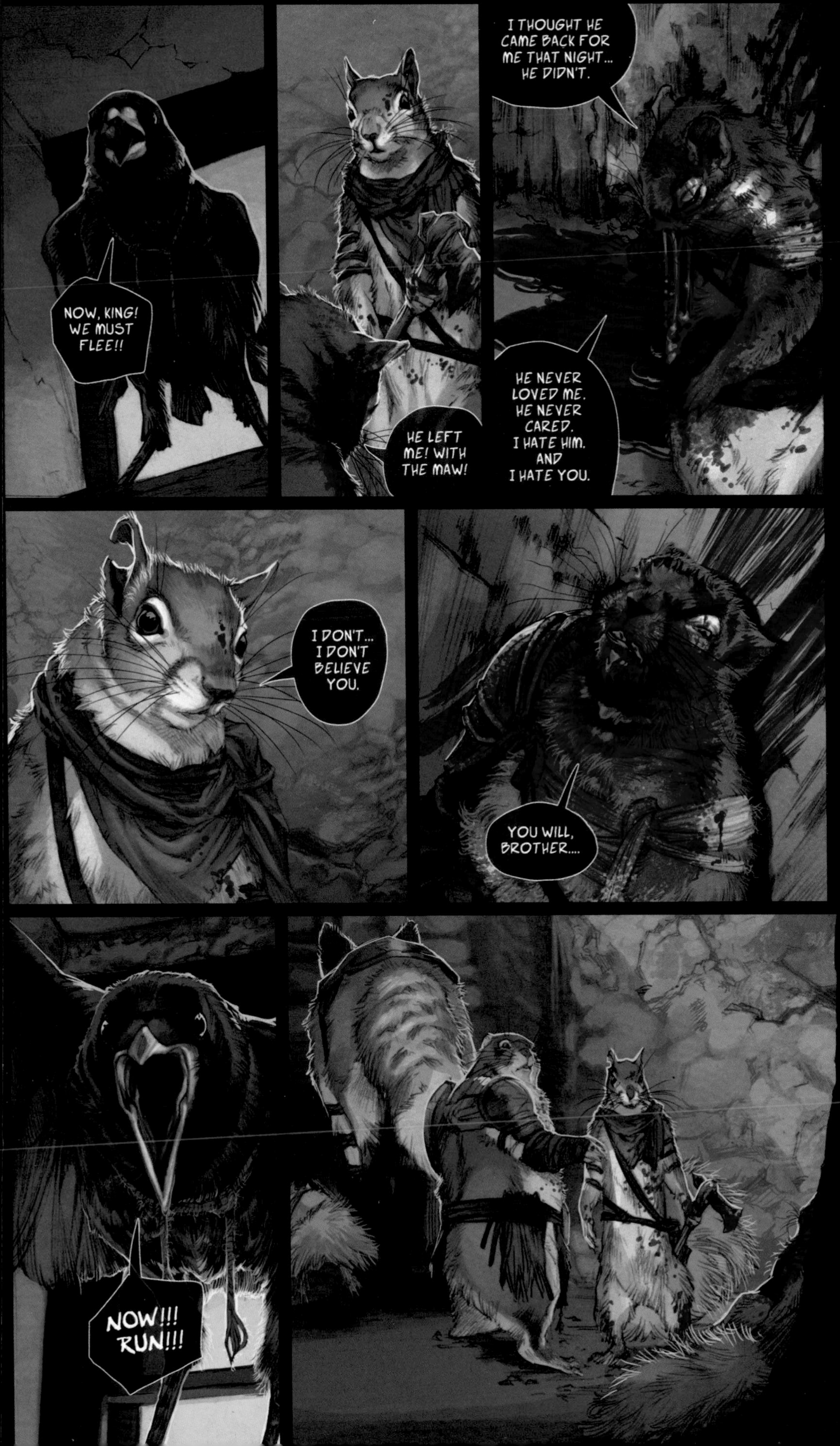
NOW, KING! WE MUST FLEE!!
HE LEFT ME! WITH THE MAW!
I THOUGHT HE CAME BACK FOR ME THAT NIGHT... HE DIDN'T.
HE NEVER LOVED ME. HE NEVER CARED. I HATE HIM. AND I HATE YOU.
I DON'T... I DON'T BELIEVE YOU.
YOU WILL, BROTHER....
NOW!!! RUN!!!

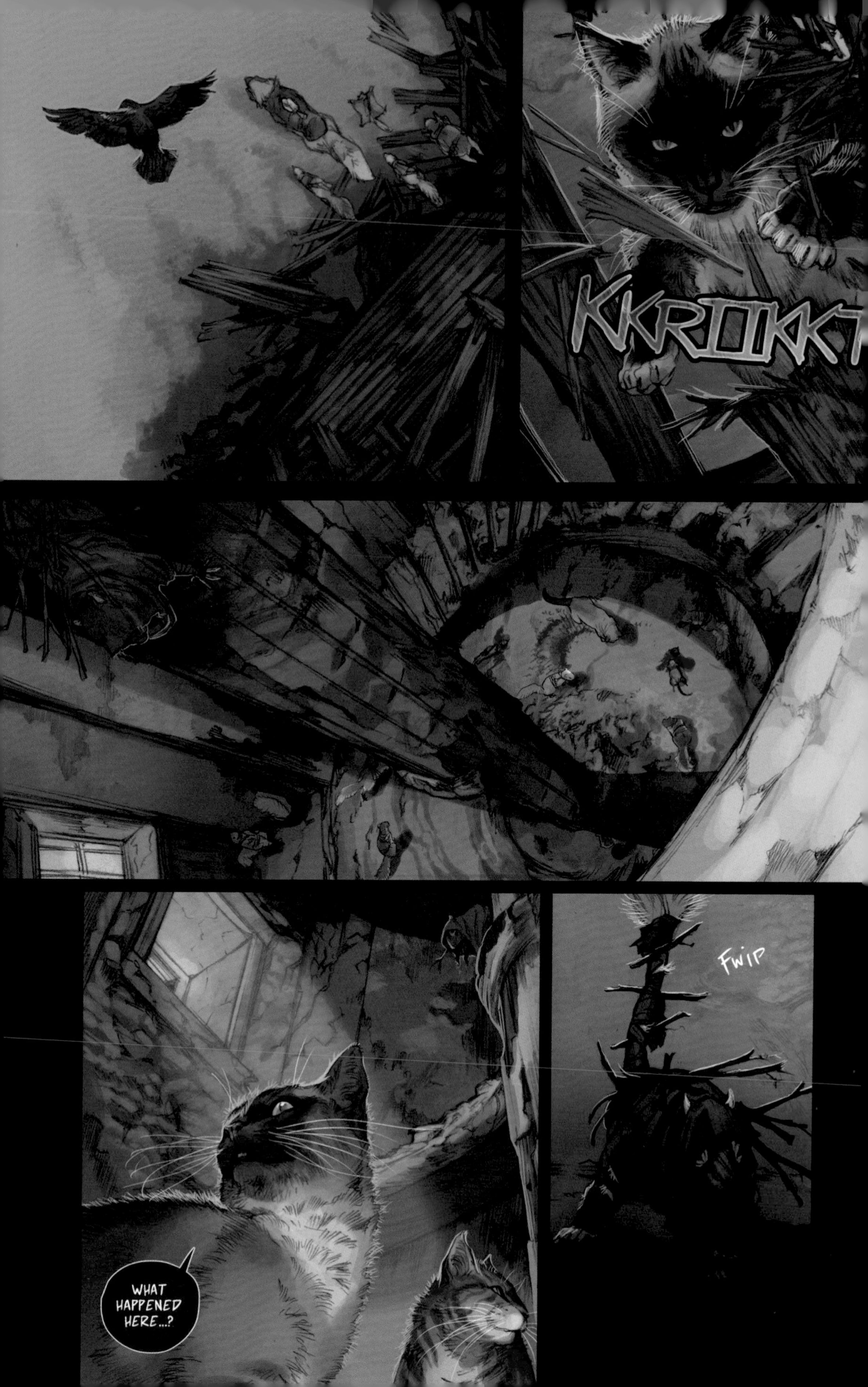
KKRIIKKT
FWIP
WHAT HAPPENED HERE...?

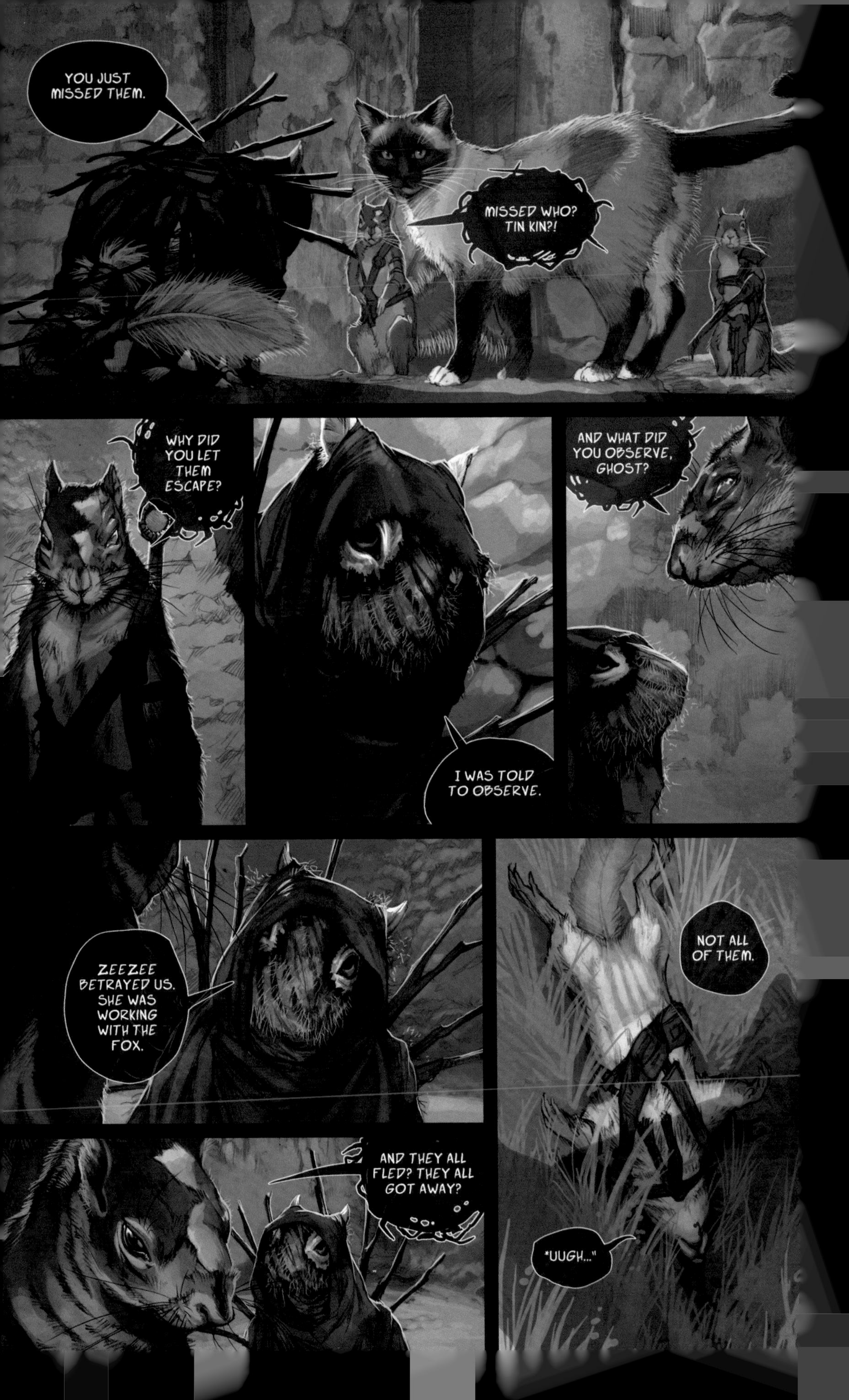
YOU JUST MISSED THEM.
MISSED WHO? TIN KIN?!
WHY DID YOU LET THEM ESCAPE?
I WAS TOLD TO OBSERVE.
AND WHAT DID YOU OBSERVE, GHOST?
ZEEZEE BETRAYED US. SHE WAS WORKING WITH THE FOX.
AND THEY ALL FLED? THEY ALL GOT AWAY?
NOT ALL OF THEM.
UUGH...

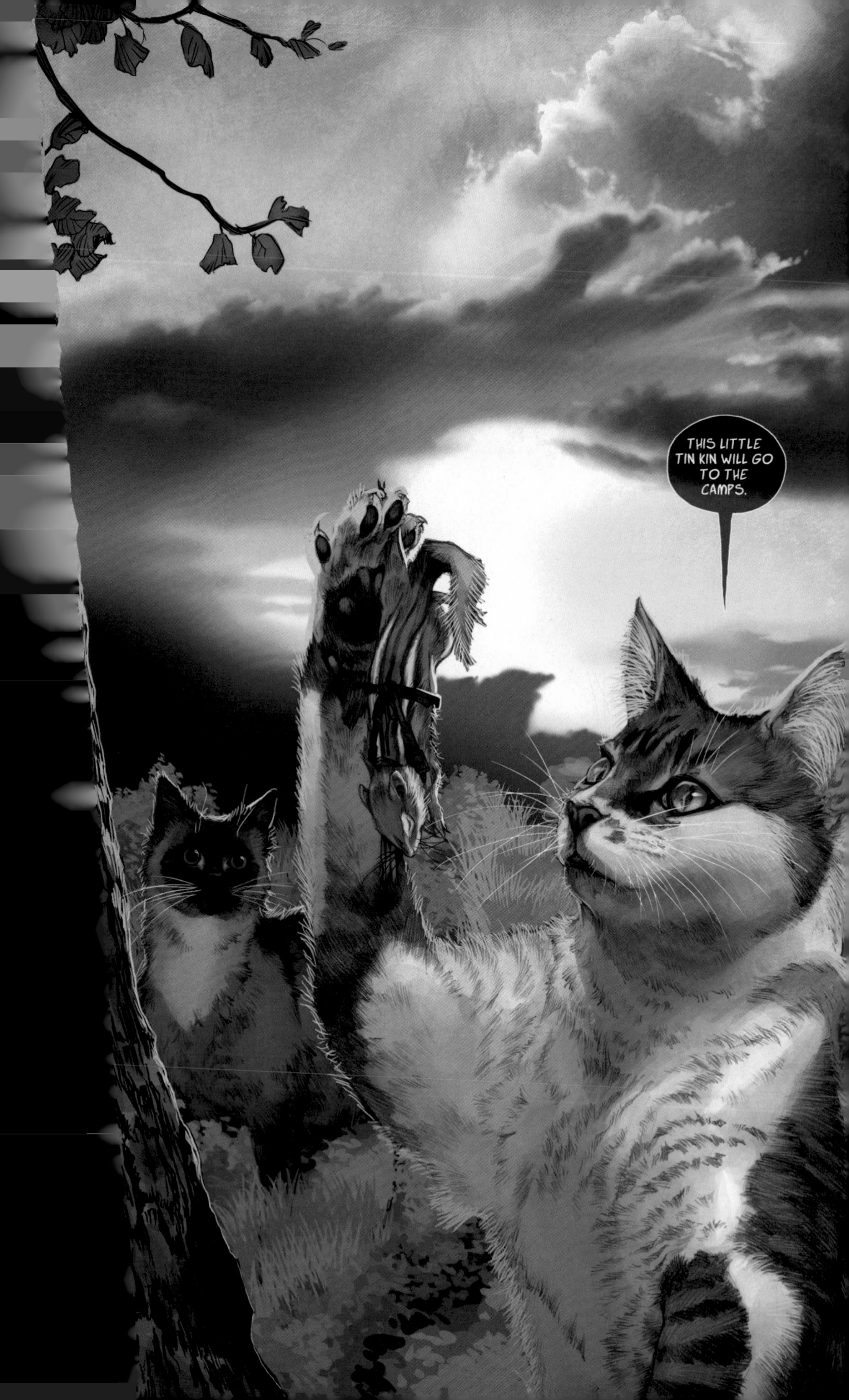
THIS LITTLE TIN KIN WILL GO TO THE CAMPS.

THE TIN KIN

The Tin Kin are a collective of over forty animals led by the squirrel known as King. Among his most trusted companions are fellow squirrels Cheeks, Jacko, Jobe, and Tree Jump, Eli the fox, and a mouse name Meo.

Long before the Tin Kin, shortly after humanity passed, a large animal collective known as the Amoni ruled over the land.

The Amoni followed the ways of their ancestors, embracing their animal nature of war and "survival of the fittest" mentality. However a small pack of these animals began to believe that with their unexplained new intelligence came a responsibility to act more rational and civil.

Denounced by their leaders, this pack of animals fought a short war against the Amoni before finally being driven to the edges of the land. Here they began their own, semi—peaceful, order known as the Tin Kin.

The leaders of the rebellion were two squirrels, King's father, Brand, and Redcoat. Brand was a charismatic, natural leader and a dreamer who was obsessed with animals' recent spark of rational thought. He would often approach the Amoni leaders with his ideas and philosophies.

Brand preached about a new world where animals would embrace their intelligence and use it to develop a peaceful utopia. He feared that if animals continued to follow the old ways of instinct, they too would find themselves removed from the planet, like the human civilization before them. As Brand persuaded others, the ranks of the Amoni began to degrade and quarrel; those defending the old ways against those seeking to move into a new order.

Such is the story of Squarriors, the Tin Kin, and their rival nemesis, the Maw. Found in the soon to be released pages of the Squarriors comic book series by Ashley Witter and Ash Maczko from Devil's Due Entertainment.

KING

SPECIES: SQUIRREL

AFFILIATION: TIN KIN (ALPHA)

GENDER: MALE

AGE: 5

COLOR/MARKINGS: GREY

RELATIVES: BRAND (FATHER), LINDY (MOTHER), KERA (SISTER).

BIO: KING IS THE CURRENT ALPHA OF THE TIN KIN. KING'S FATHER, BRAND, THEN THE ALPHA OF THE TIN KIN, WAS KILLED BY REDCOAT WHEN KING WAS A PUP. AT THE TIME, KING'S MOTHER AND SISTER WERE ALSO MISSING, LEAVING KING ORPHANED. JOBE, BRAND'S BROTHER, TOOK OVER CARING FOR AND RAISING KING. KING IS FUELED BY THE DEATH OF HIS FATHER AND THE SEARCH FOR HIS MOTHER AND SISTER. HE ADAPTED EXCEEDINGLY WELL TO THE CODE OF WILL, AND FOLLOWING THE LEGACY OF HIS FATHER, BECAME THE TIN KIN'S ALPHA.

Cheeks

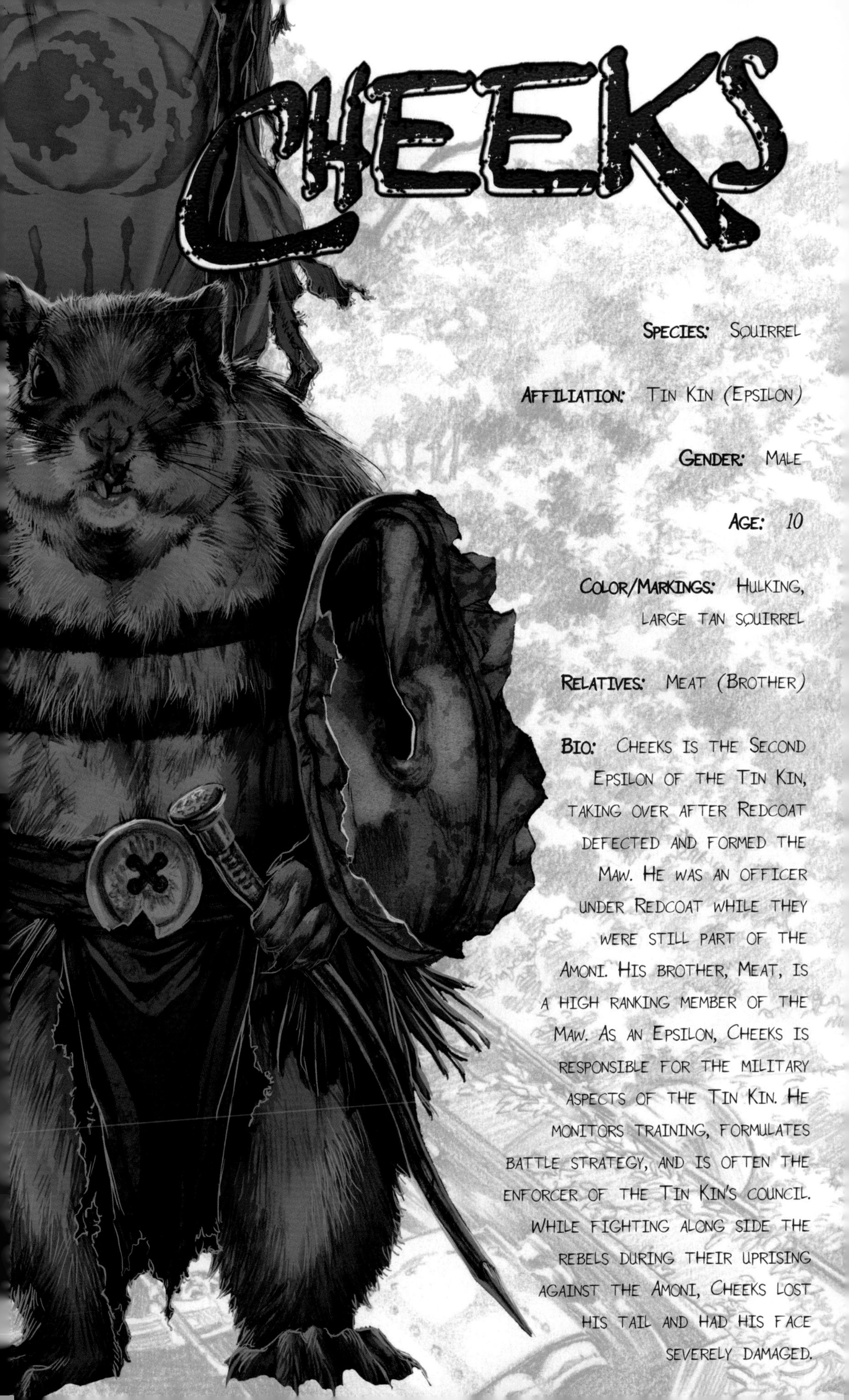

Species: Squirrel

Affiliation: Tin Kin (Epsilon)

Gender: Male

Age: 10

Color/Markings: Hulking, large tan squirrel

Relatives: Meat (Brother)

Bio: Cheeks is the Second Epsilon of the Tin Kin, taking over after Redcoat defected and formed the Maw. He was an officer under Redcoat while they were still part of the Amoni. His brother, Meat, is a high ranking member of the Maw. As an Epsilon, Cheeks is responsible for the military aspects of the Tin Kin. He monitors training, formulates battle strategy, and is often the enforcer of the Tin Kin's council. While fighting along side the rebels during their uprising against the Amoni, Cheeks lost his tail and had his face severely damaged.

JACKO

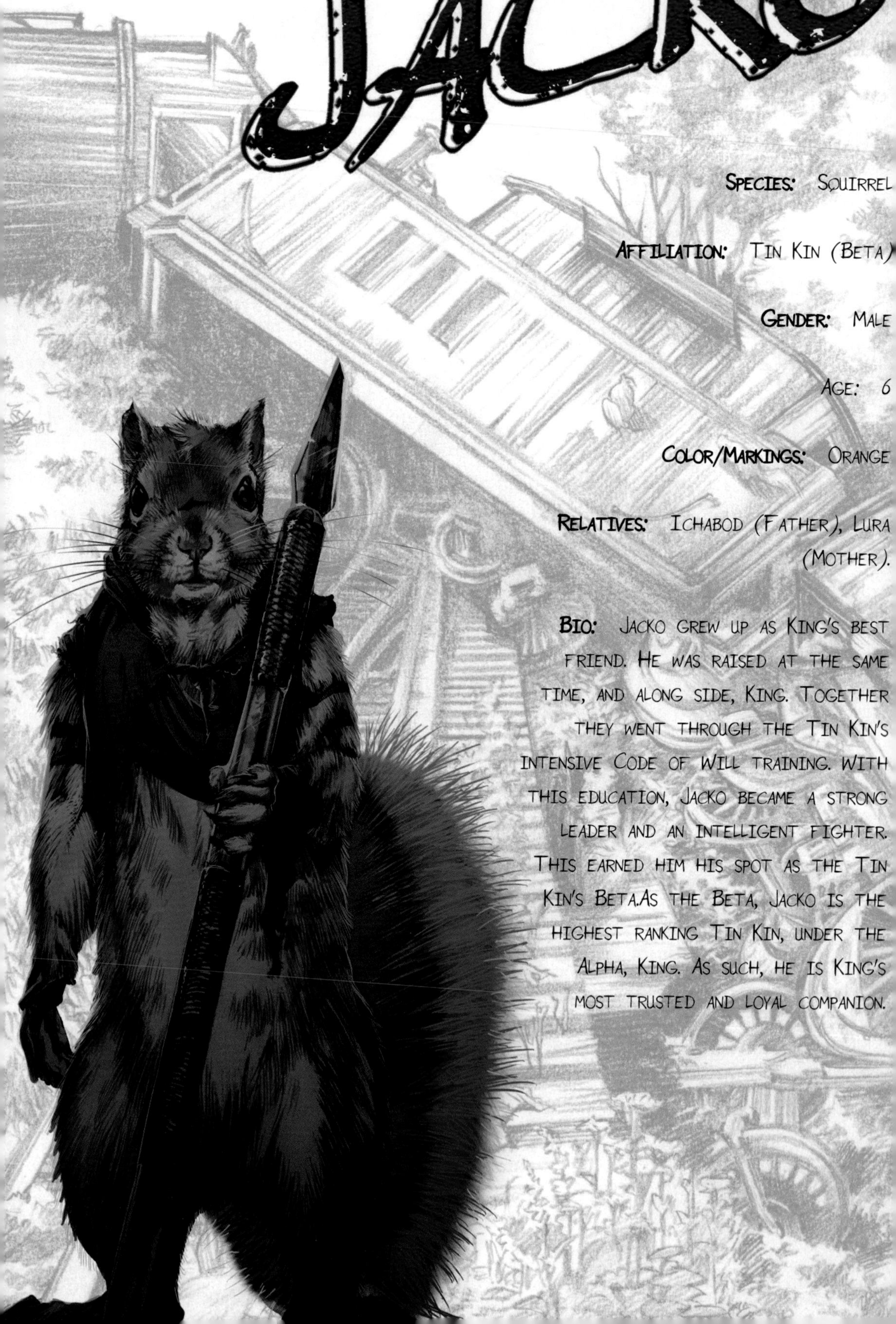

SPECIES: SQUIRREL

AFFILIATION: TIN KIN (BETA)

GENDER: MALE

AGE: 6

COLOR/MARKINGS: ORANGE

RELATIVES: ICHABOD (FATHER), LURA (MOTHER).

BIO: JACKO GREW UP AS KING'S BEST FRIEND. HE WAS RAISED AT THE SAME TIME, AND ALONG SIDE, KING. TOGETHER THEY WENT THROUGH THE TIN KIN'S INTENSIVE CODE OF WILL TRAINING. WITH THIS EDUCATION, JACKO BECAME A STRONG LEADER AND AN INTELLIGENT FIGHTER. THIS EARNED HIM HIS SPOT AS THE TIN KIN'S BETA.AS THE BETA, JACKO IS THE HIGHEST RANKING TIN KIN, UNDER THE ALPHA, KING. AS SUCH, HE IS KING'S MOST TRUSTED AND LOYAL COMPANION.

JOBE

SPECIES: SQUIRREL

AFFILIATION: TIN KIN (GAMMA)

GENDER: MALE

AGE: 19

COLOR/MARKINGS: GREY

RELATIVES: BRAND (BROTHER).

BIO: JOBE IS THE TIN KIN'S PRIMARY ADVISOR. THIS ROLE IS KNOWN AS THE GAMMA. HE RAISED KING AFTER THE DEATH OF KING'S FATHER, AND JOBE'S BROTHER, BRAND. AFTER BRAND'S PASSING, JOBE SPENT A FEW YEARS AS THE TIN KIN ALPHA AND PERSONALLY TRAINED KING IN THE WAYS OF THE CODE OF WILL. WHEN KING WAS READY, HE WAS VOTED IN AS THE NEW ALPHA AND JOBE TOOK THE POSITION OF THE TIN KIN'S GAMMA. JOBE SHARES HIS WISDOM THROUGH HIS CODE OF WILL TEACHINGS, WHICH IS REQUIRED LEARNING FOR ALL TIN KIN WARRIORS.

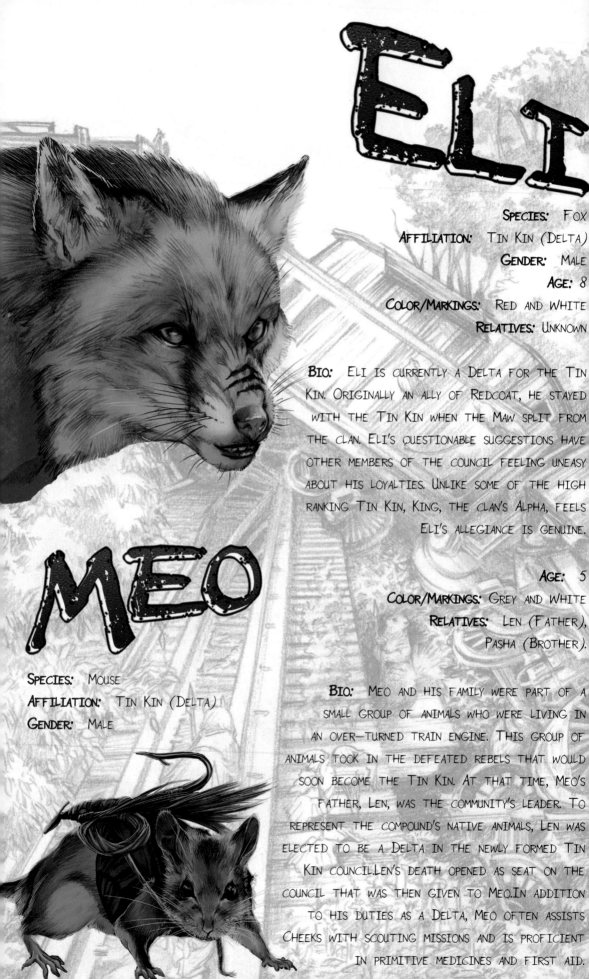

Eli

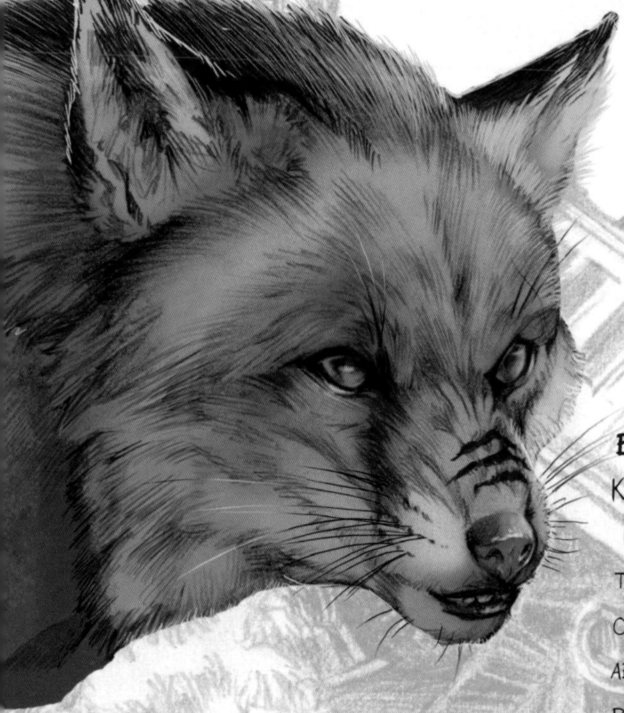

Species: Fox
Affiliation: Tin Kin (Delta)
Gender: Male
Age: 8
Color/Markings: Red and White
Relatives: Unknown

Bio: Eli is currently a Delta for the Tin Kin. Originally an ally of Redcoat, he stayed with the Tin Kin when the Maw split from the clan. Eli's questionable suggestions have other members of the council feeling uneasy about his loyalties. Unlike some of the high ranking Tin Kin, King, the clan's Alpha, feels Eli's allegiance is genuine.

Meo

Species: Mouse
Affiliation: Tin Kin (Delta)
Gender: Male
Age: 5
Color/Markings: Grey and White
Relatives: Len (Father), Pasha (Brother).

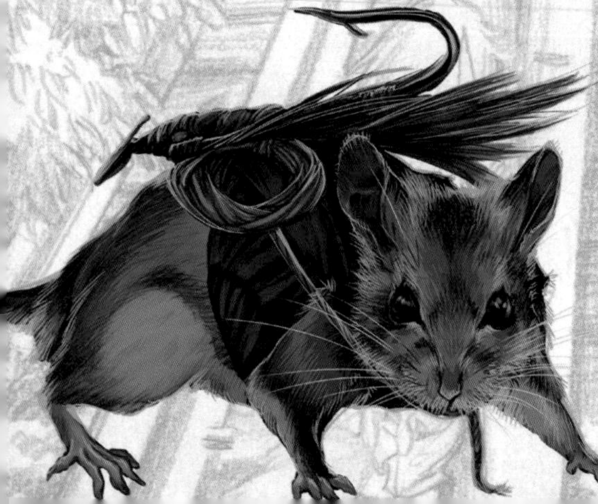

Bio: Meo and his family were part of a small group of animals who were living in an over-turned train engine. This group of animals took in the defeated rebels that would soon become the Tin Kin. At that time, Meo's father, Len, was the community's leader. To represent the compound's native animals, Len was elected to be a Delta in the newly formed Tin Kin council.Len's death opened as seat on the council that was then given to Meo.In addition to his duties as a Delta, Meo often assists Cheeks with scouting missions and is proficient in primitive medicines and first aid.

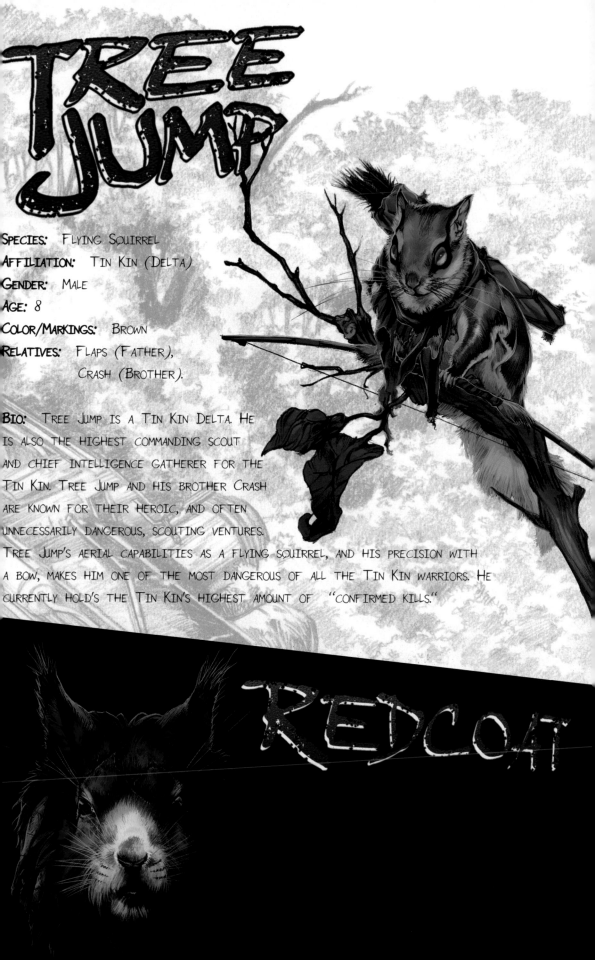

TREE JUMP

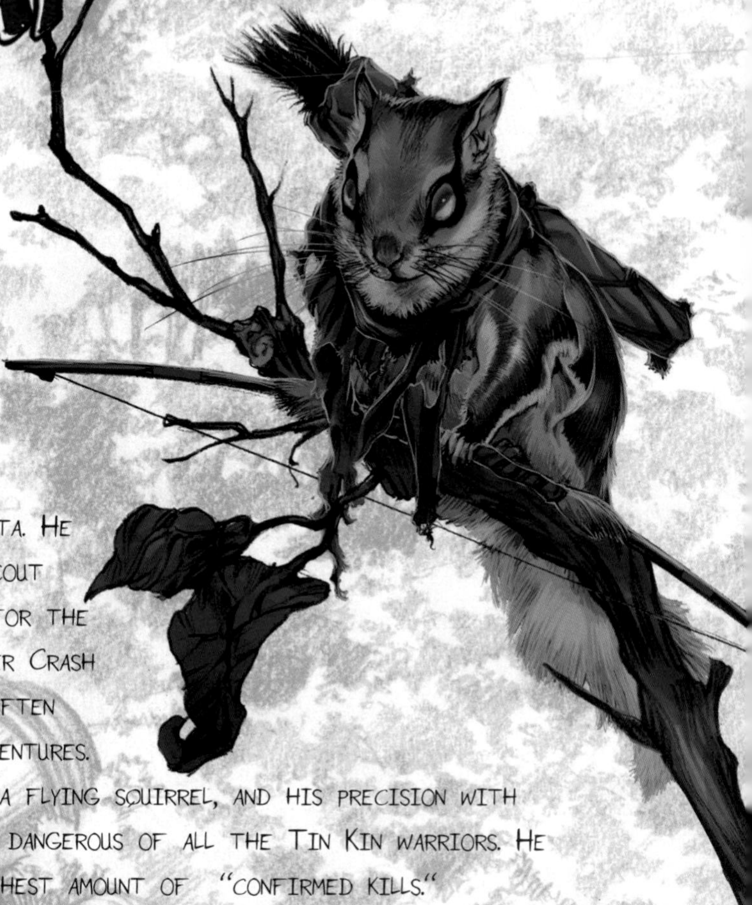

SPECIES: Flying Squirrel
AFFILIATION: Tin Kin (Delta)
GENDER: Male
AGE: 8
COLOR/MARKINGS: Brown
RELATIVES: Flaps (Father),
Crash (Brother).

BIO: Tree Jump is a Tin Kin Delta. He is also the highest commanding scout and chief intelligence gatherer for the Tin Kin. Tree Jump and his brother Crash are known for their heroic, and often unnecessarily dangerous, scouting ventures. Tree Jump's aerial capabilities as a flying squirrel, and his precision with a bow, makes him one of the most dangerous of all the Tin Kin warriors. He currently hold's the Tin Kin's highest amount of "confirmed kills."

REDCOAT

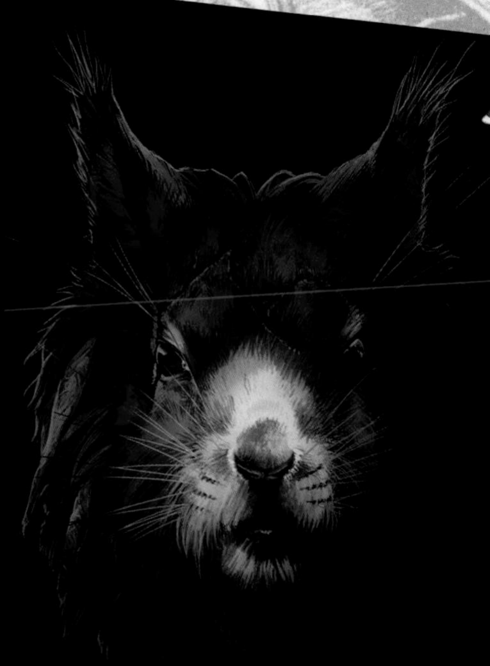

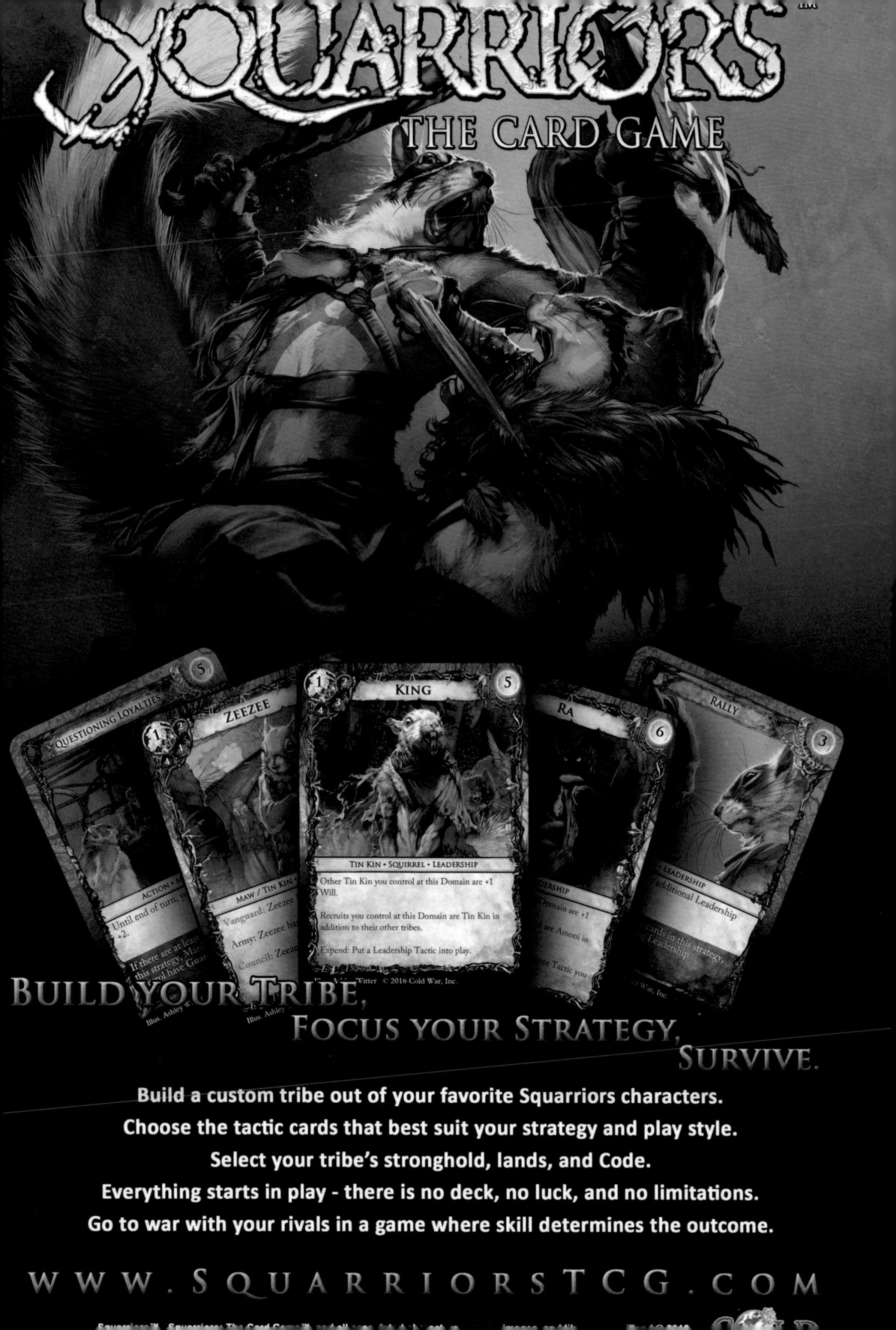
SQUARRIORS™
THE CARD GAME
QUESTIONING LOYALTIES
ZEEZEE
KING
TIN KIN • SQUIRREL • LEADERSHIP
Other Tin Kin you control at this Domain are +1 Will.
Recruits you control at this Domain are Tin Kin in addition to their other tribes.
Expend: Put a Leadership Tactic into play.
© 2016 Cold War, Inc.
RA
RALLY
BUILD YOUR TRIBE,
FOCUS YOUR STRATEGY,
SURVIVE.
Build a custom tribe out of your favorite Squarriors characters.
Choose the tactic cards that best suit your strategy and play style.
Select your tribe's stronghold, lands, and Code.
Everything starts in play - there is no deck, no luck, and no limitations.
Go to war with your rivals in a game where skill determines the outcome.
WWW.SQUARRIORSTCG.COM

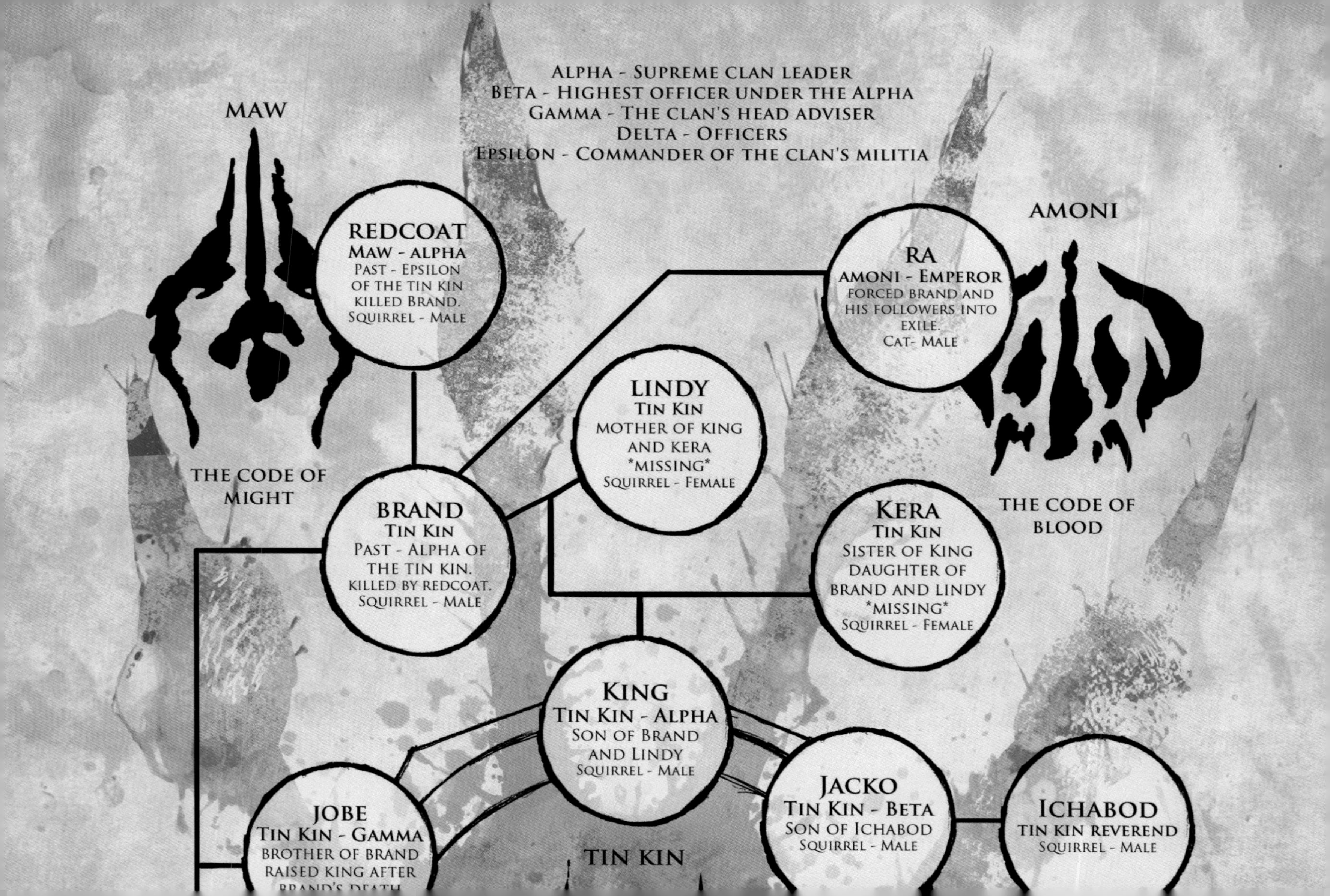

Alpha - Supreme clan leader
Beta - Highest officer under the Alpha
Gamma - The clan's head adviser
Delta - Officers
Epsilon - Commander of the clan's militia
MAW
THE CODE OF MIGHT
REDCOAT
Maw - alpha
Past - Epsilon of the Tin Kin killed Brand.
Squirrel - Male
AMONI
THE CODE OF BLOOD
RA
Amoni - Emperor
Forced Brand and his followers into exile.
Cat- Male
LINDY
Tin Kin
Mother of King and Kera
Missing
Squirrel - Female
BRAND
Tin Kin
Past - Alpha of the Tin Kin.
killed by Redcoat.
Squirrel - Male
KERA
Tin Kin
Sister of King
Daughter of Brand and Lindy
Missing
Squirrel - Female
KING
Tin Kin - Alpha
Son of Brand and Lindy
Squirrel - Male
JOBE
Tin Kin - Gamma
Brother of Brand
raised King after
JACKO
Tin Kin - Beta
Son of Ichabod
Squirrel - Male
ICHABOD
Tin Kin Reverend
Squirrel - Male
TIN KIN

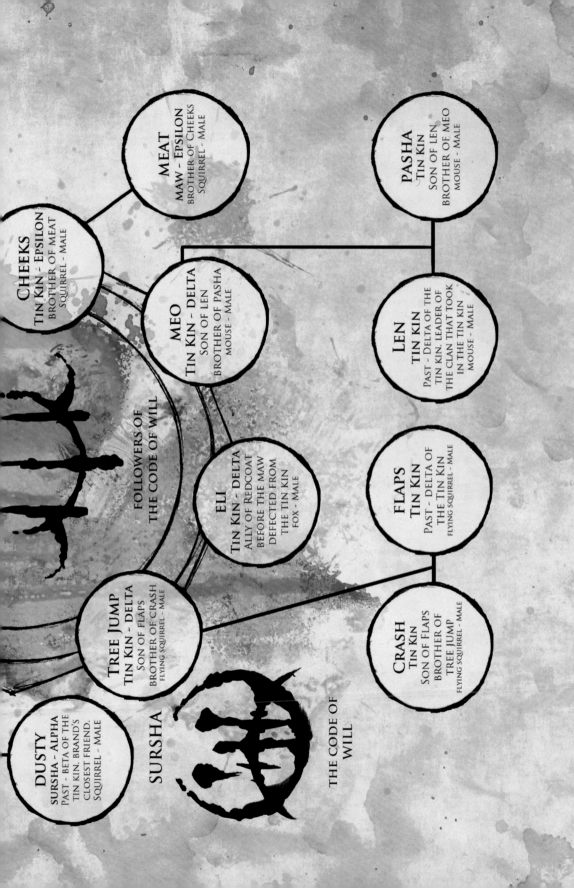

CHEEKS
TIN KIN - EPSILON
BROTHER OF MEAT
SQUIRREL - MALE

MEAT - EPSILON
MAW - EPSILON
BROTHER OF CHEEKS
SQUIRREL - MALE

PASHA
TIN KIN
SON OF LEN
BROTHER OF MEO
MOUSE - MALE

MEO
TIN KIN - DELTA
SON OF LEN
BROTHER OF PASHA
MOUSE - MALE

LEN
TIN KIN
PAST - DELTA OF THE
TIN KIN. LEADER OF
THE CLAN THAT TOOK
IN THE TIN KIN
MOUSE - MALE

FOLLOWERS OF
THE CODE OF WILL

ELI
TIN KIN - DELTA
ALLY OF REDCOAT
BEFORE THE MAW
DEFECTED FROM
THE TIN KIN
FOX - MALE

FLAPS
TIN KIN
PAST - DELTA OF
THE TIN KIN
FLYING SQUIRREL - MALE

TREE JUMP
TIN KIN - DELTA
SON OF FLAPS
BROTHER OF CRASH
FLYING SQUIRREL - MALE

CRASH
TIN KIN
SON OF FLAPS
BROTHER OF
TREE JUMP
FLYING SQUIRREL - MALE

DUSTY
SURSHA - ALPHA
PAST - BETA OF THE
TIN KIN. BRAND'S
CLOSEST FRIEND.
SQUIRREL - MALE

SURSHA

THE CODE OF
WILL

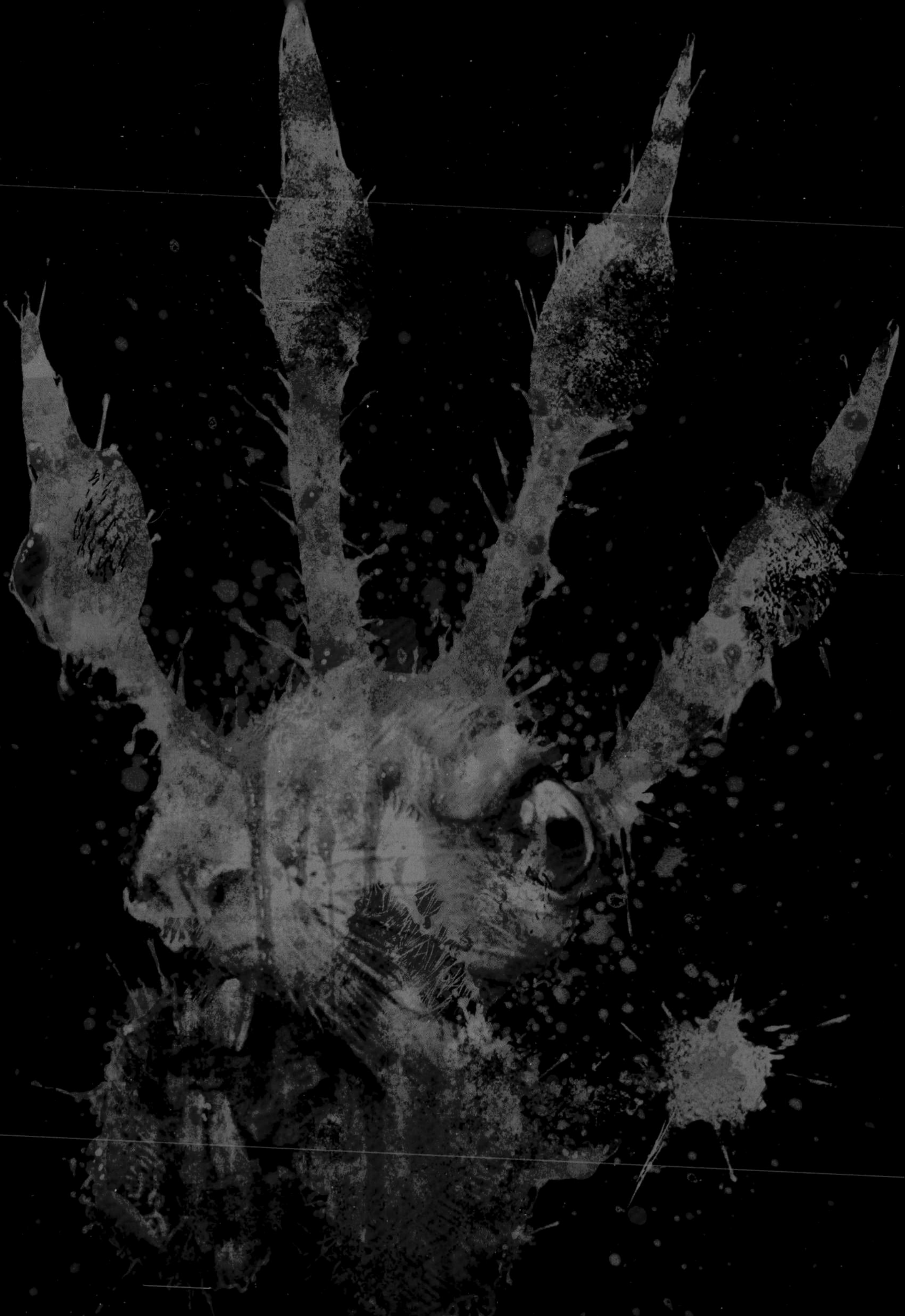